INSTALLING & SERVICING ELECTRONIC PROTECTIVE SYSTEMS

By Harvey F. Swearer

TAB BOOKS

Blue Ridge Summit, Pa. 17214

FIRST EDITION

FIRST PRINTING—JUNE 1972

Copyright © 1972 by TAB BOOKS

Printed in the United States
of America

Hardbound -   International Standard Book No. 0-8306-2605-X

Paperbound -   International Standard Book No. 0-8306-1605-5

Library of Congress Card Number: 72-80559

Contents

Preface

The all-out effort to effectively combat crime finds the rapidly expanding security system business falling far short of the current demand for reliable installations. Even though solid-state devices have come to the rescue, they still require proper maintenance. Competent personnel are simply not available in sufficient numbers to adequately staff central alarm companies, and only a trickle of technicians and trainees are switching to this phase of electronics. More training programs are needed because the surface has been barely scratched at this time. And for those interested in an exceptional opportunity for a prosperous future, a careful review of what is being offered here should be more than worthwhile. You can't go wrong helping friends and neighbors protect their property, and the demand for the well-trained security specialist far exceeds the supply! Truly, the rewards of security electronics are exceptional, and the following comprehensive coverage of the burglar alarm business will show you why as we review each type of system step by step with concise explanations, illustrations, diagrams and other technical information to insure a complete understanding of each and every one.

Although many may enter the business of installing and maintaining the systems of various manufacturers, there will be an even greater number with their roots in electronics who will select the servicing of the many complex systems offered as their ultimate goal. Chapters 10 and 11 are geared to train the latter group and prepare them for the technical duties and "know how" involved in filling the job of security technician. Even the more expensive systems are useless unless they perform as designed, and continue to do so 24 hours a day, every day in the year. Although honest people take a holiday—sometimes—the thief operates every day around the clock.

No experience is required for the installation of most systems, merely the aptitude to follow detailed, though simple, directions. Such ambitions are well-rewarded because the field is now wide open. Many are making big money installing alarms every day, so why not you? The early chapters of this manual explain just what is involved in the alarm system, how to select the one for the job at hand, types available, estimating costs, how to build and expand your business, train your help, finance the operation and line up, install, and check out components. Descriptions, operational explanations, specifications, typical installations, testing, and troubleshooting procedures are included.

During the preparation of this material, the unselfish technical assistance from many manufacturers of security systems and related components was tremendous. This fact shows all the way through the text, and as a direct result, we were able to come up with a more informative and helpful manual. Special thanks to Robert M. Ballinger, Systron-Donner Security Devices Div.; P. I. Corbell, Johnson Service Co.; and D. T. Heckel, GTE Sylvania Electronic Systems Group (Western Div.). The complete list of cooperating firms follows. For a complete listing of manufacturers and suppliers, see the appropriate section in the back of the book.

Adcor Electronics, Inc.; Alarm Products International, Inc.; Alarmtronics Engineering, Inc.; American District Telegraph Co.; Arrowhead Enterprises, Inc.; Artronix Surveillance; A.T.A Control Systems, Inc.; Benedict Electronics Technology, Inc.; Bourns Security Systems, Inc.; Delta Products, Inc.; Detector Industries; Detectron Security Systems Inc.; Fire-Lite Alarms, Inc.; Functional Devices, Inc.; GBC Closed Circuit TV Corp.; GTE Sylvania Electronic Systems Group; Holobeam, Inc.; Honeywell, Inc.; Johnson Service Co.; Kolin Industries, Inc.; Lear Siegler, Inc.; Lectro Systems, Inc.; Linear Corp.; Mallory Distributor Products Co.; Metrotech Electronics, Inc.; Morse Products Mfg. Co.; Motorola Communications & Electronics, Inc.; M.R.A. Associates, Inc.; MRL, Inc.; Multra-Guard, Inc.; Multi-Elmac Co.; National Alarm Products Co., Inc.; Northern Electric Co.; OMW Electronics, Inc.; Optical Controls, Inc.; Poly-Scientific, Litton Systems, Inc.; Pulse Alarm Detection Systems, Inc.; Rusco Industries, Inc.; Sontrix Distributing Co.; Schulmerich Electronics; Systron-Donner Security Systems; Tapeswitch Corp.; Teledyne Geotech; and Three B Electronics, Inc.

Harvey F. Swearer

Chapter 1
Basic Alarm Systems

What is a burglar alarm system? Nothing more than a complete facility for detecting the unauthorized entry or trespassing of an intruder in a given area as determined by the owner, lessee, or designated person in charge thereof, including the responsive action to such detection in the form of an alarm, light or other indicator. There are several types of burglar alarm systems from the standpoint of the method of detection, and these may be roughly summed up as electro mechanical, photoelectric, ultrasonic, microwave, proximity, audio and visual.

Each type is discussed in detail in later chapters, but for the time we are concerned only with the grouping from the standpoint of the method used to sense or detect a violation. Fire detectors use a type of heat-sensitive device such as a thermocouple or even a thermistor which varies in resistance with heat. The ambient temperature of the device causes its contacts to close, in the case of the thermocouple, when the heat exceeds a fixed value or to change the resistance in the latter device to trigger a solid-state amplifier or SCR. Numerous other electronic circuits may be used, but all for the purpose of activating a relay or switching device to initiate an alarm or warning signal in the form of a buzzer, bell, blinking light or some other form of indicator to alert personnel in the area of the condition.

Incidentally, there are many reasons for detecting temperature variations aside from fire, such as manufacturing processes where complex mixtures and reactions occur in a comparatively short time. These conditions dictate the urgent need for indicating devices to monitor the activity at a central location. Indicating devices may even be utilized to control conditions by initiating the correction of an error by lowering the temperature or retarding an activity in the manufacturing plant. These central control centers often include visual monitoring equipment for inspection of remote areas in the plant.

Wasteful practices often result in unnecessary plant expenses which may be drastically reduced by specific measurements and indications readily offered by temperature-sensitive devices. An additional plus offered by such systems is the safety factor—always an important consideration in industrial work. Many manufacturing processes necessitate conditions that could hardly be less than hazardous for human visual or proximity operation; atomic energy or "hot" areas are a specific example of the demand for reliable instruments to take the place of human senses to warn against the dangers of radioactivity, extreme pressure, heat, or other factors. Such coordination is a segment of quality control and its importance is certainly worthy of considerable expense.

Oftentimes, a chemical reaction produces appreciable heat which may be beneficial in the speeding up of a process, although excessive heat could result in the breakdown of the ultimate product. Instruments can continuously monitor the heat level and actuate equipment for its removal or correction by retarding the addition of materials in order to reduce the action at the proper time.

In industrial processes, the major variables are temperature, pressure and flow, so numerous types of electrical and electronic means of converting, transmitting, and presenting the information required to remote locations are currently utilized. Such systems operated less efficiently in the past with mechanical or hydraulic capabilities. Since electrical characteristics parallel dominant physical changes occurring in many processes, the capability of monitoring with electronic devices offers an inexpensive and simple means.

The junction of two dissimilar metals exposed to changes in temperature will induce a voltage if a closed circuit is formed, and this potential is readily measurable in small fractions of a volt or millivolts. These tiny voltage changes are directly proportional to the differences in temperature between hot and cold junctions. A useful thermocouple provides a potential output that may easily be applied to a voltage amplifier for even greater sensitivity to minute changes.

Pressure may be measured with a simple float to provide movement of a variable resistor for relaying the desired information to recording instruments or monitoring devices. This could include the flow of gases or liquids that are pressure related and measurable by magnetic methods such as passing a conductive fluid through a pipe encircled by a magnetic field. The amplitude of the voltage produced would be a linear measurement of the fluid flow when amplified and displayed or recorded on a suitable indicator. An extremely sensitive temperature-indicating circuit utilizing a thermistor is shown in Fig. 1-1.

PRELIMINARY EVALUATION

No home or business is safe from burglary or even violence with the current wave of disregard for law and order. Drugs, unemployment and inability, or lack of interest in earning a legitimate living actually trigger the criminal brain. Effective prevention circles around the weapons of electronic technology, so ably offered in our modern security systems. The criminal's ignorance should not be over-estimated in evaluating his vulnerability to the elements of surprise, time and fear. In dealing with amateur or small-time burglars, we may assume that their skills are quite limited or they wouldn't be playing for small stakes. This means that good locks and properly installed safes usually provide adequate protection for most items of average value such as small property of less than a few hundred dollars. Since time is so important to the small-time thief, the difficult forced entry is out of the question, and even a simple, inexpensive alarm system is all that is needed. This is especially true where the locks are of more than the "love tap" variety.

As we move up to businesses or homes with items of far greater value within, the safeguards must be more sophisticated. Security systems may be used in combinations where a simpler arrangement is backed up by a more complex system. This will often fool the semi-pro who is still looking for the easy touch, and not quite confident or capable of the major league job. Often the noise of an alarm bell, siren or horn will cause him to run, because he can't afford to be caught in ac-

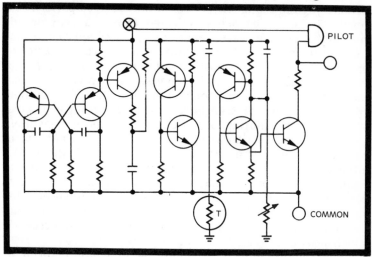

Fig. 1-1. Temperature alarm circuit using a thermistor.

tion now. Where locations are isolated during "after hours," the security system must be backed up with some type of signaling device to advise the authorities of the attempted burglary. This may be done in many ways without warning the intruder, and although some are too expensive for the small business, others less expensive will still be satisfactory. Naturally, when round the clock surveillance is necessary, connections with police headquarters or guard services in central station locations must be maintained. Although the cost may run extremely high, insurance costs are likely to be prohibitive otherwise.

SELECTING THE ALARM SYSTEM FOR THE JOB

The building, whether home or business, must be carefully surveyed regarding layout, protection requirements, methods and extent of property to be protected. The line-up of any system boils down to sensors or detectors, control or wiring and the response or alarm device. The detection part of the system may be very simple: a magnetic switch to warn that a door or window has been opened, or foil strips applied on windows to warn that the glass has been broken. In either case, the circuit or loop is opened to the alarm relay control circuit. Photoelectric sensors using solid-state transmitters and receivers with invisible light beams are used in many cases, and ultrasonic or radar type detection devices also have proven quite popular, although more expensive than the previously mentioned types. The latter type equipment works on the frequency shift principle where the intruder's entry is detected by the change he causes in the received pattern as a result of the waves being reflected from his body to the receiver. A change in frequency results as he approaches the transmitter or walks farther away from it. The capacity or proximity detector is most useful for protecting safes or vaults, because if an intruder approaches a protected area, these safeguards will provide an immediate alarm condition.

Audio sensors or transducers are often used in central systems for monitoring purposes, as well as in apartment buildings in conjunction with electric locks. The visual type of sensing device finds limited use in special applications and, although the arrangement usually is very costly, the end results are exceptional and can be duplicated only by live personnel. Thermostats or thermistors are quite useful for sensing fire or freezing conditions and the smoke detector has the ability to sense very small amounts of smoke (2 percent), which also affords early warning in case of fire.

Basic control units may include any type of monitoring or supervisory circuitry to trigger the alarm or response section upon proper signaling from the detection segment of the system. The control unit supplies power for the complete system, along with other selected functions such as timing, switching and programming. Capabilities in this area are unlimited, according to the complexity of the overall security system, and provisions for emergency battery power are normally included along with anti-tampering switches. In areas where power failure is other than a rarity, the battery power addition is mandatory, and in other sections where power failure hardly ever occurs, emergency power in the form of dry battery types is adequate. It is important to remember that under any condition, the power line could be cut by the intruder and unless some form of battery power is available, the system could be useless except for phone lines.

The response section of the system includes bells, buzzers, lights, phone dialing units, recorders, cameras, meters and any type of monitoring capability desired. Audible alarms may be protected by steel enclosures to prevent silencing. Such units usually are equipped with internal switches to signal or trigger an alarm condition when attempts are made to pry them open. Lights may be turned on in response to the "alarm signal" either inside the premises, outside or on a central station switchboard through leased lines. Telephone dialers, which play a recorded message, or radio control remote units are used in some installations to initiate action in the alarm condition. Other systems utilize continuous surveillance through closed-circuit television (CCTV) where the monitor provides a view of the desired area at all times. Camera systems are available where motion pictures of a protected area may be taken at preset times or on signal. The response section may cover proper action to any type of condition selected, whether it be intrusion, fire, smoke, shoplifting, freezing, liquid levels, weights, etc., as well as any desired combination of conditions.

Reviewing the types of intrusion alarms according to the detection method, the **electromechanical** is normally the least expensive, but it has limited capabilities. Various detector or switch-type devices connected in series to form a loop that completes the circuit to a simple holding relay is all that is required, except for a bell, buzzer or siren warning device. Foil on windows, door and window switches of various varieties, vibration switches, magnetic switches, etc., are used to complete the closed loop, and any break in that sensing circuit will immediately trigger the alarm. See Fig. 1-2.

The **photoelectric** alarm, or electric eye, is quite simple to understand; it provides reliable space or perimeter protection with an invisible beam of "black" or infrared light. Although

11

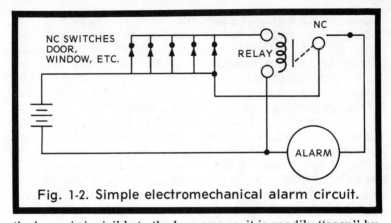

Fig. 1-2. Simple electromechanical alarm circuit.

the beam is invisible to the human eye, it is readily "seen" by the photoelectric cell receiver. The light source could be barely visible except for the infrared filter which eliminates this condition, and light from the newer solid-state light-emitting diodes is completely invisible to the eye. But if the beam is broken by anyone passing through it, the receiver activates a relay which causes an alarm. The careful positioning of a few units in strategic locations enables the user to protect quite a large area. The photoelectric system may be used to supplement or back up the usual foil and switch arrangement of the electromechanical system. Photoelectric units do find widespread use and are comparatively inexpensive; in fact, large areas around a building may be protected for a lower cost than would be possible with a wired job such as a foil and switch type arrangement, and with equivalent capability. The system may be extended considerably without additional units by using mirrors to project the beam around corners.

The **ultrasonic** detector has the capability to protect large open areas. Such a system will detect an intruder's movements regardless of where he is operating. The ultrasonic unit is usually a little more expensive than those already discussed, but it is easy to install and very reliable in most indoor locations. The transmitter sends out sound waves above the hearing range of the human ear, often around 20 kHz or higher. By tuning the receiver to the same frequency, it picks up the sound waves regardless of whether they are from the transmitter or merely echoes bouncing off the furnishings or equipment in the area. Of course, any motion in the room would change the frequency of these waves. Any change in frequency would be detected immediately by the master control system. As soon as the receiver and transmitter are not in "time" or not sending and receiving the same signal, master control detects the lack of balance between the two and automatically sets off the alarm. Thus, the system is nearly foolproof for most applications, but some have an added disadvantage in that the delicate balance required to insure adequate sensitivity restricts the location of the unit. It may not be installed near air conditioners, heat ducts, telephones, or other sources of sound or shock waves. See Fig. 1-3 for a photo of an ultrasonic detector unit.

The **proximity** or **capacity** type device is ideal for protecting a vault, safe or other critical point in an establishment against intrusion. As soon as the protected area or device is approached, the body capacity of the intruder is added to the balanced circuit, thus lowering the capacitive reactance, causing increased current flow in the monitoring circuitry which triggers the alarm condition. The theory may appear somewhat complex, but it is covered in detail in Chapter 8.

The **microwave** intrusion detector, or radar type device as it is often called, may be used to protect specific areas indoors or outdoors, and, although the cost is more than the photoelectric detector, it is usually less expensive than the ultrasonic type. The system operates on the same principle as that employed by airfields to detect approaching aircraft. The transmitted signal in the form of a radio wave bounces off the wall or other solid object and returns an echo to the receiver in the system. Any change in the wave pattern, as caused by the entry of an intruder, is immediately sensed by the receiver and the lack of balance triggers the alarm. This device is self-contained and normally purchased as a complete unit ready for immediate installation. See Fig. 1-4.

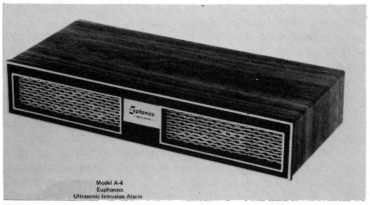

Fig. 1-3. Ultrasonic intrusion alarm device. (Courtesy Bourns Security Systems, Inc.)

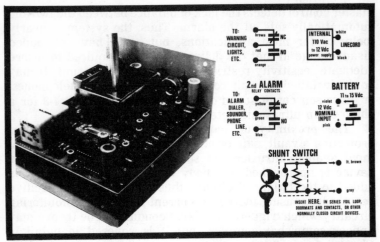

Fig. 1-4. Microwave security system, also called a "space switch."

An **audio** protective system, as used in many apartment buildings, is an intercom between the main entrance and each individual apartment. The system permits the occupant to talk to the visitor before tripping the front door lock. The electrically operated latch may be released only by the tenant, and if the party at the front door is unable to be properly identified, the lock button should not be pressed. The occupants of the building have a pass key for their own personal use in opening the door, and with reasonable cooperation between tenants, the system provides satisfactory protection for all. When opening the front door with a pass key, no one should be permitted to enter unless he is known or otherwise properly identified, and should be made to wait outside until necessary identification is provided.

A selective response from multiple audio detector networks may be provided by triggering circuits through threshold sensitivity coupling. This allows the alarm or responsive device to be triggered at preset sound levels to greatly reduce the chance of false alarms. Variations in sound levels in some areas make this system impractical because it covers too wide a range. Heavy machinery operating intermittently could provide an excessive variation and carpeted areas would result in the opposite extreme. In such cases, an audio system is useless unless numerous assists are included such as sound filters, time delay and sound cancelling circuits. If the usual low cost of the audio system had to be exceeded by too great a margin, consideration of other types of sensors would seem advisable. Where external noise is excessive, a sound balancing arrangement may be utilized through the use of internal and external sound transducers coupled to the usual discriminator, which would require the inside noise to be equal to or exceed the outside noise during any time segment. The vibration detector, although similar to the sound detector, does not have a diaphragm. Instead, its operation depends on the motion of a magnet surrounding a coil which induces a voltage in the coil as the lines of force are cut.

The video system or closed-circuit television (CCTV), as it is sometimes called, offers many additional features to overcome the limitations of sound and other types of security systems. Although the average cost figure would exceed most arrangements, the reliability and flexibility of the video method affords two major points for consideration when these features are mandatory. The closed-circuit camera and monitor loop does require continuous vigil, but even this disadvantage may easily be overcome by the addition of detection devices to signal the precise time such attention is warranted. The closed-circuit TV camera may easily be spotted by the subject to be watched, but this is often a deterrent to the thief and decoy cameras are frequently used on this assumption. Needless to say, we will not dwell on the effectiveness of simulated systems in this manual. If a dummy camera pays for itself, what would the real thing do for you? See Fig. 1-5.

Fig. 1-5. Typical closed-circuit TV camera. (Courtesy GBC Closed-Circuit TV Corp.)

Chapter 2
Business
Operations

Estimates differ greatly from job to job, but a definite rule of thumb should be applied. Since the time required will vary according to the ability and experience of the installer, your charge for labor must be somewhat flexible in the early stages. Since the rate per hour must be based on your speed, your rate per hour can be higher than average as soon as you are able to do the job faster than the average.

Consideration also must be given as to whether a monthly service fee has been included, and in such an event, the estimated installation fee would be less. Actually, it is wise to keep the installation fee as low as possible, or even skip it entirely if the monthly service charge is available. This enables you to give complete service to the prospective customer by taking care of his overall system, which includes preventive maintenance. However, if something goes wrong, it is definitely your job to repair it in short order. Of course, this entitles you to a reasonable fee, depending on such variables as the area covered and type of system involved, and should average about ten dollars per month for a local bell type system. A central station type system connected to telephone lines running either to police or central station monitors would call for a fee of around $35 to $50 per month due to the complex arrangement.

It is always wise to consider the competition, and keep your charges in line without undercutting. If a competitor is doing a good job and providing an honest service, try to keep your estimating figures in line with his as much as possible. Many small businesses as well as homes require only a basic alarm system which includes a sensing loop, control box and alarm bell, buzzer, siren or flashing light or combination. In such cases, window and door foiling, skylight lacing, system wiring, etc., involve labor costs plus material; therefore, a formula should be worked out to quickly enable you to come up with the proper figures. The installation of systems connected to a central station actually involves no additional charge because the leased lines utilized are charged directly to the customer by the telephone company. However, the monthly service charge associated with these systems are considerably higher.

Applying foil to windows, doors and other openings, along with skylight coverage (whether by lacing or sensors), wiring from other sensors or detectors, control box and responsive devices, plus the mounting of the units and their costs to the customer, should all be carefully computed. Proper estimating of foiling may be figured on the basis of the glass dimension by adding the measurement across the bottom to the sum of the two sides, based on a charge of 30 cents per running foot plus the cost of the reinforcement or 20 percent of the total for each section. Consider a glass pane of 2 ft. by 2 ft., for example, adding 2 feet for each side plus 2 feet across the bottom, the total is 6 running ft., or $1.80 total for the foiling. Then, adding 20 percent for the reinforcement, we have a figure of roughly $2.20. By the same method, a pane of glass having a dimension of 4 feet square (4 feet on either side plus 4 across the bottom) would give us a total of 12 feet at 30 cents per foot or a total figure of $3.60, plus 20 percent for reinforcements or $4.30 in round figures. In this way we can reach a fair estimate and at the same time come up with a reasonable figure that should be satisfactory to the customer and to the installer as well. Of course, we come up with a profit in material which is a way of handling overhead expense. Lacing skylights and doors, etc., should be figured on a time basis. The wire is very inexpensive and the framework should not be too high.

Obviously, preparations must be made before beginning this type of work and time may be figured on a reasonable basis, with the rate depending on the speed you have attained. Other items, such as running wires, can be approximated and you probably should set up a regular scale for running a wire to a bell or horn or other warning device, considering the number of feet and the surface material involved. The main thing when making an estimate is to cover your cost of material plus the approximate time required and allow a reasonable margin of profit for yourself in addition to these costs.

When installing a system with no service fee arrangement, the job should be figured on a contract with a profit added to cover the contract fee. However, in an installation of a system on a monthly fee basis, the profit received each month will enable you to keep the price considerably lower but yet sufficient to cover the costs of materials and time plus possible service calls or maintenance that might be required at regular periods. Emergencies will arise, but these will be few and usually you have a sufficient margin already built into the estimate to take care of normal problems of this nature. In cases where such emergences are due to area conditions of an unusual nature, special charges would have to be added to take care of above average calls that would be necessary on such installations. In all cases, a reasonable profit and a reasonable wage for the work, knowhow, etc., involved should be expected and all fees should be based on that conclusion. By keeping the fee low, the customer realizes that he is actually renting the equipment and is merely paying for service. This factor will probably insure renewal when the contract period expires. Such an arrangement will eliminate or at least reduce the chances of a competitor replacing your installation with his equipment and service.

In setting up a profit goal, the opportunities are unlimited. Good prospects for alarms may be easily located—schools, factories, industrial plants, offices, stores, apartment buildings and most types of businesses or individual locations with valuables on the premises. Your goal should be realistic, and if you're working part-time it should be figured on that basis. Considering a basis of 20 hours per week, 75 dollars would be a fair figure in the beginning, and as more experience is acquired, this figure could be increased to possibly 120 dollars for a 20-hour week. When switching to full time, the figure necessarily would probably be double; in other words, about $240 to $300 a week, which would cover such out-of-pocket expenses such as telephone and possibly a small ad in a local paper or even a small ad in the yellow pages of your local directory.

An ample margin should be available before going into it on a full-time basis and eliminating the regular job. Newcomers to the business have a tendency to become over-anxious to get started and do not allow themselves sufficient time to work the business up into a reasonable level before requiring withdrawals for living expenses week after week, which could reduce the chances of success from a business standpoint and possibly even jeopardize the whole effort. In other words, be sure of yourself and your ability to do the quality of work that would guarantee more business and improve the chances of growing by word-of-mouth advertising. Try to improve the operation, making it as efficient as possible; do a good job and at the same time don't overdo. Try to get a reasonable amount of free time and time away from the work. Your time should be figured out in advance. You should lay out a program and try to follow it through as closely as possible. By planning ahead and using your time wisely, the maximum amount of work can be done with a minimum of effort.

You will need to spend time explaining the operation of the burglar alarm system you are trying to sell your prospect, its potential and how much money it can save him in the long run. In many cases, a burglar alarm system is mandatory in order to get a decent insurance rate, and in such instances it should not be too difficult to point out the value of a good system that will meet with the approval of the insurance company. This would be especially true of a business that had been robbed previously or had sustained considerable losses. In such cases, a good system is required in order to avoid either prohibitive insurance rates or cancellation entirely.

By operating your alarm business from the home, you normally may expect the help and cooperation of the family, the wife and any older children and possibly an elderly person that may be living with you, such as an aunt or uncle, mother, father, mother-in-law, etc. The chore of keeping the books, sending bills to your customers and mailing circulars or advertising material to prospects, answering telephone calls, lining up appointments, handling the banking chores, keeping simple records, all can be handled entirely by members of the family. They can also prepare materials such as the reinforcements, wind the wire, measure various layouts, and connect wires according to your directions. By working the family into the operation you are holding your overhead expense to an absolute minimum while conserving your own time for things in the business that may be handled only by yourself. In this way, you are operating at top efficiency and your chances of success are much greater. The operation from the home in the beginning is also ideal because it eliminates the charge for rent, heat, light, and so forth that are required in an office or business place. Thus, your initial cost is held to a minimum. As the operation grows and is expanded to a full-time business, there will be plenty of time to find quarters that are larger and more desirable and at the same time not too expensive, and you will not be under any great pressure to make a change; it can be made gradually at your convenience and when your need is great enough and the profit is sufficient to handle the additional overhead of such an operation.

EXPANDING YOUR BUSINESS

Since you must make as many dollars per hour as possible you should figure your time in such a way as to use it to full advantage. This means not only the actual planning of your time, but rather exactly what you may do to get the most profit from each hour. In this way you will improve the operation to the extent desired. There is no sense in trying to sell the system to everyone in sight. Rather, you should select those businesses or persons in greatest need of your service, those to whom it would mean the most. These prospects are more capable of paying the most for a proper alarm system.

Although commercial establishments provide the most acceptable returns, in the beginning it may be best to work on private individuals in need of such protection; for example, friends of the family or even members of the family. By starting with these folks you can acquire the confidence necessary to really sell to the commercial establishments, pointing out the need and the capability of your company to do a job that is satisfactory for their specific operation. Naturally, you will find some that are just too big to handle, but there will be plenty well within your initial limited capability and many of these will prove most profitable, not only from a standpoint of dollars and cents but also for the recommendations they will provide and the doors they will open for even larger installations. There are areas where competition is limited, where it is not sufficiently competent to handle most of the businesses in the area. In these cases you may select the jobs that are best from a standpoint of time, effort and profit. Initially, you may have to take a little less money than you would expect, but as you gain experience and are able to do the job more quickly, your efficiency and speed will increase to a point where your rate per hour will increase accordingly.

Your business will grow automatically if you are careful to do the job as you know it should be done at a reasonable price. It is also vital that you stand behind your work. Guarantee it to be as represented. By gaining a good reputation for honest, proper installation, you will have more work than you can handle, and as you are able to put in more time and eventually hire help, you will find your business growing by leaps and bounds.

In hiring help, carefully screen each individual and check on references, aptitudes, etc. It may be desirable to have them go along and watch and assist you as you make an installation. When key personnel are hired who are capable of doing a job, then you can send others along to assist. As you gradually acquire several competent, dependable assistants, they, in turn, can train new personnel to do the work in the proper manner and in a way that will meet with your approval. By all means, check the individuals yourself that have been trained by others and make sure that they do the job the way you would have it done yourself according to your specifications and according to the plan adopted for the particular system.

Courteous personnel are important and all members of the firm must be carefully trained in this regard. Never argue with a customer, and if such appears to be necessary, that is, due to a disagreement with a customer, the supplementary personnel should refrain from comments and refer the customer to the owner or their immediate supervisor without making any comments whatsoever while maintaining a polite attitude at all times regardless of how far off base the customer may appear to be. In other words, you are building a business that depends on reputation. It is important to remember these simple rules: the customer is always right, and even if he appears to be wrong, we must try to pacify or compromise to his point of view.

It is impossible to keep good help without offering fringe benefits, as they are well known, in the form of insurance plans paid by the owner or employer and pension or bonus plans where an employee's benefits accrue as he spends additional time with the company. By rewarding your good employees with such plans and benefits, the reliable devoted type personnel so necessary to a business of this kind may readily be attained. The additional expense of such an arrangement should prove quite worthwhile

Service contracts are very desirable and should be your long-term goal in the business, because monthly contracts produce a steady income and make for an ideal arrangement. Nevertheless, some prospects will resist this type of agreement, such as a person in a nearby town who may want an alarm system installed in a home and the distance may be too great for regular service trips. There are conditions where a remote installation may require your services regularly and your fee would be enough to warrant the expense involved even in the routine service of such an installation. However, we should never turn down business because of the inability to get a monthly service fee, and when necessary the alarm may be installed and sold outright. In such instances, an additional fee would be required to provide the necessary profit above the actual cost of time and material. Such an arrangement would depend on your personal judgment, and just how close you were willing to work at the time, but it should be noted here that we must make a profit regardless, and any job on which a small profit is not possible is not worth the effort. It has often been said in jest, "We made nothing on this job but we hope to make twice as much on the next." However, I am sure you will not let this happen to you!

There will be cases when you wish to advise the customer that an outright sale is preferable from his standpoint as well as yours. Suppose Farmer Brown is having trouble with chicken thieves. An alarm installed in the chicken house would serve the purpose and he could easily turn off the device himself.

The monthly service fee, of course, will vary according to the installation, its size and the degree of supervision required, as in the case of a central station alarm where 24-hour supervision is necessary and a leased telephone line is involved from the customer's building. The fee could run considerably higher in such cases and should be carefully figured from the amount of responsibility required. For a simpler system, such as the ordinary electromechanical type, the fee could be as low as eight or ten dollars a month, including a routine checkout in the nature of preventive maintenance to make sure that everything is in proper working order. Calls should be made at regular intervals on such systems without the necessity of the owner calling for your service. Such preventive maintenance could be carried out on a two or three month basis regardless of call. Getting into the more complicated and vulnerable systems, a routine monthly call for maintenance would be necessary and the customer could count on this being made without his request.

As you consider expanding your business, your pricing structure and the number of service contracts should be given serious consideration. You must have a clear profit of at least 50 percent more than your regular weekly wage at your regular job before serious consideration may be given to a full-time operation. In other words, leave a reasonable margin for contingencies that are bound to arise at various times and have enough surplus to take care of such unforeseen periods that are bound to occur. The monthly service contracts may be written for a 2-year period or even longer, and you must be careful not to arbitrarily raise the fee when you do renew the contract, at least for the initial renewal. Many of your contracts will be written on a yearly basis at the beginning, but these, of course, should be worked into longer periods on renewal but not with an increased rate. If economic conditions do turn upward, it would be best to keep increases to a very small figure, not over five or ten percent tops. As you acquire more installations and more monthly contracts you will be operating on a more efficient basis and the volume of your sales will enable you to work much closer than you were able to do in the beginning.

No elaborate accounting or bookkeeping system is necessary. It is easy to keep track of installations and each estimate as you go along. As you send out bills, keep a duplicate or a record. Of course, as the business grows, more records, inventory, and bookkeeping will be necessary.

INSTALLATION TECHNIQUES

The installation of foil on the window glass should be preceded by a careful check of the fit of the glass or pane. If the glass is loose, tighten screws that are available but do not tighten the screws too much that would result in cracking the glass. Putty should be used where missing or loose and the old putty may easily be replaced with fresh putty. Window foil installation may be somewhat improved by proceeding as follows: Clean the window with ammonia and water, rather than a commercial cleaner which leaves a residue. Windows must be tight in their frames because foil will not stick on wet windows. Mark guidelines on the reverse side of the glass with chalk or water soluble ink, allowing a 3-inch space from the window frame. If you are using self-adhesive foil, you may disregard the application of a coat of foil varnish. If the foil is not self-adhesive, apply the varnish along the guidelines with a $\frac{3}{8}$-inch brush. By using a clear varnish, the excess may be easily removed after foil application. The varnish should be partially dry when the foil is applied in order to permit quick adhesion. In the beginning it may be advisable not to apply too long a strip of foil at one time. The ability to apply the foil in a straight line as desired will become easier with practice. In the beginning it may be necessary to apply small amounts of varnish at a time due to the length of time required for the careful application of the foil, but later on as your speed increases you can probably apply the varnish to the entire window area and then begin applying the foil immediately.

If a quick drying adhesive is used instead of varnish to apply the foil, the excess should be removed as soon as the foil has been attached before the adhesive has a chance to dry. A clean rag dampened with naphtha can be used to remove the excess. Since the foil may be applied rapidly after practice, the damp naphtha cloth may be used to smooth the foil while cleaning away the excess adhesive. Where varnish is used, the excess may be removed with benzine solution as a separate step.

At the beginning, the foil should be long enough to permit tacking it into the wood sash. The foil must be applied, without any air bubbles, perfectly smooth to the window with no bumps or ridges, and you should be able to apply a straight line of foil to the varnish line each time.

Of course, the foil is a good conductor and on windows and doors it acts just like wire and can be short-circuited, cut or grounded the same as a wire. There will be times when insulation is necessary. Of course, glass is not a conductor, nor is the wood frame, but where the foil crosses the metal frame of a window or door it must be insulated. When such is the case, you must use adhesive tape under the foil and if using the standard foil the ¾-inch adhesive tape may be used to allow sufficient margin where the foil crosses a metal frame or where it crosses from one window pane to another. If it crosses itself, be sure to insulate the one strip from the one crossing it. Cinder blocks, bricks, plaster and the like may act as a conductor in wet weather and it is advisable to run adhesive tape under foil whenever it comes in contact with these materials.

Now you're ready to apply varnish on top of the foil after permanent connections are made where the foil was torn or overlapped and where reinforcements were put in. Reinforcements are needed wherever the foil leaves the glass and goes on to the window frame and wherever the foil crosses a piece of wood or metal separating the panes in a multipane window. Be sure to prick holes in the reinforcements before varnishing. This is to provide positive contact between the layers. Never attempt to apply foil while a window is wet or damp or even frosted. In warm climates it is common practice to apply the foil with a type of water glue. Tinned shim brass or shim stock may be used to reinforce the foil where it leaves the glass and comes in contact with the window frame or goes from one pane to another over wood or metal cross members. The length of shim stock will depend on how far the cross member is away from the surface of the glass. The shim should be long enough to extend two inches in each direction past the cross member onto the glass after it is glued down.

The ultrasonic detector is very effective and widely used, although some are subject to false triggering. Causes of these nuisance alarms may be summed up briefly and in most instances quickly corrected. The most important and easiest to correct is the tendency to set the sensitivity control too high. Start at the lowest setting and gradually increase the sensitivity to get the exact area coverage desired and nothing extra. Check the setting under various conditions while keeping the detector away from drafts as caused by heat ducts, air conditioners, open windows or light weight movable objects, as well as pets. The ultrasonic detector will actually detect any motion including air, and even a fire in the fireplace can be detected. Ultrasonic signals in the area within range of the detector **must** differ in frequency or they could activate the unit. So if it's necessary for more than one motion detector to operate in the area, be sure they use different frequencies. Proximity to air-purifiers, ultrasonic cleaners, telephones or television receivers may also offer trouble and should be avoided.

The ability of the installer to follow a standard list of simple directions is all that is required. The installation may be made by carefully following directions and using the devices as explained in the manuals or brochures which normally accompany the shipment. Sloppy wiring or poor foil installation present a shabby appearance and the contacts may require considerable patching in order to get the system operating properly. In such an installation, considerable reliability is sacrificed. By taking your time until you become familiar with the type of work and making sure the runs and connections are neat and tight, customer satisfaction will provide the best form of advertising and the amount of business acquired as a result should be most rewarding. In the beginning, cutters, diagonals or a type of pliers, screwdriver and hammer are just about all that are needed. The testing meter, volt-ohmmeter as it is often called, which permits measurement of current, voltage and resistance with a sufficient accuracy, may be purchased at a very reasonable price: I would say under $10, possibly less than $5 in many cases. You will also need a soldering iron, and an electric drill may be purchased for under twenty dollars.

Chapter 3
Sensors & Detectors

Mercury switches have proven quite useful in loop applications where tilting windows or openings are being protected, but their inability to withstand shock or a bump greatly increases the chance of false alarms. The button-type switch as frequently installed behind a door will trigger the alarm or light a light the minute the door is opened and it is not susceptible to shock or bumping. The magnetic switch is a reed device that may be activated by a magnet attached to the window or door while the contact portion is attached to the jamb or door frame. There are two reeds or magnetic leaves that close the circuit when the magnet on the moving member pulls them together and completes the loop continuity.

A microswitch operates on a principle similar to the button type, although both sensitivity and cost are higher. This type switch is normally enclosed for protection against the weather and other adverse conditions, and the pressure required to activate it is quite small. Since overtravel is also small (less than one 100th of an inch), a roller type actuator is used. Sensitivity and low price are favorable features and most microswitches have the additional plus of easy installation, since only a screwdriver is needed. Vibration detectors are self-contained units, hardly larger than a microswitch, that may be mounted in the ceiling or wall to detect vibrations resulting from attempted break-ins through a wall or ceiling. This switch has a weight that is adjusted according to the sensitivity required on the contact. Since the contact is closed normally, jarring by the intruder will open the loop to set off the alarm.

One residential type door alarm provides reliable protection at low cost with an easy-to-install door-type alarm. An intruder opening the door sets off the alarm by tripping a magnetic actuator which triggers the alarm circuit, producing a shrill warning horn which can be silenced and reset only with the use of a key. This compact self-contained unit works equally well on in-swinging or out-swinging doors. The door is always available as an emergency exit, but the device will produce an alarm only when set. No wiring is required.

A quality home-type fire alarm is available from one manufacturer. The unit operates from house current with automatic transfer to a 6-volt standby battery in the event of power failure. As power is restored, the system automatically switches back to the house current operation. It also meets all UL requirements for supervision. The built-in trouble signal sounds if the thermostat wire breaks, power fails, or the system malfunctions. There is no limit to the number of thermostats that may be installed and connected to the unit. The manufacturers say more than half a mile of No. 18 wire may be used for the loop if necessary. A selector switch inside the locked cabinet serves several important functions. It silences the warning signal in the event of trouble, shuts the alarm off when necessary, and tests the complete alarm system including bells from the power line and standby battery. This invaluable test makes certain the standby is in working order. Pilot lights on the front of the cabinet warn when the control is either in trouble or in the "off" condition.

A smoke type alarm protects a home and family from house fires with an early warning smoke detector. Most fires produce smoke prior to the heat, and smoke is the principal killer. By fastening the smoke detector six to 12 inches from the ceiling and plugging it into the house power, any condition of 2 percent smoke density will sound the built-in horn type alarm. Smoke is detected as it enters a light source photocell optical path arrangement. When the light is reflected from the smoke into the cell, the alarm sounds. The case measures 4¾" x 8" x 2½" deep and weighs 2¾ lbs. The cost is comparatively low for this essential type of unit for home use.

Another alarm system detects smoke and heat from a fire. In this self-contained unit, a photocell light detector is triggered by an accumulation of no more than 4 percent smoke in the protected area, or a temperature over 135 degrees. The unit is ideal for homes or small businesses, and may be hung on the wall and plugged into the nearest receptacle. Operating on 110 volts AC with about a 10 watt power consumption and finished in white enamel, the unit is 8" x 4" x 2¼" and weighs about 2¾ lb. It comes complete with 9 feet of cord, all ready to plug in.

An economy fire alarm is available to fill an acute need for an effective warning of fire in the home. Being compact yet highly efficient and easy to install, the streamlined cabinet contains all necessary components including a specially designed, earsplitting blast horn, a relay and battery. The heavy duty 6-volt battery is normally good for a year. Practically any number of thermostats may be used and connected to the enclosed terminal strip. Provision is made to connect an outdoor bell where needed, in which case a 6-volt extra-heavy duty battery is used externally to replace the above battery. Periodic checks may be made by pushing a test switch, which tests all components, including the blast horn and relay and indicates if battery replacement is needed.

An inexpensive portable fire alarm which is completely mechanical and simple to hang on a nail or hook is available. No batteries or wiring are required. A permanent bi-metallic thermostat senses the temperature. The alarm is a 7-inch bell audible for a quarter of a mile. This is a mechanical device and requires no electrical power whatsoever. It weighs only 3 pounds and several are recommended for the average home.

A gas-powered fire alarm system is designed for simple wall installations for the home, office, or a public building. It requires only two screws to attach. The alarm is rated at 135 degrees F and is contained in an attractive unit. This unit also requires no wiring, batteries or external power. Two cylinders of Freon F12 provide the energy necessary to emit an alarm signal when abnormally high temperatures occur. The fusible metal plug melts to release the Freon and the resulting alarm signal, which is a piercing whistle with a duration of at least four minutes at a sound level of no less than 85 decibels. The alarm is packaged in a gold-colored case and locations are unlimited. A built-in visual indicator cautions the owner if the energy pack is getting low on gas. The alarm measures 4½" x 4¾" x 2¾" deep and weighs merely 2 pounds.

A professional type ultrasonic intruder detector utilizes three ultrasonic channels and is capable of six hours operation on a rechargeable standby power. It is completely tamper proof and UL listed. This type detector is designed for use by professional installers in either commercial installations or homes. It fills a trap zone with an ultrasonic screen that cannot be seen, felt or heard. Walls and furniture reflect the energy to the receiver and the slightest frequency shift caused by movement, such as an intruder in the protected zone, actuates the output alarm relay. When the trap zone or protected area has been selected, the unit may be placed anywhere, such as on a desk, table, on the wall, or even on the ceiling. The output may be connected to any type of an alarm system. Normally closed relay contacts can trigger local alarm bells, high intensity lights, horns, actuate a telephone dialer, or signal a central switchboard. A 12-volt AC transformer provides external power. The nicad standby batteries are continuously charging from the AC power and take over automatically when the power fails. If the battery becomes discharged, the unit will go into an alarm condition.

Up to three units may be operated in the same room area using three different frequency channels. The nominal trap zone is 18 feet in range, 14 feet wide, depending, of course, on the reflecting qualities of the room. A range or sensitivity control is located in a tamper proof rear compartment. An adjustment allows the range to be reduced to half of normal. The alarm is packaged in a solid walnut external case with an internal one-sixteenth aluminum rear access plate. Tamper switch protected, the unit measures 9¾" wide by 8¼" deep by 3¼" high and weighs 6 pounds. Input power is 12 volts AC at 10 volt-amperes, 60 Hz, or 18 volts DC at 100 ma. The standby nicad battery has a typical 6-hour discharge capacitor and 24-hour recharge. Ultrasonic frequencies: channel A, 39-39.5 kHz; channel B, 41-41.5 kHz; channel C, 37-37.5 kHz. The normally closed output relay contacts are designed to switch currents ranging from .5 to 200 ma.

The subminiature infrared intrusion detector is a highly efficient system which may easily be concealed in any indoor protected area. It is small enough to blend into the background and thus defy detection. It may be installed in pictures on the wall, receptacles, plaques, door jambs, radios and mirrors. Using the interrupted beam principle, facing units provide an invisible infrared protective screen. The compact transmitter and receiver units may be either battery powered or operate from a 110-volt AC source. The transmitter emits short pulses of infrared energy to the detector. If the chain of pulses is interrupted, an alarm results. Alignment is quite simple due to the wide beam width on both units. Other features include a solid-state infrared source and low false alarm rates. The unit is not sensitive to lightning flashes, power failures, and spoofing attempts have no effect. The range is 75 feet and angular alignment adjustment is 40 degrees, both vertical and horizontal. The units do not have to be opposite each other. The input power may be either a Neda 904 dry cell battery, which is capable of one year of life, or a power pack operating from 120 volts AC with a 24-hour standby rechargeable battery. Both are offered as options. Transmitter and receiver each are a compact 2¾" x 1⅞" x 9-16" (less the flange) and weigh 6 ounces. A galium arsenide infrared source is used with a beam width of 5 degrees minimum. Power supply size is 2¼" by 3¾" by 2¾" including batteries and weighs 12 ounces. One power supply can operate both transmitter and receiver, or separate supplies may be used. The alarm output actuates a normally open, normally closed momentary closure nonlatching relay with a one second hold. The unit comes complete with the false duplex receptacles on both units.

A self-contained infrared type intruder detector senses movement and is not affected by sound, air turbulence or radio interference. The A-2 infrared detector utilizes infrared or heat radiation to detect intruders. A non-transmitting passive detector senses infrared radiation from the walls, floors, and all objects within the protected area to establish the nonalarm, reference condition. If an intruder enters the protected area, his body heat creates a rapid change in the infrared radiation which is detected by the A2 infrared detector. Infrared will not penetrate construction materials, including glass, and this passive sensor will not detect radiation outside of the protected area, which eliminates the possibility of false alarms from this cause. The unit is capable of detecting the infrared energy from a human moving one foot per second or faster over an area 20 feet square.

No range or sensitivity adjustments are required, and the unit is easy to install. Mounted usually 8 to 10 feet above the floor on a wall or ceiling, the infrared detector provides surveillance of a 74' x 74' area. The cover and the cables are tamper proof. The detectors diameter is 2½" by 4½" long and is mounted on a swivel base. It comes complete with a step-down transformer to provide 24-volt AC from the 115-volt AC 60-Hz source. The current draw is 0.5 watts maximum. The alarm relay output is rated at 2 amps, 115 volts AC or 0.1 amp, 130 volts DC. Both normally closed and normally open contacts, single pole, double throw, are contained in the unit. Ambient temperature range is -20 degrees F to +140 degrees F. Optional nicad batteries are provided for four hours standby and may be mounted in the base where a trickle charger maintains them at full charge.

Automatic photoelectric light controls are popular and useful fixtures for the home owner or small business man. The indoor model, in an attractive housing, needs only to be connected to the power line. Then any lamp plugged into the control will turn on at dusk and off at dawn. The outdoor version is weather resistant, designed for outdoor post lamps, entrance lights, floodlights and displays. The unit has a 300-watt capacity to safeguard your property against burglarizing, vandalism, and accidents. These units are UL approved.

An economy 2-unit photoelectric warning system consists of a light source and receiver. When the beam is interrupted, the receiver relay activates and supplies 110 volts AC (up to 300 ma) to a bell, alarm, counter, light or other responsive device. The sensitivity amplifier in the receiver may be adjusted in intensity and the infrared filter on the light source provides an invisible beam. The unit is very useful around the home or business as a burglar alarm, in stores for surveillance and door openings, or in plants or warehouses for counting, sorting, and protecting restricted areas. Each unit is packaged in a strong metal case measuring 5" long by 3" wide by 4" high.

A mini-microwave detector offers a high level of intrusion security at low cost. It detects very slow movement and precise area coverage. The self-contained unit sounds an alarm from small and slow intruder motions by sensing frequency changes due to the Doppler effect between the transmitted and received signals. It is designed for space protection of small to moderate sized areas, such as offices, storerooms and small retail stores and provides trap protection of key areas in large buildings. The unit detects very slow movements and does not react to air turbulence, drafts, noise, temperature change or humidity.

Using the X-band radio frequency, the antenna pattern may be precisely controlled to limit coverage, and this often permits operation near moving objects without interference. The mini-microwave antenna normally covers a 20-foot wide by 30-foot long area and has an optional antenna adapter providing a pattern about 15 feet wide by 50 feet long. Depending on the range control setting, the device is capable of detecting a man-sized target moving from 3 inches per second to 10 miles per hour. A walk test light aids in range control adjustment prior to actual operation. The fail-safe circuit monitors operation and goes into an alarm condition if a malfunction occurs. A special circuit filters electrical noise, random motion and transience. Tamper-proof features cause an alarm if signal or power wires are cut or if voltage drops and it is powered by 115 volts AC through a 12-volt plug-in transformer. The transmitted power is 2 milliwatts at 10.525 GHz (X-band). Operating temperatues are -30 degrees to +140 degrees F. Output relay contacts are rated at 2.0 amp at 115 volts AC, 0.1 amp at 130 volts DC. Both normally closed and open (SPDT) contacts are included. This potent low-cost detector is only 2½" in diameter by 4½" long mounted on a hinged base, with a back cover designed to fit a standard electrical box. An optional power pack provides four hours of continuous standby operation in the event of power failure and contains sealed lead dioxide batteries with charging circuit to recharge and maintain the charge. Switchover is automatic, insuring uninterrupted operation. The power pack uses 1.8 watts and the battery voltage is 12 volts DC at 0.25 amps, with a capacity of 1.8 amps. The weight is 2½ lbs. and provides high quality compact protection.

The radar space switch type of unit provides microwave penetration of roof, doors, walls and windows. It operates on AC or battery power and is a compact solid-state unit utilizing a two-stage filter to minimize false alarms. This unit is an all solid-state microwave UHF Doppler radar system providing wall-to-wall and floor to ceiling protection and covers as much as 3500 square feet or a 30-foot radius. The microwave transmissions penetrate most non-metallic structures such as plaster, wood and concrete but are reflected by metal. Thus, an entire premise may be protected and movements such as an intruder makes will set off an alarm circuit, while a digital filter rejects movements by small animals. The movement by an intruder triggers the first alarm stage within seconds. If no further movement is detected, the unit resets. Further movement, however, triggers a second stage in the alarm. The alarm duration is adjustable from seconds to several minutes.

Installation requires only power and alarm connections unless a larger system is required. The on-off switch is tamper proof, and since tampering with the shunt switch circuit produces an alarm, this series circuit can include window foil, magnetic and vibration contacts as well as floor mats. The antenna coverage is omnidirectional, and the transmission is 4 milliwatts at 400 MHz. The alarm duration is adjustable from 5 to 200 seconds and the single-pole double throw (SPDT), output relay is rated at 1 amp at 250 volts, normally open and normally closed. The device is 3¾" high by 6" wide by 7" deep without the antenna, and the weight is 4 lbs. Input power is 115 volts AC at 3 VA or 12 volts DC at 80 ma, battery optional. It is mounted in a steel cabinet with two 2¼" x 20" nuts.

One system uses pull traps in a low-cost reliable constant duty switch. The alarm goes off when an intruder pulls out the clip by touching the wire. Fine black wire or nylon fishing line may be run at knee level in protected areas. The traps have cast brass for contacts. They are available in closed-circuit non-insulated pull traps with brass trap clips included, or closed-circuit insulated pull traps with a clear plastic base and brass trap clips included. Open circuit insulated pull traps, clear plastic base, fiber trap clips are included and replacement brass or fiber clips are available.

Microswitches are offered in a variety of sizes and different degrees of actuator travel and operating forces. They provide easy and reliable answers for tamper switches on doors, boxes and windows. Quality installations rely on these tiny, unobtrusive units. They can be connected for normally open or normally closed circuits, and terminals are generally three 6-32 screws with cap washers on the bottom. Standard size switches have an electrical rating of 15 amps at 125v AC and 0.5 amp at 125v DC. Some units are available in plastic packages 1.940" long by .94" high by .687" deep, with two mounting holes on 1-inch centers.

Reed magnetic switches with rhodium contacts are UL listed and shock resistant. They're low cost, easy to install and have revolutionized the installation industry. Since they're essentially free from false alarms, reed magnetic switches offer a simple way to protect most every opening. When the magnet is located 1 inch or less from the switch, the switch is pulled in. When the two are separated, the switch resumes its normally open or closed position. They replace many limit or plunger type switches and may be mounted in any direction. The reed magnetic contacts are self-insulating and mounted in modern, slim housings only ½" x ½" x 3⅞" and are molded of high temperature, impact resistance, gray metallic polystyrene. The rhodium contact material eliminates contact freezing in a hermetically sealed switch. The finest Alnico No. 5 magnet insures indefinite life under continuous operation. Powerful 3-inch magnets are used for locations near steel. Maximum contact ratings are 15 watts or 400v DC at 1 amp. The contact resistance is .060 ohms. The switches are available with a 2-inch magnet or a 3-inch magnet and in normally opened or normally closed configuration.

All types of movable windows and doors such as sliding windows and doors, French, tilt, double-hung windows, etc., may be connected to an alarm system by combination magnetic contacts. The switch consists of a magnetic contact and coiled two-conductor cord. Foil or other circuit connections made on movable portions of doors or windows connect directly to terminals provided on the contact housing, eliminating the need for separate flexible cords. A coiled cord extends four feet and is only 9 inches retracted. The magnetic contacts are the same as previously mentioned for reed type. The recessed magnetic contacts are practically invisible with proper installation and merely require drilling and gluing. This new widely accepted switch frustrates intruders or stay-behinds. It is next to impossible to locate or shunt because of concealed installation. The sensor consists of a single-pole normally open switch which is sealed in a black cylindrical type package with 6-inch leads. The switch is rated at 10 watts to 100 volts DC at 0.5 amps maximum and the contacts are rhodium to eliminate sticking. A powerful magnet is included of Alnico V designed for optimum magnetic force. Both units are 7/16" diameter by 1⅛" long and may be easily recessed with a 7/16" drill. As the magnet is moved away from the switch, the switch will open to trigger the alarm. It should be used with normally closed systems.

VIBRATION DETECTOR

Vibration detectors are designed to sense crowbar and hammer burglary attempts through walls and ceilings. These quality vibration detectors may be used on all kinds of construction such as hollow tile, plaster and lathe, brick, concrete, metal ceilings or wood. After mounting, the desired pressure can be set. The detector can take terrific abuse without damage and they are widely used for high security applications such as central stations and banks. Construction is of stainless steel with a chrome finished cover. The size is 3½" long by 1" wide by ⅞" high.

RIBBON SWITCHES

Ribbon switches are available with built-in contacts along its entire length. This modern, all-purpose continuous strip momentary contact switch solves alarm, signal and control problems easily, reliably and inconspicuously. It is constructed of clad spring tempered conductors with primary Mylar insulation, and the extruded Vinyl jacketing is tough and highly resistant to acids, alkalis and oils. The switches will withstand hammer blows and the cable grade polyvinyl jacketing will withstand the toughest abrasion. They are quite versatile and can be operated by hand, foot or vehicle wheels. The switches are flat and inconspicuous (⅛-inch thick), appearing as a neat plastic strip that blends quietly with decors. The ribbon switches bend around sharp radii and may be coiled like cable. The material may be cut to any desired length with shears and installation made with adhesive, staples or special moulding. Connections are made by soldering or available fittings. Several finger pressure sensitivities are available and countless applications in many fields can be served. The switch is designed for currents up to 1 amp at 117 volts AC or 28 volts DC. The 12- and 40-ounce varieties are provided with moulded terminals, while the 8-ounce sensitivity type has heat-sealed ends. All have 24-2 lead wires 18 inches long on one end. The switches are usually available in various lengths.

ANNUNCIATOR KIT

A complete entrance signal system is actuated by a footstep on the mat, which strikes a pleasant dual note chime.

Offices, stores, homes and institutions will value this system comprising a Tapeswitch mat (18 inches by 24 inches), dual note chime, plug-in transformer, 30 feet of wire, plus hardware and operating instructions. It operates on 115-volt AC power.

UNDER-CARPET SWITCHING RUNNER

A low-cost area detector switch can be made to fit any need from continuous runner material 30 inches wide and only three 32nd-inch thick. Roll stock may be cut to any length. The wire connections are tinned for easy soldering or twist connections may be easily made. A 5-pound pressure activates the switch and ribbon switch elements on 2⅞" centers are wired in parallel and encased in polyethylene. It is easily installed and concealed under carpeting, floor tile or rubber runner. Runner is supplied in 5 or 25 foot rolls that may be cut with scissors to lengths that cover the desired area. Especially suitable for home alarms, annunciators, vault or safe areas, or safety warning. See Figs. 3-1 and 3-2.

TAPESWITCH MATS

For entryways and floor switching, a grid of ribbon switches on 2¾-inch centers is bonded between vinyl sheets to allow area switching. This thin, sensitive mat, shown in Fig. 3-3, may be overlaid with carpet, plastic floor covering or entrance mats. A 5-pound pressure activates this 17-inch by 23-inch by three 32nd-inch thick detector. Suitable for 24 volt circuits, the contacts are rated at 1 amp, 117 volts AC, and a 6 foot 24-2 wire is included. Fig. 3-4 is a diagram of a complete closed circuit protective system.

Fig. 3-1. Under-rug runner switching device. (Courtesy Tapeswitch Corp.)

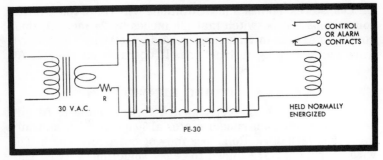

Fig. 3-2. Drawing of the PE-30 (Fig. 3-1) under-rug switch circuit.

CASH REGISTER PROTECTION KIT

Cash register protection is available with a package designed for areas where the register cannot be opened from the customer's side of the counter. Only an authorized person behind the counter stepping on the concealed mat may open the register. It is easy to install by plugging the register into the relay provided at the power outlet and concealing the mat near the register which increases the security considerably. The kit includes a 6-inch by 23-inch mat with 6 feet of lead wire and miniature plug, plug-in relay (5A at 117 volts AC) and instructions.

Fig. 3-3. Tapeswitch mat. (Courtesy Tapeswitch Corp.)

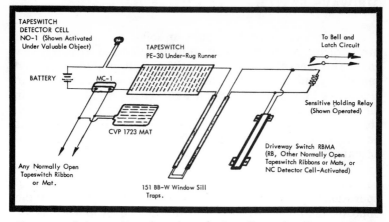

TAPESWITCH
DETECTOR CELL
NO–1 (Shown Activated
Under Valuable Object)

TAPESWITCH
PE-30 Under-Rug Runner

To Bell and
Latch Circuit

BATTERY

MC–1

Sensitive Holding Relay
(Shown Operated)

CVP 1723 MAT

Driveway Switch RBMA
(RB, Other Normally Open
Tapeswitch Ribbons or Mats, or
NC Detector Cell-Activated)

Any Normally Open
Tapeswitch Ribbon
or Mat.

151 BB–W Window Sill
Traps.

Fig. 3-4. Schematic of a closed circuit protective system.

FOOT SWITCH

A foot switch is perfect for a concealed alarm, door opening, counting or a safety switch. It is rated at 100 watts with a 5-pound nominal foot pressure, and uses ribbon switches, both momentary and normally open, sealed in a moisture proof flat pad 2 inches by 5 inches by ¼-inch thick. May be taped or cemented to the floor and has leads 18-2, 6 feet long.

ANTI-SHOPLIFTING WAFER SWITCH

The small flat switches in Fig. 3-5 will sound an alarm when objects placed on them are removed, and their small size (1½ inches in diameter by 3/16 inches thick) makes them hard to see. Nominal sensitivity is 2 pounds with 22-2 leads, 18 inches long. They are available normally open or normally closed.

Fig. 3-5. Wafer switches designed to prevent shoplifting.

AIR-WAVE SWITCH

An air-wave switch is able to solve a wide variety of mechanical sensing and controlling problems at extemely low cost. This versatile, highly sensitive unit provides unusual sensitivity and durability. The switch body is divided into two chambers by a sensitive diaphragm where slight changes in air pressure are connected to the switch through two $\frac{1}{8}$-inch stems. An air pressure wave as light as one inch of water is adequate. Even breathing on the open pressure stem will actuate the switch.

A pair of adjustable spaced silver contacts can be left normally open or brought together for normally closed operation. A pressure wave on one chamber, or vacuum on the opposite chamber, will operate the device. Applications include auto treadles, individual safety switch or automatic door opener. In perimeter alarms, one switch is capable of detecting disturbances on inexpensive plastic or rubber tubing to several hundreds of feet. Contact rating is 1 amp at 300 volts AC, actuation pressure from 1 to 16 inches $H20$ (adjustable pressure or vacuum), and the actuation time is less than 20 milliseconds. The case is made of thermoset plastic 2.2 inches high by 1.2 inches wide by 2.25 inches long and weighs about 3 ounces.

CIRCULAR CONVEX DETECTION MIRRORS

Convex mirrors installed in stores, business and service stations will detect shoplifters or intruders and provide wide-angle vision to permit seeing around corners. They're available in 16- or 26-inch diameters with indoor type quality glass mirrors.

ONE-WAY VISION MIRRORS

One-way mirrors appear as regular mirrors from the front but permit photography through glass from the rear. They are of proven value to reduce theft in factories and stores. However, the rear viewing area must be darker than the area being observed.

FIXED TEMPERATURE DETECTORS

These widely used, inexpensive units are self restoring, reliable and snap acting when a preset temperature is exceeded. The electrical contacts close with heat and are self restoring when the heat is removed. Some units are designed to cover 400 square foot with a normal temperature pattern, using 136 degree F unit to 200 degree F unit for boiler rooms or attics. Each device is 2 1/16 inches in diameter and 15/16 deep and the normally open contacts are rated at 6 to 125 volts AC, 6 amps, or 6 to 28 volts DC, 3 amps.

FIXED TEMPERATURE & RATE OF RISE DETECTORS

These units provide two distinct fire detection capabilities with a carefully calibrated rate of rise element that senses an abnormal rise in air temperature as produced in flash fires. Upon removal of heat, the contacts restore themselves, but if a factory preset temperature is exceeded, the fusible link is melted, the contacts close and the detector must be replaced. Most locations are 136-degree F units; abnormally hot areas require 190-degree F units. They're 3 3/16 inches in diameter by 2 3/16 inches long with normally open contacts.

SMOKE SWITCH

Available is a smoke switch designed for remote actuation of alarm signals. Abnormal accumulations of smoke will trigger the alarm which results when a 2 to 4 percent condition exists. The photocell circuit operates to close the normally open switch and pull in the relay. Contacts are rated at 120 volts AC at 1 amp and it operates on 115 volts AC. The switch is 7¾ inches high by 4⅜ wide by 2¼ deep and weighs 18 ounces. Complete with indicator light, mounting plate, template, instructions and wiring diagram.

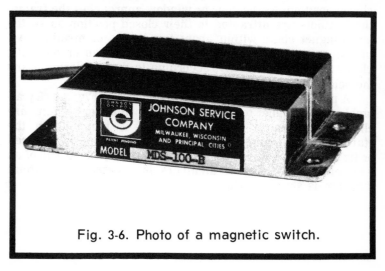

Fig. 3-6. Photo of a magnetic switch.

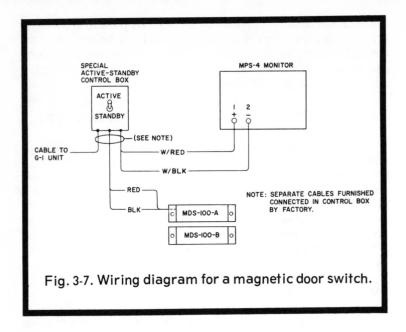

Fig. 3-7. Wiring diagram for a magnetic door switch.

MAGNETIC CONTACTS

Magnetic contacts are probably the most popular for adequate protection of doors and windows. The magnetic element attached to the movable (door-window) member causes the switch element on the stationary (frame) member to be attracted from its normally open position and assume a closed position. As the door or window approaches the frame, the contacts are attracted to their closed position as switch and magnet come within about two inches of meeting. Applications and variations of the normally open or normally closed contacts are many, according to the requirement and the selected use by the installer.

A photo of a magnetic switch is shown in Fig. 3-6. By attaching the magnet to the door, all movable connections are eliminated because the switch itself is mounted on the stationary door frame. The magnet must be properly centered or its pulling power will not be sufficient; only about 1/16 of an inch clearance between members is necessary. A circuit diagram is shown in Fig. 3-7.

Chapter 4
Electromechanical Alarm Systems

The electromechanical system functions by opening the circuit in the "sensing" mode. It is a normally closed circuit holding a relay in its energized position. Thus, the relay contacts are held open to prevent power from reaching the alarm (response circuit). The normally closed contacts resume their natural position when power is interrupted to the relay coil and the alarm is triggered immediately. Any break in the sensing loop, caused by opening of the switches or other sensors therein, will open the relay holding circuit by removing its power source.

The sensing switches or other devices used in the sensing loop may be any of the common variety such as microswitches, mercury switches, button switches or other pressure types, foil circuit around the glass to protect the premises against glass breakage, or any of the more complex types as is discussed later. A solid-state circuit utilizing a single transistor may be used in the relay loop to trigger a silicon controlled rectifier or similar device to trigger the alarm or relay directly or through a relay holding circuit arrangement.

These systems are quite simple and inexpensive but have quite a few limitations. They are usually overcome by a skilled burglar since the foil on the windows is quite noticeable and a more professional thief can easily manage to cut the glass without breaking the tape or he may even bypass the tape with an improvised jumper arrangement. Another problem is the difficulty in protecting all possible means of entry such as the ceiling, walls, floor and windows or doors, and once the intruder gains entry the system is of little value. However, the inexperienced thief can often be discouraged by such a system and the low cost is well worthwhile for the limited value of the system. One of the major advantages of the electromechanical system is as a backup for a much more sophisticated arrangement. Although the inexperienced burglar may be discouraged by the threat of even this simple system, the skilled burglar or professional type would feel safe in defeating the system while overlooking the more complex system that is used in addition to the electromechanical type. In other words, he may fall prey to the ultrasonic or

Fig. 4-1. Detectron 410 signal processing module with two pulsors.

microwave type system which is used in conjunction with the electromechanical type and would discover his mistake too late to escape.

Electromechanical systems all utilize sensors or transducers of various types which actuate the communication link that triggers responsive action. Spot protection covers obvious points of entry such as windows or doors, which have foil and magnetic or button switches to signal a break-in or opening. Pressure mats, panic buttons and heat sensors all are connected to the centrally located control box, which is in itself protected with a set of tamper contacts. The control box takes care of the appropriate responsive action, which may include several extremely complex actions.

PULSOR LOAD CHANGE DETECTION SYSTEM (DETECTRON, MODEL 410, 412)

The solid state "load change" type transducer used in this system insures positive indoors or outdoors intrusion detection, since it is not affected by environmental conditions such as humidity, temperature, age and other variables. Easily installed, these pulsors detect the intruder's movement by electrical pulses which are amplified in the 410 signal processing module. The signal processing module operates on

12 volts DC at 30 ma with the ability to handle up to 16 individual pulsors. It provides relay closure in the alarm state and may be wired directly into the security perimeter loop.

Each pulsor consists of a microscopic transducer crystal encapsulated in polyurethane for optimum protection, and it may be epoxied to strategic places such as floors, walls, stairs, and porches where the intruder probably would walk (see Fig. 4-1).

Parts of the building that support weight would offer the proper location for pulsors. The best way to select locations is to check doors, windows, halls while observing traffic patterns and tracing the most likely route for the intruder to take. This will help to pinpoint the exact location and the pulsor may be cemented to the midpoint of the longest span of a structural member, as shown in Fig. 4-2. Specifications for both models are listed below:

Model 410, Signal Processor

Electrical requirements:	12 volts DC, 30 ma
Pulsor input:	Up to 16 pulsors
Pulsor output	C-Form relay closure, 1 amp contacts
Dimensions:	4" long, 2" wide, 2" high
Weight:	6 ounces
Construction:	Blue steel case

Model 412, Pulsor

Electrical resistance:	1,000 ohms (nominal)
Excitation voltage:	1.5 volts DC max. (from signal processor)
Mounting:	Epoxy (included)
Dimensions:	3½" by ⅝" encapsulated
Weight:	2 ounces

DETECTOR INDUSTRIES SENTRY ALARM

This small, inexpensive, self-contained unit with a temperature sensor will set off the enclosed siren at 135 degrees F in case of fire. Window and door type switches may be connected to the unit to provide an intrusion warning alarm. It affords protection against fire and burglary, and operates from enclosed batteries (Fig. 4-3).

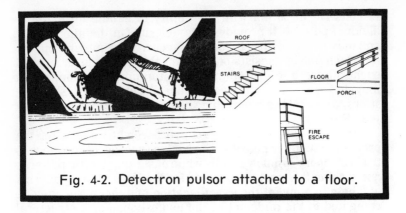

Fig. 4-2. Detectron pulsor attached to a floor.

DETECTOR REFLECTOR

A convex mirror, providing a panoramic vision of the installation area, makes complete coverage of a store, office, factory or room area possible at a single glance. Sturdily constructed and handsomely finished, the reflected image is clear and bright. Models are offered in round shapes for indoors or outdoors and from 13 inches in diameter to 36 inches. Rectangular and unbreakable acrylic plastic models are also available. Indoor units are made with a white rim; outdoor

Fig. 4-3. Detector Industries Sentry alarm provides fire and intrusion warning.

units have a waterproof rubber rim and weatherproof backing. The Detector Reflector mirror carries a lifetime guarantee and his proven most successful for stopping inventory shrinkage.

THREE-B ELECTRONICS ALARM

The TBE103 alarm system (Fig. 4-4) is a solid-state system offering a built-in fire alarm and preset timing controls. The TBE103 operates on AC power and transfers automatically to battery operation if power fails. The device functions as a closed or open circuit loop, with a separate open-circuit loop for thermostats and a fire warning horn. Remote control stations are available, too.

The TBE 103 has a built-in fire alarm which will sound the siren when a temperature of 135 degrees F is reached. A red and black wire in a plastic jacket is provided for fire-stats and horns. This circuit should be used only where a separate warning signal is necessary. Connect a 12-volt battery (TW-2 or equivalent) to the red and black wire as shown in Fig. 4-4.

To set the alarm, check all protected openings to see that they are closed. Turn the switch to the **on** position. The green light will come on to indicate that all openings are closed.

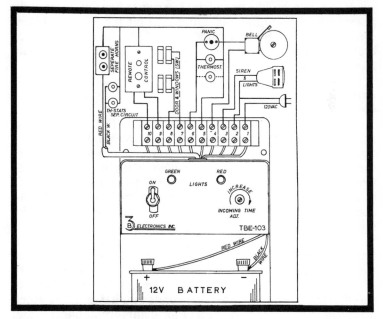

Fig. 4-4. Wiring diagram of the Three-B Electronics Model TBE 103 alarm system.

Fig. 4-5. Kolin Industries, Inc., Model ES-900 electronic siren.

Time alloted is 30 seconds from the time the switch is in the **on** position. If the red light comes on, put the switch in the **off** position and recheck doors and windows.

When entering the premises, the owner has approximately 15 seconds to go to the panel and shut off the alarm. (Timer can be adjusted from 0 to 30 seconds.) When an intruder breaks in and the protective circuit opens, a bell will ring and 30 seconds later a siren will follow.

KOLIN INDUSTRIES, MODEL ES-900, ALARM

This electronic siren warning device (Fig. 4-5) emits a loud attention-getting penetrating, rapid yelping sound quite similar to the new sirens used on police, fire and emergency vehicles. Tone varies from low to high automatically. The ES-900 is completely transistorized with the entire electronic circuitry and rust-proof anodized aluminum trumpet built into a single integral unit which is waterproof. The unit actually functions under water, according to the manufacturer.

Power required is 12 volts DC at 750 ma and it will continue to operate when the battery drops to lower voltages. The frequency sweep is 500 Hz to 1,600 Hz with a sweep duration of 0.5 seconds. The device is 6 inches long, 5¾ inches high with 5¼-inch trumpet; it weighs 1½ pounds and has a heavy steel, black finish mounting. It is ideal for commercial burglar and fire alarm systems, pleasure craft, stores, factories, banks, commercial vehicles, military and police applications.

Chapter 5
Photoelectric Alarms

Perimeter protection systems, operating on beams of invisible (infrared) light, with coded pulses to eliminate the risk of false alarms from small animals or falling objects, offer reliable coverage to distances as great as 500 feet. The use of properly mounted mirrors allows protection to be extended around corners without the use of additional light transmitters or receivers.

All types of motion-sensing systems may be used to offer adequate volume protection under a wide range of conditions, and since all may be triggered by authorized persons as well as the intruder, they are more susceptible to false alarms. In an effort to furnish a truly reliable intrusion system, features from each have been combined to achieve that ultimate result. Light-emitting diodes (LEDs) are now available to insure a margin of safety never before possible. LEDs have an infinite life expectancy as well as an amazingly low operating cost. Their invisible rays are used in more inexpensive photoelectric systems for the home or small business than ever before. Although it is quite possible for the "pro" to avoid the light beam, his movements may be somewhat restricted as a result, and this factor could make him more vulnerable to other backup detectors.

BASIC PHOTOELECTRIC SYSTEM

A beam of light on a photocell causes a relay to close and the alarm contacts remain open as long as the light is maintained on the photocell receiver. As soon as the beam is interrupted for any reason, the relay drops out, which closes the contacts and energizes the alarm. In other words, the relay contacts for the alarm circuit are normally closed (NC), and as long as the relay coil is energized the NC contacts remain open and the source of power to the alarm bell or horn is not connected.

The visible light beam is no longer useful and even the invisible infrared beam has far too many limitations, since it can be blocked by external light and other methods. The modulated light beam bypasses the flashlight approach easily, and by offering a reference signal to the phase detector, ample DC output is available only when the received light is in phase with that reference signal. In any other case, the relay will drop out, and trigger an alarm immediately. Using this approach in conjunction with such solid-state devices as the LEDs, results in a system that is practically impossible to defeat. As with all current alarm equipment, vacuum tubes are passé and solid-state devices are used throughout to ensure lower cost and far greater reliability.

INSTALLATION

The installation of these units is quite simple, and by following the plain language of the instruction sheet, few if any problems are likely to result, except in the most unusual circumstances. This type of device is quite widely used where an inexpensive system with fairly good efficiency is required. The receiver and transmitter must be aligned, which dictates a location at a point where the beam would be broken or interrupted only by an intruder.

If the location is outdoors, the beam must be high enough that small animals crossing its path would not trigger the alarm, and this suggests a height of two to four feet as being most desirable. You should decide how many light sources are needed to adequately cover the area desired and how many receivers or electric eyes as well. A rough sketch of the premises often assists in reaching a correct decision, and a top view will enable the use of mirrors in some cases to reduce the actual cost of the installation. The actual distances covered by each beam may be long as possible. The beam should pass the important sections to be protected such as showcases, cash registers, safes and other sections of the premises where valuables are ordinarily kept. The light source and receiver should be high enough to permit the beam to pass over the tops of counters so that an intruder would have to cross the beam, which in turn would trigger the alarm. Electric eyes, as they're called, must be mounted securely so that they are not easily moved, and the light source should be aligned with the detector and solidly mounted so that its beam will remain in line with the photocell receiver.

Ordinarily the light source and the photocell are safe from many of the dangers that normally affect outside installations. Falling branches and wind, small animals, etc., often affect the outside installation and even a slight movement of the light source could easily throw the beam out of line with the receiver a couple of hundred feet away and keep the light from striking the cell, which would trigger the alarm. A good solid wall provides a good place for mounting either indoors or outdoors. A solid shelf on inside installations or the side of a cabinet will provide an ideal mount. It may be necessary to have a post in the ground with a concrete foundation on some outside installations in order to provide the stable mounting required.

The receiver and light source should be hidden or at least covered and made as inconspicuous as possible so that the intruder or even a prospective intruder who may be looking the location over would have difficulty spotting the exact location. If the location is known in advance, it may be possible for him to crawl under the beam or step over it when the time arrives for his attempt. The light source may be mounted inside a closet or case, or any type of enclosure, and a small hole drilled in the door, which would not even be visible during business hours, yet when the door is closed would be quite satisfactory after closing the shop. A mirror can be located inside a case or shelf and shielded from view so that an intruder would not realize its true purpose. Oftentimes the receiver may be mounted in a recessed position and remain hidden from the average passerby. The light source requires no special wiring other than AC power in most cases. The light source should be installed in the proper position, then the 117-volt power source may easily be run to the light afterwards. There will be some cases where some phases of the installation will fall under jurisdiction of the electrical code even though the main circuit does not, since it is normally operated from battery voltage. Before connecting into the AC circuit, local or city codes should be checked to find out just what is required. There will be many cases where the light source may be operated from an ordinary plug-in type arrangement inside, which would hardly be against any of the local codes, but the outside installation could easily require careful consideration of the code requirements since the dangers are much greater due to weather and other conditions. In such instances it may be necessary to secure the assistance of a licensed electrician. Naturally, in some cases, such personnel will be available within the organization.

For outside installations, it may be necessary to run the wire underground in a conduit or use heavy waterproof cable. This is no problem as long as regulations are observed. External power runs should always be in pipe or conduit to protect children and animals in the area who could easily be in danger with less adequate arrangements. There must be no chance whatsoever of water getting to the power circuit, since this could be extremely dangerous. In outside installations a housing may be necessary over both the light source and receiver to protect them against the elements. Aside from the protection offered by the housing, they will also hide the installation from the general public, which is also an advantage.

Normally, instructions are included with the electric eye and all that is necessary is to simply follow these instructions; no specific electronic technical skill is required. Although the receiving unit or photocell in the outside installation is connected only to a small DC source such as a 6-volt dry cell, the wires from the battery to the unit should be weatherproofed at least to avoid possible short circuits in the future.

Normally, the wire to the photoelectric cell should be an 18 gauge weatherproof pair; one wire is connected to each terminal on the receiver and the other end of the pair into one leg of the line (DC line) at any point inside the building. These wires should normally be underground, and when crossing a driveway or walkway some ingenuity is required to avoid the danger of being disturbed at some future date. Sometimes it's possible to run the wires from a pole to the side of a building above the normal traffic, pedestrians and even motor vehicles. In any event the wire must be high enough where it will not be bumped or broken by cars or trucks, allowing for the highest trucks in the area and also the antennas on automobiles and smaller trucks. When fastening wires to a building or pole, you must use an insulated staple at frequent intervals, and it is important that the wires are fastened securely to protect the installation against weather, wind, etc., to which it will be subjected over a period of time.

Of course, the inside installation presents no real problem. The only headache is the careful consideration of the best place to install the unit where the longest straight line is available between receiver and transmitter in order to provide the maximum coverage with the two units. Consider carefully how the burglar would manipulate in order to get around the beam or to get around the premises, and govern your installation accordingly, always remembering that you have the advantage, since you know the paths that he must necessarily take in order to achieve his results, and he will be unaware of the exact location of your installation as it is set up to protect your customer. In the home you will find many ideal locations for efficient coverage with a photoelectric unit, and by careful planning, the installation will provide the coverage desired with a minimum of expense. Hiding the units is usually quite simple in the home, and there are many tricks of the trade that you will soon pick up as you go about making your installations.

Since the outside light is greatly reduced late in the day, final adjustments on the precise angle of the light source may best be made at that time. When distances covered are long, a very slight change in the position of either unit could make quite a big difference in the point where the beam is received and whether or not the photocell is getting sufficient light to guarantee reliable triggering of the circuit. When an infrared filter is attached to the light source, it should be removed for the purpose of making the alignment job more accurate. After completing alignment of the units, the filter can be replaced without disturbing the alignment adjustment.

ARROWHEAD ENTERPRISES, MODEL 1700-3R

This system is a signal-initiating device for use in security installations. It operates on the photoelectric principle of detecting interruptions in a completely invisible light beam. The light beam is modulated to render it unsusceptible to ambient and other external light sources, and there are no interconnections required between transmitter and receiver. A receptacle outlet appearance and recess mounting (Fig. 5-1) makes the unit well suited for home or commercial use where its inconspicuous appearance enhances its value. An operating range of 125 feet and a self-contained 72-hour standby power supply adds to the overall reliability of the 1700-3R.

The system emits a pulsed-modulated infrared beam from a solid-state (gallium arsenide) light-emitting diode (LED). The receiver is tuned to the narrow band frequency of the transmitter. The installation is not vulnerable to false alarms or malfunction resulting from undesirable ambient conditions or countermeasures. Alignment is simple; all adjustments are internal with a 90-degree horizontal and 40-degree vertical range (Fig. 5-2). The electrical outlet box with its chrome wall plate makes the system appearance ideal for home, office or store. The standard 2-receptacle wall plate may be replaced with any desired color to match the decor of the individual surroundings. The system is designed with supervised circuits, and connections are conveniently located on terminal blocks.

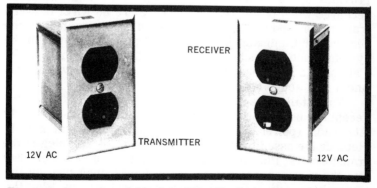

RECEIVER

TRANSMITTER

12V AC

12V AC

Fig. 5-1. Arrowhead Model 1700-3R photo-electric system.

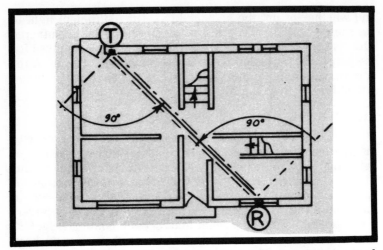

Fig. 5-2. Installation sketch showing adjustment range of the Arrowhead Model 1700-3R photoelectric system.

The signal-initiating alarm relay is a "Sigma" single pole, double throw (SPDT) type, UL Listed for burglary protection equipment. The relay is internally mounted in the receiver, and normally open and normally closed contacts are provided on the terminal strip with a selection of momentary or "lock-in" performance. Mirrors may be used to bend and reflect the beam, but each mirror will reduce the range by about 30 percent.

The input power to transmitter and receiver units is 12 volts AC from a Model 1596-3 plug-in transformer (Fig. 5-3) or equivalent (115v to 12v AC, 60 Hz). Standby power from an internally mounted rechargeable lead-dioxide battery (gel-cel) is included in both the transmitter and the receiver and provides up to 72 hours standby operation and automatic recharge when power resumes. There are no wires between transmitter and receiver. A small meter mounted in the receiver unit indicates proper alignment and operation of the system. Each recess box is 3¼" high, 3" deep and 2¼" wide. Care should be taken to provide rigid mounting between 2 feet and 4 feet above the floor.

To install the system, remove the assemblies from the receptacle boxes and mount the recess boxes. Connect the 12v AC leads (power off), battery leads, and alarm circuit. Replace the assemblies into the recess boxes and plug-in the transformers. Plug the alignment light fixture (Model 1690) into the receiver, hang in on the receiver, then turn on the transmitter. Adjust the transmitter optical system. Plug the alignment light fixture into the transmitter, hang it on the transmitter, aim it and illuminate the receiver, then adjust the receiver optical system.

The Model 1700-3R is designed for indoor use and appropriate applications are across windows, inside perimeters, traffic areas, hallways, work areas, stairways, across and through doorways and openings, near doors that will interrupt beams, rooms, places where valuables are stored, vestibules, storage areas, and others where reliable protection against intruders is desired. The versatility of the system is shown in the sketch of Fig. 5-2.

The next three modular design photoelectric systems are completely solid-state with rechargeable standby batteries and optional alignment accessories. The 7570 Series features an infrared eye with automatic gain control. It is approved for outdoor applications because it is housed in an all-steel chassis and cabinet treated with a resistive coating to protect its circuitry from corrosion and harsh temperatures. The 1000-foot indoor range and 500-foot outdoor range provide a 4-to-1 safety factor in compliance with UL standards. The other two systems are designed for indoor protection. The OG-75 is useful up to 75 feet, and the Model 1600 Series is capable of a mid range of 400 feet.

MORSE PHOTOELECTRIC

The completely solid-state McCulloh circuit burglar alarm transmitter, Morse Products Mfg., Model SST-170,

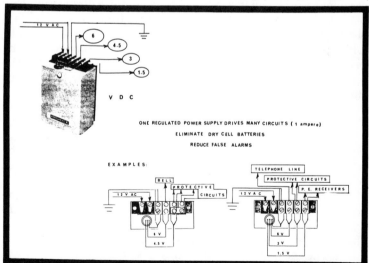

Fig. 5-3. Power supply for the Arrowhead Model 1700-3R.

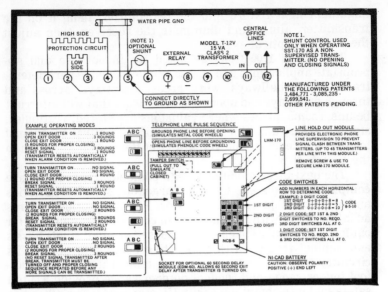

Fig. 5-4. Operational diagram of the Morse SST-170 burglar alarm transmitter.

offers a digital slide-switch binary code system, a selectable one, two, five or seven round closing sequence, 3-position mode switch, plus an optional plug-in holdout module and exit delay module. The SST-170 terminal strip along with a description of the operating modes and telephone line pulse sequence are shown in Fig. 5-4. The schematic diagram in Fig. 5-5 covers the SST-170, and the 60-second time delay module is shown schematically in Fig. 5-6. The line holdout module, LHM-170, provides electronic phone line supervision by preventing signal clash between transmitters (Fig. 5-7). The following alignment procedure will reveal further details on the operation of the system.

1. After the units have been installed, apply power to both the exciter and receiver, but DO NOT connect the batteries.

2. Mount the alignment telescope on the receiver chassis with the cover off and center the exciter on the cross hairs by adjusting the unit mounting plate. Then remove the alignment telescope.

3. Mount the telescope on the exciter chassis with the cover off and center the receiver on the cross hairs by adjusting the unit mounting plate. Place the screen up against the telescope out of the optical path.

4. The receiver meter should display an upscale reading at this time. The following procedures may be used to align the exciter:

A. Station one person at the receiver to call out the meter reading and another person at the exciter. The reading should be increased by adjusting the exciter horizontally and vertically. When the meter reads full scale, the screen on the telescope is lowered until it is against the body of the unit. If the meter is still full scale, raise the screen until the meter reading is less than half scale. Continue the adjustments until the maximum possible signal is obtained. If necessary, continue raising the screen to keep the meter reading below full scale.

Note: The telescope cross hairs may not be in perfect alignment with the optical beam, and it may be necessary at long ranges to scan vertically and horizontally within the telescope view to obtain a meter reading. As soon as a reading

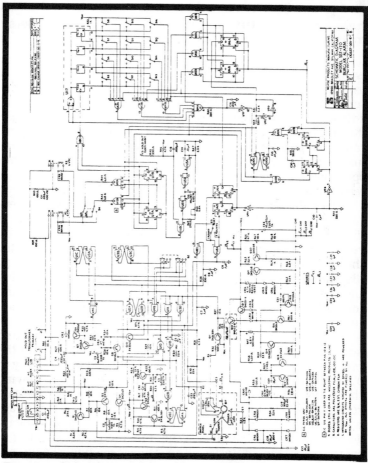

Fig. 5-5. Schematic of the Morse SST-170 alarm system.

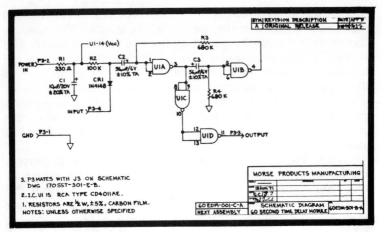

Fig. 5-6. Schematic of the Morse SST-170 time-delay module; it provides a 60-second delay.

is obtained on the meter, all further alignment is performed using the meter to show increasing signal strength and the screen to keep the meter reading below full scale. The vertical adjustment may give a maximum reading over a wider angle than the horizontal adjustment. This is especially true at short range, so position the unit in the middle of this vertical adjustment for optimum results. This will insure reliable operation even if the units move because of settling or as a result of thermal changes in outdoor installations.

Lock the unit in place, connect the battery and momentarily disconnect the AC to test the battery. The AC may be disconnected at the plug-in transformer rather than by removing the connector, as the latter procedure could disturb the alignment. The meter reading may change when disconnecting the AC, but not more than 20 to 30 percent. Plug the transformer back in, remove the alignment telescope, and install the cover on the exciter, which is now completely adjusted.

5. Mount the alignment telescope on the receiver and adjust the screen to obtain about a half-scale reading on the meter. Adjust the receiver both vertically and horizontally to obtain a maximum signal reading on the meter while moving the screen when needed to keep the meter below a full-scale reading. When the alignment is complete, lock the adjustments and connect the two batteries. Momentarily disconnect the AC and observe the meter to check the operation of the batteries. The meter reading should not change more than 40 to 50 percent when the AC is discon-

nected; the amount of change depends on the state of charge of the batteries. Reconnect the AC power and move the screen down against the receiver chassis. The screen in this position provides a loss of 75 percent of the received signal. Underwriters' Laboratories requires that no alarm occur under

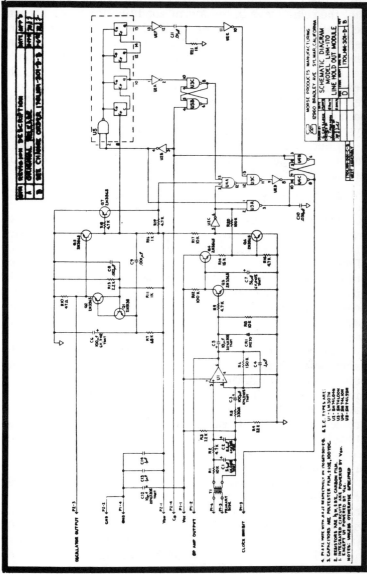

Fig. 5-7. Schematic of the Morse SST-170 line hold-out module, LHM-170.

this condition for an approved installation. For most installations, even at 1,000 feet, the meter will show a reading of from 2 (two) to full scale with the screen in this position. If operation is satisfactory, remove the alignment scope.

6. Break the beam momentarily with your hand or some solid object while observing the relay alarm condition and see that the relay stays in the alarm condition for 1 or 2 seconds before it automatically resets. If the latching feature is being used, open the latch circuit for a few seconds, then close the circuit. Now break the beam. The unit should remain in alarm until the latching circuit is again opened, even though the beam is no longer broken. The monitor circuit provides for a remote indication of the system's operation if desired. A DC voltage of 6 to 9 volts appears across this circuit when the system is set and drops to zero volts in the alarm condition.

Caution: Do not draw more than 3 ma from this circuit to maintain proper operation. If the alarm circuit is working properly, replace the receiver cover.

OPTICAL CONTROLS, INC., OG-1000

The OG-1000 system includes a light-weight infrared transmitter (Fig. 5-8) that emits short, invisible pulses which are picked up by an extremely sensitive receiver. Interruption of the pulse chain by an intruder passing through or disturbing or tampering with the system in any way will promptly trigger an alarm or other responsive device as a result. The system is designed for operation during daytime or nightime hours, regardless of adverse weather conditions, such as fog, rain, or snow.

The output beam can be bent around corners at will by using simple reflectors to permit perimeter protection with only a single transmitter and receiver. In some applications, multiple beams from one transmitter, with receivers at various heights, actually provide an invisible "fence" of protection against intrusion. The unit operates from regular 110-volt AC power lines. It also contains a rechargeable 72-hour capacity standby battery pack to automatically take over in case of power outages.

A gallium arsenide diode is used to provide an infrared beam. The system incorporates modern PC design, plus advanced optical components to make possible the highly collimated pulses of difficult-to-detect infrared energy. Narrow-band filters, sensitive detectors, and pulse modulation techniques eliminate the false alarms from such unusual sources as radio frequency interference, lightning flashes, flickering sunlight, and inclement weather. The wide beam emission and large field of view of the receiver provide freedom from nuisance alarms resulting from severe vibrations. Normal causes of equipment malfunction, often a cause of false alarms in the past, have been eliminated through the use of reliable components, conservatively rated and operated; see Fig. 5-8, which is a view of the transmitter. The range of the unit is 1,000 feet at temperatures from -30 to 150 degrees. Overall dimensions are 3'' by 5'' by 4½''. It weighs 1.7 pounds. The optical system is 2.5 inches in diameter.

The receiver uses a silicon diode detector, has the same dimensions as the transmitter, and weighs 2 pounds. It has enclosed DPDT relay contacts and is compatible with all existing alarm systems. The normally open, normally closed alarm circuit contacts offer momentary closure or latch capability. Other features include nonlatching operation, 1 second hold, automatic reset, tamper and fail-safe provisions, with electronically supervised housing and alarm circuits.

The OG-75 subminiature photoelectric detection system may be installed behind pictures, or mounted on any type wall surface, and it comes with false duplex receptacles for mounting in standard electrical outlets. The system may be operated from AC lines or batteries and is easily concealed. Typical installations for home or business are shown in Fig. 5-9.

HOLOBEAM LASER FENCE INTRUSION ALARM

The laser fence is an invisible, automatic protection system for any indoor or outdoor area. All units use infrared

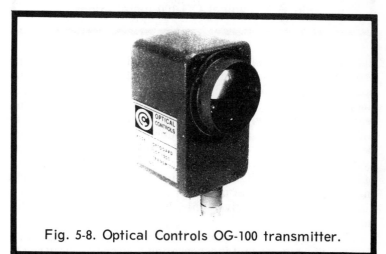

Fig. 5-8. Optical Controls OG-100 transmitter.

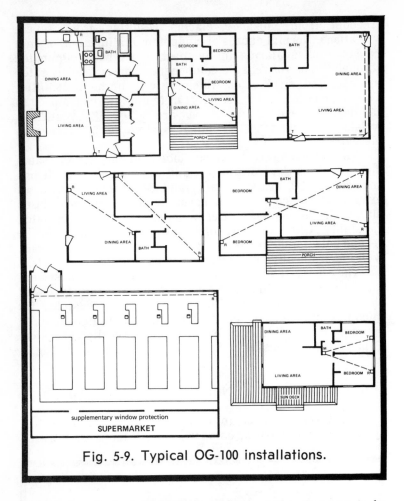

Fig. 5-9. Typical OG-100 installations.

light to create invisible "fences" around the property to be protected and can span a distance from 0.5 to 50,000 feet. Units operate under all weather conditions such as rain or fog and in the presence of disturbances caused by animals, birds, falling leaves and the like without triggering false alarms. Solid-state light sources are used in all models, as well as solid-state detectors. Only severe physical damage can disable the system and then only by creating an alarm condition. The use of lasers as infrared light sources in LF50, LF500 and LF50,000 means that distances of up to 10 miles can be covered with a single transmitter-receiver pair. Fig. 5-10 shows the master unit.

The outdoor Laser Fence system, shown in Fig. 5-11, consists of a master unit incorporating a laser transmitter (T) and a receiver unit (D), with the master unit located at control point (CP). There are eight repeaters, R1 to R8, and the system operates as follows:

As soon as the master unit is turned on, the transmitter starts sending a narrow invisible beam of infrared light toward the first repeater R1. The repeater receives the light signal, restores it to its original level by amplification and sends it to repeater R2. This action—reception, amplification, and re-transmission of the light signal along the chain of repeater units—continues until the originally transmitted signal is received by receiver D, which triggers an alarm whenever it fails to receive its proper input. In this system, Model LF5000 units are used throughout to insure optimum reliability even in heavy fog. Although the LF5000 is conservatively rated at 5,000 feet under normal conditions, experimental tests indicate that only 500 feet may be reliably protected under heavy fog conditions.

It may be noted that repeater R6 is located at the midpoint of the 480-foot leg because of a change in ground elevation. Since the Laser Fence is a line-of-sight system of detection, the narrow beam must pass between three and five feet above the ground, and any change of ground elevation beyond these limits would leave a "hole" in the protective fence.

The simplified installation and flexibility of the Laser Fence is due partly to the fact that each station from the master unit to the final repeater is designed to operate on rechargeable batteries or standard line power. Thus, each fence may be easily assembled by the user from standard Holobeam modules. Any changes in the perimeter to be

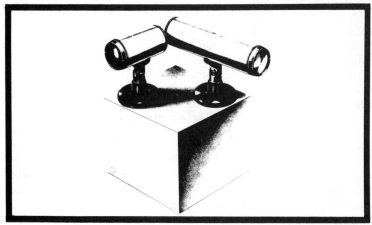

Fig. 5-10. Holobeam "Laser Fence" master unit LF5000.

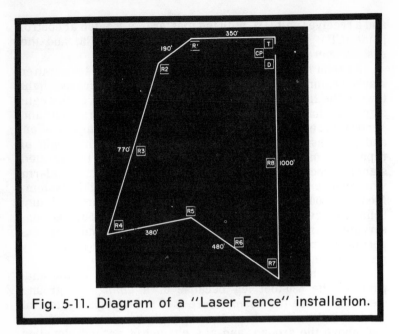

Fig. 5-11. Diagram of a "Laser Fence" installation.

protected require only a simple realignment of the repeaters. The batteries need charging after about three months and this may be handled on a scheduled maintenance assignment to avoid any possible interruption in coverage.

Reliance on active electronic light repeaters, rather than such passive devices as mirrors, provides the user with many important advantages. Alignment problems, a big headache with mirrors, are non-existent in the laser system due to the predetermined divergence of the laser light beam and the fact that locating the repeater anywhere within that area will afford normal reception. Precise angular positioning required in reflector-type systems does not apply here. The light beam will be sensed by the Laser Fence detector even if it falls at an angle as great as 110 degrees.

The light intensity transmitted by each repeater is identical to the original transmitted beam, with the direction of each repeater determined solely by aiming the transmitting head instead of depending on the incident light. Automatic display of the intrusion point is provided on the control panel with audio or visual indicators for each span between the repeaters. As soon as an intrusion occurs, the first repeater that failed to receive its proper signal sends an alarm to the control point which identifies that repeater.

Brief interruptions of the beam caused by falling objects or birds will not trigger an alarm due to the repetition rate of the light pulses. An alarm condition will exist only after a preset number of pulses from the transmitter fail to get through to the receiver, thus minimizing nuisance alarms. The semiconductor lasers used in the Laser Fence system operate well within the limit of safety to the human eye as established by U.S. military medical authorities.

The failure of any component within the system will automatically result in an alarm condition to insure reliable operation, and the solid-state components make the space requirements of master or repeater units very small, typically about 4 inches by 6 inches by 4 inches, including battery pack. This facilitates concealment with the surrounding decor. As the alarm condition produces the closure of relay contacts, any desired responsive action may be used, whether it be bell, horn, buzzer, automatic gate or door, CCTV, central station, telephone dialer or any combination of those available.

The master unit and the repeater include three parts: transmitter, receiver and power supply. A gallium-arsenide laser is the heart of the transmitter and the receiver uses a silicon photodetector diode. The power supply section consists of alarm logic circuitry, regulators and converters for generating DC levels for the entire unit plus the battery pack to supply the power. The repeater unit provides the role of the optical transponder by detecting the incoming laser signal and generating another laser beam in any desired direction. The master unit has its own signal source and logic circuit to generate the alarm, while the repeater is triggered whenever a signal is received.

The transmitter uses a GaAs laser diode. The peak power is 1 watt; the repetition rate is 30 Hz. The batteries are NiCd rechargeable types capable of 2500 hours operation. The operating temperature range is -0 to 120 degrees F.

In addition to perimeter protection, windows and doors may be protected with a single transmitter and receiver covering a row of windows along a 500-foot building, eliminating the taping of windows. In some critical areas, the Laser Fence may be combined with CCTV to monitor disturbed areas from the guard house.

The door application is virtually impossible to defeat, unlike magnetic or mechanical devices, with the solid-state light source mounted on the inside of the door. A miniature photodiode and associated module is placed on the door frame directly facing the light source. With the alarm in operation, the door may not be opened, even the width or thickness of the door, without reducing the light input to the photodiode and creating an alarm condition.

Chapter 6
Ultrasonic Detection Systems

The 20-kHz ultrasonic sound waves generated by the oscillator in these systems fills the area to be protected. Some of this energy is reflected back to the receiver, but most arrives directly from the transmitter. The signals from the direct path and those from the reflected path are combined in the receiver to be added or subtracted according to their phase relationship, and as long as the protected space remains without motion, the signal at the receiver is steady. However, any motion at all will alter the frequency of the reflected signal which, in turn, will affect the combined signal at the receiver. The resulting amplitude modulation causes the detector to respond with an alarm condition. The ultrasonic intrusion detector has the capability of protecting large open areas regardless of the intruder's segment of operation. The system will detect his movements by the resulting frequency shift and the output of the phase detector will automatically set off the alarm. Even the slightest motion alters the reflected pattern sufficiently to be readily detected by the discriminator. The shift in frequency of the reflected wave gets higher as the intruder approaches the transmitter or lower as he walks away. Any frequencies above or below the triggering segment of the band are screened out by bandpass filters.

An ultrasonic detector should be placed on a table or shelf, near the front edge with a clear view of the area to be protected and about two to five feet above the floor level. All surfaces should be free of vibration and the unit must be reasonably removed from telephones, doorbells, buzzers, heat ducts, open windows or other sources of air currents. The ultrasonic detector is intended for indoor use only, and if additional units are required to adequately cover an area, different operating frequencies are necessary.

Most units need only be plugged into the 115-volt AC power outlet, and the lamp and-or alarm sounding device plugged into the back of the unit. Sensitivity controls are easily adjusted where necessary and a few simple walk tests should pinpoint the correct level for any specific location. By all means, **never** increase the sensitivity even a hair's width above the required level for proper response in the selected space. Also, dogs and other pets will trigger the alarm if they are allowed to enter the protected area. Some alarms offer an automatic sensitivity control (ASC) which protects the user from possible nuisance alarms caused by longer duration noises. The sensitivity is quickly though temporarily reduced, then recovers very slowly.

Even greater protection is possible with the ultrasonic intruder alarm system described in detail below with its capability to detect an intruder's presence in your home from the home next door. This remote receiver enables the neighboring home or business to be signaled immediately of an alarm condition in or on your premises. No wiring is required; simply plug in the remote receiver in any room or location within 300 feet or so of the basic system, and turn it on.

NORTHERN ELECTRIC CO., MODEL 1702, 1703 ULTRASONIC ALARM

The transmitter unit fills the area to be protected with invisible, inaudible sound waves that are picked up by the receiver. The intruder entering the protected area disturbs this sound pattern and the receiver immediately senses this change. The receiver unit contains a loud horn as well as provision for plugging in a lamp so that both go on to startle and scare any intruder who enters the covered area. In ad-

Fig. 6-1. Northern Electric Co. ultrasonic intruder alarm, Model 1703.

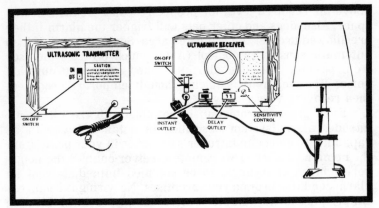

Fig. 6-2. Rear view drawing of the alarm system shown in Fig. 6-1.

dition to the transmitter and receiver units as included in the Model 1702, the 1703 provides a remote receiver unit (all 3 units are pictured in Fig. 6-1). The remote unit will receive an alarm in any room outside the protected area, even a neighbor's house, over the house wiring. If any intruder enters the protected area, the remote receiver signals to warn you of the intruder's presence.

The units feature solid-state circuitry, and invisible, inaudible (ultrasonic) sound waves are used to detect the presence of any intruder movements, setting off a loud horn and-or lights. It provides wide area coverage, exceeding 750 square feet, and includes a "double check" circuit to prevent false alarms. No wiring is required; simply plug in and turn on.

The transmitter operates at an ultrasonic frequency of 23 kHz. Both receiver and transmitter operate on 120 volts AC. The transmitter draws 2 watts and the receiver 10 watts. The lamp outlet is rated at 120 volts AC, 150 watts maximum. The remote receiver signaling frequency is 175 kHz. The remote signaling transmitter (contained in the ultrasonic receiver) has an internal supply voltage and also operates on 175 kHz with a modulation frequency of 200 to 900 Hz.

Study the area to be protected and the likely route an intruder would follow. The unit must be near the front edge of a table or shelf, about 2 to 3 feet above the floor, and units should not face each other. Locate the units on the outer edges of the protected area. Plug the transmitter and receiver into any 110-120 volt AC outlet and plug the lamp into the instant outlet on the back of the receiver and turn the lamp on. Continue with operating, testing and sensitivity adjustment as required. See Fig. 6-2.

To get the system in **operation**, turn the transmitter on and move the switch on the back of the receiver to the "horn and both outlets" position. Any movement will turn the lamp on for 1 to 1½ minutes to indicate the unit is working. A second motion, 7 to 10 seconds or more later, will turn on the horn. The horn and light will automatically turn off together after the 1 to 1½ minute alarm period. The instant outlet position is the same as above except that horn does not sound. When turning on the system to protect an area, always start from off the position because the horn will come on at once if you switch from "instant outlet" to "horn and both outlets." You now have 7 to 10 seconds to leave the area before the horn sounds. The light turns off automatically and the system is ready.

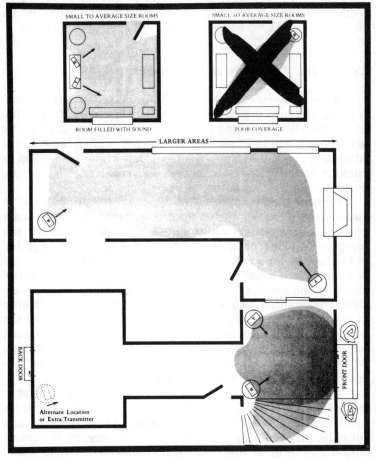

Fig. 6-3. These drawings show various room arrangements for the Model 1703.

When re-entering the room, the light will come on at once and you have 7 to 10 seconds to go to the receiver, where the lamp is plugged in, and move the switch to off before the horn sounds. There are two outlets on the receiver, the instant outlet which comes on at first motion detection and which can be used for a table lamp, and the delay outlet which comes on when the horn sounds and which may be used for an extra responsive device as desired. The 7- to 10-second delay between the time the lights come on and the horn sounds is adjustable if longer or shorter periods are needed.

Avoid pointing the transmitter toward air conditioners, hot air blowers, fire places, drapes or other areas of considerable air current activity. Don't place the units too close to the floor and never have transmitter and receiver facing in rooms less than 20 feet. The front grill of units must not be obstructed, and keep pets out of the protected area (see Fig. 6-3).

Testing and Sensitivity Adjustment

Move the switch (back of receiver) to the "instant outlet" position and turn the switch on the back of transmitter to the on position. While moving around the area to be protected, the alarm lamp will light up as soon as your motion is detected. After 90 seconds the lamp will go out, but while it is still on, a clicking sound will be noticed in the receiver. This is the normal sound when motion is being detected.

To check the range of the system, leave the protected area (with the system on) for at least 90 seconds, and then walk back into the area normally, noting your position when the lamp lights. The transmitter and receiver have been adjusted at the factory for a room approximately 12 feet by 15 feet, and if a change in sensitivity is desired, the sensitivity control (back of the receiver, right) may be adjusted. If more sensitivity is required, turn control clockwise toward high, a little at a time. If the sensitivity needs to be decreased, turn the control counterclockwise toward low. In either event, do not adjust this control higher or lower than necessary; too high will result in false alarms from air currents, pets, etc., and too low may result in the failure to detect a careful intruder.

The Model 1703 has a remote receiver to permit the user to monitor the protected area from a distance of 300 feet or so, and it may be placed anywhere within that perimeter. The unit must be plugged into the same power source as the transmitter and receiver units because the detection signal is sent through the normal house wiring. The remote receiver light should go on as soon as motion is detected by the regular receiver and remain on according to the remote switch position. When testing the remote unit, if it fails to pick up signals, try another outlet or another room. The remote unit should be left on continuously, since its current consumption is less than an ordinary electric clock. There is an outlet plug on the back of the remote receiver which may be used for plugging in any desired 110-volt AC alarm device as bell, buzzer, siren, flashing light, etc. Switching positions for remote and main receiver are shown in Fig. 6-4.

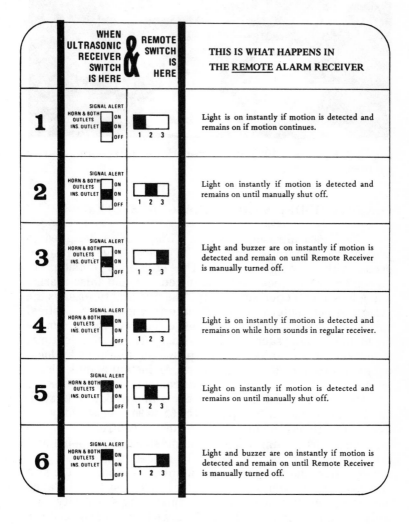

Fig. 6-4. Northern Electric Co. Model 1703 switch functions.

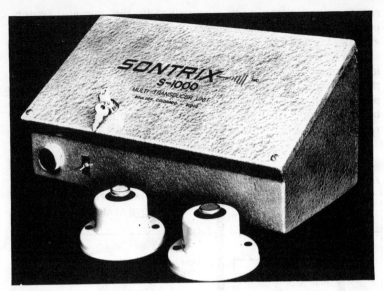

Fig. 6-5. Sontrix S-1000 multi-transducer ultrasonic alarm system.

SONTRIX MODEL S-1000 ULTRASONIC SYSTEM

The S-1000 ultrasonic system (Fig. 6-5) is designed to provide simultaneous protection to many large and small areas with a single control. The effects of outside environmental influences are minimized to avoid false alarms and a loss of detection sensitivity. The manufacturer says the system is completely free of RF interference and acoustical saturation. An air turbulence cutoff circuit allows for sundry air motion without sacrificing sensitivity. The system features a supervised transmitter circuit providing alarm relay lockout in the event of equipment failure. An instant audible signal is omitted if the AC power to master control is interrupted.

Thirty hours of Gen-Cel battery standby power is standard, but optional battery packs for 60 or 90 hour standby are available without modification of master control.

The S-1000 system includes the master control panel and the required number of remotely placed transmitter and receiver transducers; the actual number depends on the size and contents of the area to be protected. The system balance and detection threshold may be adjusted by sensitivity controls in the master control panel, as well as in each receiver transducer. The system is fully protected against tampering and offers a double set of alarm relay contacts. A local walk test capability is provided and controlled by a front panel switch which prevents reset. The remote test may be made by the addition of a remote test transducer to one or more of the protected areas. However, multiple area tests must be sequential and systems making use of several master controls are synchronized by a simple 2-wire interconnection.

The master control unit generates the 26-kHz transmitted signal, interrogates the received signal, and initiates an alarm when the two signals are different in frequency to a prescribed degree. The master control will operate up to 200 transducers, with transmitters outnumbering receivers, since greater efficiency is normally possible with multiple transmitters around a single receiver. The result is an improvement in signal-to-noise ratio.

Transmitters and receivers located in the protected area are interconnected to the master control. The transmitters produce and radiate 26-kHz ultrasonic energy into the area, while receivers convert the detected energy into electrical energy to be fed back to master control for interrogation. Transducers must be located on a vibration-free surface, and if the ceiling height is greater than 10 to 12 feet, transducers may be mounted on walls about 10 feet above the floor. The use of a swivel mount is recommended in this case, allowing the transducer to be pointed down somewhat.

Proper installation of the ultrasonic system requires consideration of the sound characteristics of the area to be protected, both from the absorption and reflection standpoints. As the ultrasonic energy or waves are confined to the area to be protected by walls, floors and ceilings, total coverage is possible by the reflection of the transmitted energy from these hard surfaces. The more and better the reflecting surfaces, the fewer the number of transducers required to do the job. Hard floors, walls and ceilings as well as windows are considered to be excellent reflectors of ultrasonic waves. Most drapes (cloth), clothing, carpeting, cardboard, acoustic paneling and similar materials are sound absorbing, which makes additional transmitters and receivers necessary for full coverage. Pointing the wall-mounted transmitting transducers toward the floor will increase their efficiency due to the highly reflective surface.

Transducers may be placed 25 to 45 feet apart according to room conditions and dimensions. Where the room is full of absorbing materials, spacings as low as 15 feet may be necessary. The transducer has a plastic edge cover for insulation purposes and this should not be removed. When mounted on a metal or masonry type surface, the cover insures proper protection against grounding the device.

The units are of a two-piece "semi-snap-on" design, permitting easy removal for adjustment purposes. Transducers are mounted by attaching the crossbar with extending machine screws to the mounting surface. After making the wire connections, the transducer grommets are pressed over the machine screw threads. The plastic grommets hold the receivers while gain adjustments are made. The transmitting units may be permanently installed by attaching the knurled nuts. After gain adjustments are complete, the knurled nuts should be attached to the receivers as well. The sensitivity control (potentiometer) on each receiver is set to maximum (fully clockwise, right) at the factory, but this adjustment may need to be changed to meet specific conditions as explained later.

Although most installations are not affected by wire size, in very large installations involving 100 or so transmitters on a line, No. 16 wires should be used to the first transmitter and No. 18 to the rest. If only 10 transmitters are on a line from the master control and the distance to the last one is 500 feet or less, No. 22 wire may be used on each line up to 10 lines of 10 transmitters (100). If the last transmitter is 1000 feet from master control with 10 transmitters on a line, No. 20 wire should be used, and here again up to 10 lines of 10 transmitters may be used on each (100). Always use **twisted pair** wires. Since line loss on receivers is negligible, No. 20 or No. 22 shielded wire may be used for any number of receivers on a line and at any distance required. Transmitter or receiver heads with the tamper feature will require two additional wires which need not be shielded in either case. Although shielded wire offers no performance advantage on transmitter wiring, it may be used, but the shield **must not** be connected to the panel or individual transmitters. Transmitter and receiver tamper may be on the same line, but it must be **twisted**. Most tamper lines are not twisted and will not work.

The master control may be placed on any flat surface such as a shelf, and requires an outlet to plug-in the 120-to-115v AC transformer. No. 18 zip cord may be used to connect the transformer secondary to the master control, but do not connect until the wiring to the panel from all transducers has been checked for shorts! In a large installation where different businesses or departments require protection in a common building, multiple control panels may be used, providing interconnection is made to synchronize the units. Using a single cable shielded wire, the units are connected in parallel with master control (terminal 14 of each to the shield and terminal 15 of each to the center conductor); see the sketch in Fig. 6-6. As many slave units as required may be used, but the "patchcord" should be pulled from each.

The S-1000 offers an automatic sensitivity control throughout the detection range of any transducer as long as the system is properly installed and adjusted according to the following instructions:

The master sensitivity control affects all receivers equally and should be adjusted once for the largest or least sensitive room. A sensitivity adjustment is provided on each receiver and the adjustment of one does not affect the others. If the control is at minimum (counterclockwise, left) and less sensitivity is still needed for an individual receiver, increase the size of the red "dot" on the face.

If a thorough check of coverage is desired prior to regular transducer placement, a T0-10 transmitter and R0-20 receiver may be connected to the master control by 100 feet or so of line and the test transducers placed or taped in selected positions. Walk test the area while observing the 50 microamp meter to check for possible problems, thus allowing evaluation of placements before running lines. Overnight observation is possible using the 50 microamp chart recorder SCR-1. The wide-angle directional characteristic of the transducers will allow troublesome areas to be avoided while still affording complete coverage.

After all transducers have been wired and tested for shorts, grounds and polarization, the total system is adjusted as follows:

1. Turn on the master control switch (B in Fig. 6-7), located on the circuit board inside the cabinet. The system wiring may be checked at this point by measuring the AC output at the master control and also at the most remote transmitting transducer of each branch circuit. Use a Simpson 260 or equivalent 20,000 ohms-per-volt (VOM) meter capable of measuring 26 kHz. Normal readings at the control panel are about 9 to 12 volts AC on the transmitter and 10 to 12 volts DC on the receiver.

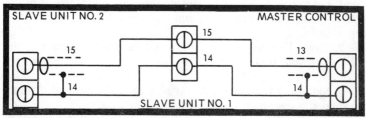

Fig. 6-6. Slave unit connections to the master control, Sontrix S-1000 system.

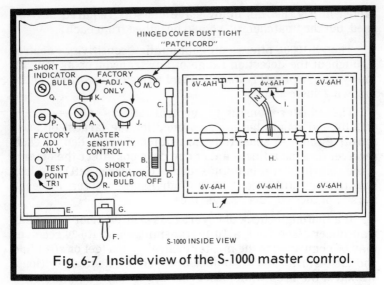

Fig. 6-7. Inside view of the S-1000 master control.

(a) With a VTVM or oscilloscope attached across the extreme end of the transmitter line, at least 12 volts AC should be indicated. A small number of transducers on a short line could show a reading of as much as 28 volts peak to peak (20 volts RMS). This test is necessary only on large installations.

(b) Short verification bulbs, as shown in Fig. 6-7, indicate a short wired or induced in the receiver cable by lighting small bulb Q (upper left), or in the transmitting cable by lighting large bulb R in front. The bulbs may be quickly checked by shorting terminal 19 to 20 to light bulb Q, or terminal 12 to 13 to light bulb R.

Connect the meter negative (-) black lead to the Sonalert or tamper switch frame, set the meter scale to 50 microamps and then connect positive (+) red test lead to TP-1. The meter indicates the Doppler signal and provides a direct check on system stability. It should read 45 to 50 microamps during an alarm condition. Continuous noise and disturbance as shown by ¼-scale deflections are acceptable, but intermittent pulses must not exceed ½ scale deflection, or 25 microamps. A properly installed system should always be set up at "0," regardless.

2. Turn the walk test monitor switch F on the front of the cabinet to on, and when out of hearing range of "Sonalert" have someone signal you.

3. Selecting the softest or largest room in the installation, remove the receiver caps in that room only.

4. Check the sensitivity of each receiver for maximum setting (fully clockwise, right) in that room.

5. Adjust the master control sensitivity (A) until motion is detected, three steps at a rate of one per second, in the room of Step 3.

6. If the room in question is acoustically coupled to your next area (such as an archway), recap the receivers before proceeding with that area.

7. Adjust the adjacent area receiver controls until you locate the 3-step test setting **without readjusting the master control.**

8. If more than one receiver is used in any of the areas starting with Step 7, adjust only one receiver at a time. As soon as one is adjusted satisfactorily, proceed to the next and, after removing the cap, adjust it. If a room or section cannot be protected by adjusting the receiver sensitivity control, then the following conditions probably exist:

(a) The area is softer and less reflective than the area selected in Step 3, or

(b) An insufficient number of transducers have been used to properly protect it.

By going back and adjusting this "softer" room with the master sensitivity control as described in Steps 3 to 5, the decision may be verified by now adjusting the originally selected room receiver sensitivity controls over again for this new master control position. However, if this fails, additional transducers must be installed in the second soft room and followed by readjusts in both rooms, beginning with Step No. 3.

The sensitivity of one area may be adjusted differently from that of another if so desired. One room may be adjusted for 2-step sensitivity while another is adjusted for 4-step without affecting the overall stability of the system.

Walking through the entire installation with the walk test switch in the on position enables a check of the total performance. This is a good time to trim the master control sensitivity setting, but overall sensitivity may best be adjusted finally after 24 to 48 hours of system operation. After the system has stabilized, it may become more efficient and sensitive.

In extremely turbulent areas, the Sontrix SP-500 signal processing miniature unit may be used with the S-1000 master control. The SP-500 is highly immune to such turbulence as caused by overhead heaters, air conditioners and other types of ventilating blowers. Its 26-kHz signal may be synchronized with the S-1000 system so it will be matched with the total installation. The SP-500 is connected in the following manner: From terminals 13 and 14 on TS-1 of the master control, run a single shielded cable to the SP-500 terminal strip as designated on the inner back. Connect the relay output from the SP-500 in

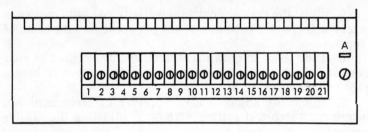

Fig. 6-8. Layout of the Sontrix S-1000 S-1000 terminal connections.

the normal manner. Pull the patch cord on SP-500 board for slave operation, checking the manual included for location.

S-1000 Terminal Layout (TS-1, Back View, Left to Right), Fig. 6-8.

A. Matching Circuit

1. Tamper
2. Tamper
3. Tamper
4. Relay contacts NC (alarm condition)
5. Relay contacts C (common)
6. Relay contacts NO
7. Relay contacts NC
8. Relay contacts C
9. Relay contacts
10. 15 volt AC, 36 va input
11. Contact rating: 5 A at 120 volts AC or 28 volts DC
12. Transmitter signal
13. Transmitter signal
14. Ground, multiple unit sync
15. Contacts (Sec. A, Part H)
16.
17. } Factory connections
18.
19. Receiver signal -
20. Receiver signal +
21. Shield, receiver only

Tamper connections (transducer):

T0-10 transmitter (blue dot) terminals 2 to 4
R0-20 receiver (red dot) terminals 2 to 4

Troubleshooting

To test for shorts in transmitter lines with the wires disconnected from master control, using Simpson 260 VOM or equivalent, set the meter on a high or medium resistance scale. Measure the resistance between 1 and 5 of the transmitter transducer (normally connected to 12 and 13 of master control). There should be no reading (very high resistance), although there may be a capacitive charging indication depending on the meter scale used and the number of transmitters on the line. Measure from both leads above to a suitable ground, conduit, water pipe or metal building with the above meter scale and there should be no reading; in other words, infinity or extremely high resistance.

To test for shorts and polarity in receiver lines:

1. Measure the resistance between the receiver transducer line, connected to terminals 1 and 5 (normally connected to 19 and 20 of master control), and ground. There should be no reading. Resistance to ground should be infinite (open circuit).

2. Attach the red (+) lead from meter to No. 5 (20 on master control) and the black lead (-) to No. 1 (19 on master control) and you will get a fairly low reading on the R X 10,000 scale. This reading, of course, depends on the number of receiving heads in the line. Reversing the meter leads should indicate infinity or a high resistance reading, depending on the number of receivers. (This simulates a front-to-back measurement of a diode.) If you get a fairly low resistance reading in both directions, it usually shows that the leads are reversed to one or more of the receiver heads.

3. Again using the VOM resistance scale, check the resistance between No. 1 and the shield and No. 5 and the shield. They both should read infinity (open).

4. Measure from the shield to an electrical ground, conduit, water pipe or metal beams. There should be no reading because there is no path; it is open. The shield should be grounded at master control **only**.

5. If the shield on the receiver cable is grounded to any part of the building electrical system, very severe problems may result!

Master Control Panel Designations

A. Master sensitivity control
B. Master control power switch
C. 3 amp slo-blow fuse (AC power)
D. 1½ amp fast-flow fuse (battery supply)
E. "Sonalert" signals AC power loss, and walk test
F. "On-off" switch to control walk test
G. Master cabinet tamper switch
H. Battery cover (Remove two screws to release batteries)

I. Plug-in strip for battery packs
J. Do not adjust
K. Do not adjust
L. 12v, 12AH batteries (two per pack)
M. "Patch-cord" (synchronizing multiple units)
N. Battery pack plug-in
O. Positive hook-up point
P. Do not adjust
Q. Short indicator bulb (receiver line)
R. Short indicator bulb (transmitter line)

DETECTRON SECURITY SYSTEMS, MODEL 350

This ultrasonic detector is completely transistorized and offers highly reliable intrusion detection which may be used in conjunction with Detectron Master Controls or any alarm device which accepts a dry closure. Operating on a frequency of 35 kHz, utilizing the Doppler principle, only objects in motion are detected and virtual freedom from nuisance alarms due to noises, line surges and other disturbances is afforded. The beam width is approximately 90 degrees horizontal and 45 degrees vertical in open space. The beam shape as well as the detector's sensitivity to motion is considerably altered in confined areas like one filled with furniture, equipment or stock. Although coverage in a confined space could well be limited to 15 feet by 15 feet (225 sq. ft.), an open area of 25 feet by 25 feet (625 sq. ft.) may be adequately protected. Even larger areas may be properly protected by employing additional ultrasonic detector units. More reliable service is possible by operating additional units at lower levels of sensitivity rather than fewer at maximum. The total number of detectors used in any given area is limited only by the power supply; for example, a series 110 master control can comfortably handle ten or more model 350 detectors.

Many unusual features identify the Model 350 as an ideal unit for protecting small areas against intruders, such as the C form alarm relay which provides contact closure or contact opening when triggered. A control determines the length of time which the relay is energized after an intrusion, and it may be adjusted to hold for 15 seconds to 2 minutes. The sensitivity control permits the adjustment of coverage and uses a built-in time delay to allow the user to leave the premises prior to becoming fully armed. The detector is shown along with other system components in Fig. 6-9.

Specifications

Operating frequency: 35 kHz
Circuit design: All solid-state

Output circuitry: C Form, DPDT, 100 watts
Controls: Sensitivity, alarm hold-time on-off
Power requirements: 12 volts DC, 20 milliamperes
Range: To 400 sq. ft.
Size: 10½" long, 3" high, 3" deep
Weight: 1½ pounds

SYSTRON-DONNER, MODEL UD-6 & UD-18

This system will accommodate up to 6 pairs of transducers on the UD-6 or as many as 18 pairs of transducers with the UD-18 model. Installation is simplified with a bracket, quick-connect wire terminations and a snap on-off lid. The integrated solid-state circuitry provides effective turbulence control for stable, maintenance-free system operation.

The capacity of the basic system extends to 7,500 square feet when using six transmitting and six receiving transducers. Larger coverage to 18,000 square feet is available with the UD-18 model. Under maximum load conditions a minimum of 4 hours standby time is provided by the batteries, and this time may be lengthened when fewer transducers are used. If circuit tamper protection is broken, the protection

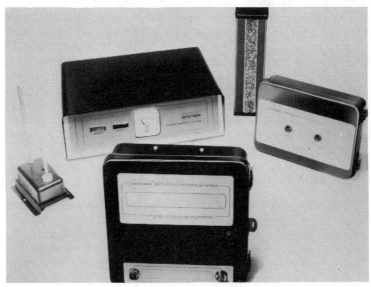

Fig. 6-9. Shown here are: the Detectron Series 110 Master Control (foreground); 305 Radar Detector; Series 105 Master Control; 350 Ultrasonic Detector; 210 Fire Monitor (background l to r) manufactured by Detectron Security Systems.

loop is opened and the unit goes into an alarm condition. Any failure or malfunction of the unit will also result in the alarm condition. The detector is compatible with all conventional alarm equipment, and to facilitate easy installation, the MB-1 mounting bracket is included. Either model may be mounted using the two keyholes and a round hole provided in the back of the case. The cover merely snaps on when the unit is in place. Both models provide the most effective turbulence compensation circuit available in any ultrasonic intrusion detector.

The operating temperature range is 32 degrees to 140 degrees F or zero to 60 degrees C. Circuit components include IC operational amplifiers with such features as short-circuit proof inputs, anti-latchup circuits and supergain transistors. Short-circuit proof test points are conveniently provided for monitoring power supply voltage, Doppler signal and battery voltage. A double-pole relay is available for additional monitoring of the relay contacts, allowing the customer to utilize his own custom alarm devices. Turbulence compensation circuitry using a precision voltage comparator automatically compensates for air turbulence, maintaining the same sensitivity with the heaters on or off. An adjustment is needed only under extreme conditions.

Wire terminations are provided through special quick-connect barrier strips using no lugs or special connectors. Power is supplied by the 110-volt to 16.5 volt AC, 50-60 Hz transformer that plugs into the wall outlet. Standby power is supplied by two 6-volt, 1 ampere-hour rechargeable batteries. Electrical tamper protection is provided by a lid-actuated microswitch. Transducer line supervision is incorporated by series connection to this switch. Mechanical tamper protection available in the form of an optional key lock. A layout diagram of the UD model detector is shown in Fig. 6-10.

FUNCTIONAL DEVICES, MODEL A-5, T-2P

No wiring is required between parts of the alarm system when using this method of transmitting the alarm signal over existing house wiring, thus eliminating a major cost in the overall system. Most alarm systems require wire connections between the sensor or detector and the alarm responsive device. No wiring problems with this system; just plug it in to the wall receptacles and you are ready to operate. The A-5 detector and the T-2P transmitter detect the adverse condition and transmit the coded signal along existing household wiring to the receiver alarms. Intrusion is signaled by a pulsating alarm and fire by a steady alarm.

The ultrasonic intrusion alarm (Fig. 6-11) or movement detector (A-5) plugs into any household receptacle (120v AC) and may be controlled by its off-on switch or wall switched receptacle. It allows 15 to 25 seconds for safe exit, then detects movements up to 18 feet away with adjustable sensitivity. When triggered, power is applied to lamp outlet (120v AC, 6A max.) and after 10 to 20 seconds, power is applied to the "bell" outlet (120v AC, 1A max.) for 1 minute. The alarm then resets automatically with the alarm stopping until the next movement. The system offers a closed-loop circuit capability and requires a Model T-2P to transmit. Pulsating transmitter T-2P plugs into the "bell" or "lamp" outlet of A-5 or other ultrasonic intrusion alarm and transmits a pulsating signal whenever A-5 is in the alarm condition.

The smoke and heat detector-transmitter, Model HST, plugs into a household receptacle and detects smoke or heat. When initiated it sounds a loud, penetrating alarm and transmits a continuous signal. It automatically resets (turns off) when smoke and heat cease.

A peripheral intrusion alarm plugs into any household receptacle (120v AC) and is wired to normally closed (NC) window or door switches. Momentary opening of any switch initiates 1 to 3 minutes of pulsating transmission, automatically resetting 1 to 3 minutes after the switch is reclosed. It may also be reset with the on-off switch as the alarm cycles 2 minutes on and 3 minutes off if a door is left open (PIA-1).

The panic alarm plugs into a household receptacle and can be moved from room to room. The PA-1 has a panic button

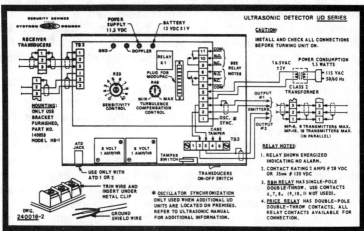

Fig. 6-10. Functional layout diagram of the Systron-Donner UD Series.

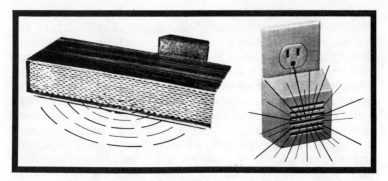

Fig. 6-11. Functional Devices A-5 detector-transmitter (left) and receiver alarm RR-1.

which may be pushed momentarily to cause a pulsating alarm to be transmitted for 1 to 3 minutes. The unit has a cancel button as well and is equipped with a 10-foot cord.

The receiver alarms are triggered when the transmitted signal is received through the AC power line following its transmission by the detector-transmitter. A single transmitter will activate all receivers that are plugged into that same side of the line transformer supplying the wall receptacles.

The remote receiver-sound, Model RR-1, when plugged into the 120v AC receptacle, picks up the transmitted alarm signal from the house wiring and actuates the medium intensity alarm enclosed in the unit. This compact model receiver-alarm is intended for installation in the bedroom. See Fig. 6-11.

A remote receiver with switched receptacle (Model RR-1SR) plugs into a 120v AC receptacle and actuates any responsive device, light or sounding alarm, that may be plugged into the unit's receptacle for 120-volt AC power, providing it does not exceed the capacity of the switching contacts (700 watts maximum).

A remote receiver with horn (Model RR-2) is exactly the same as RR-1, except it contains a very loud horn in place of the medium intensity alarm. It is recommended for a central area to frighten the intruder.

A remote receiver with dry contacts (Model RR-1DC) plugs into a 120v AC receptacle and provides a dry contact which is closed whenever the transmitted alarm signal is received. The contact rating is 6 amps at 120 volts AC or 28 volts DC. It is useful for triggering other alarm systems.

Power failure alarm, Model PFA, plugs into a wall receptacle (120v AC) and sounds a tone alarm in the event of power line failure. The unit is powered by a self-contained 9-volt battery which will last for more than 4 hours in continuous alarm condition. The battery has a normal shelf life in absence of alarm as no power is used in the circuit. A horn, Model H-1, plugs into the "lamp" or "bell" outlet of the A-5 unit or the outlet of the RR-1SR unit and sounds a loud alarm whenever the outlet is powered.

Transmitters in the alarm condition will transmit a special coded signal which is superimposed on the AC voltage as carried in the normal power wiring of the location. In other words, the AC acts as a carrier for the information transmitted and eliminates the usual wiring required between alarm detectors or sensors and control panels as well as the actual alarm responsive devices that follow.

The A-5 ultrasonic intrusion alarm unit must have the T-2P pulsating transmitter plugged into its "lamp" outlet for immediate response or plugged into the "bell' outlet for delayed response (10 to 20 second). The T-2P provides the pulsating signal transmission whenever power is applied to its plug-in terminals by the A-5 detector.

The PIA-1 peripheral alarm unit must be plugged into an AC receptacle that is always "live." Turn the unit switch to off and plug into the top duplex receptacle with screws at bottom. Wire the normally closed window and door switches in series to form a closed loop and connect the two ends of the loop to the screw type terminals on the bottom of the PIA-1 unit. Turn the unit switch on and check the loop switches by opening a door or window which should activate the alarm. The signal will continue until 1 to 3 minutes after a window or door switch is reclosed. The unit will reset automatically or may be reset by turning the unit switch off then on. The alarm will cycle if the loop switch remains open by sounding for 2 minutes and quiet for 3, then continue with this pattern. All receivers have an intentional delay of 4 to 15 seconds before triggering an alarm to avoid nuisance or false alarms.

Receivers are adjusted for reception of coded signals as generated by the system transmitters only, but instances such as several light dimmers of the solid-state type operating simultaneously have resulted in an alarm signal. Although cases of this type are very rare, if nuisance alarms show up at any time in the system, a careful check of these or similar sources should be made. Periodic checking of the transmission-reception should be included on your regular preventive maintenance service tips.

Line coupler C-1 is supplied with each receiver, and ensures the proper conduction of the transmitted signal throughout the AC wiring of the protected premises. Only one is required for each location and is simple to install by removing the plug of an electric range or dryer from the outlet and cleaning the excess rubber from the base of the prongs to permit proper electrical contact before slipping the line coupler over the 220-volt prongs and replacing the plug in the socket. If an electric range or clothes dryer is not available, a licensed electrician may remove the staples from the line coupler and install the capacitor across the 220-volt AC line on the house side of the circuitbreakers or fuses inside your main service box. Breakers or fuses must be open during such installation to avoid dangerous electrical shock or hazard.

The HS-T smoke and heat detector-transmitter should be tested at least every six months as follows:

1. The red light must be on for the detector to function!

2. After the unit has been turned on for 15 minutes, the small heating element produces a chimney effect to pump air through the smoke detection chamber, and by introducing smoke from a cigarette or smoldering string into the hole in the bottom of the housing, a loud alarm should result if the unit is detecting smoke properly. The alarm should continue for many minutes, but may be silenced by unplugging the unit for about 5 minutes.

3. Check for heat by placing a cigarette lighter or lighted match close to thermostat (round metal object above the lower front of the unit) from below. This will activate the thermostat and cause the alarm to sound. Unplug for 2 minutes, then plug in again.

4. Make sure that all remote receivers have been triggered to alarm by the HS-T, but remember that there will be a delay of 4 to 15 seconds. Difficulty with any single remote receiver could probably be corrected by checking the line coupler connection. Actually, the best installation for the coupler (capacitor) would be in the circuit breaker or fuse box for most reliable performance. The capacitor offers a low resistance path to the higher frequency of the transmitted signal while displaying an extremely high resistance to the low (60-Hz) AC power frequency.

MALLORY ULTRASONIC ALARM SYSTEM CA1A & ACCESSORIES

The Mallory CA1A ultrasonic alarm plugs into the 120-volt AC line and sends out invisible, silent unavoidable ultrasonic waves that blanket the protected area. Even the slightest movement by anyone 18 to 20 feet away will immediately activate the unit to an alarm condition. A loud audible alarm which may be switched on or off is built into the CA1A unit. Following activation, the alarm may be stopped and reset by lockswitch RS1, automatic timer CAT100 or the manual reset switch on back of CA1A

Several options are available in conjunction with the ultrasonic unit, and since the power line is used for communications between the various units, the only requirement is that all devices plugged into the line outlets are on the same side of the power company transformer.

Accessories include the outdoor horn RSR2, receiver switch RSL1, which activates a lamp or other warning device, security switch SST with an extension button for shut-ins or the bed-ridden to signal for help, receiver horn RSR1 for indoor use, power failure alarm for use with freezers and pumps to sound an alarm when power (AC) is lost (LCM1), and warning devices (bell 60006, horn 87600, and rotating red light RRL1). The CA1DC ultrasonic alarm unit automatically changes to battery operation in case of power failure and powers the motion detector plus a special bell (60007). The three Mallory M915 batteries will power the CA1DC for over a year and the bell for at least 8 hours. Pictorial views of the Mallory CA1A ultrasonic alarm and RST1 remote signal transmitter are shown in Figs. 6-12 and 6-13, respectively.

MODEL MS-200FM

The MS-200FM is a revised design of the MS-200, using an FM detection system. The battery charging circuit eliminates the need for a battery test terminal. A solid-state walk test light is provided, plus improved channel selection frequencies, according to the manufacturer.

The MS-200FM projects an ultrasonic signal into the area to be protected. Any moving objects will activate the alarm relay if the movement continues for a brief period and they approximate the size of a human body. Filtering and delay

Fig. 6-12. Mallory ultrasonic alarm, CA1A.

Fig. 6-13. Mallory remote signal transmitter RST1.

circuitry virtually eliminate false triggering of the system by small animals or sonic booms. The rechargeable nickel cadmium battery provides at least 8 hours of standby operation in case of power failure. An internal tamper switch provides complete security because the alarm signal is actuated when one of the cover plate screws is removed. Maximum range extends to about 30 feet, depending on room acoustics and fixtures, with a range selector to permit adjustments down to about 6 feet minimum.

Input power is 24 volts AC from a T-24V plug-in type UL approved transformer (24v at 20va). The internal power supply is a rechargeable 12-volt nickel cadmium battery, 180 mah, 8 hours minimum standby in case of power failure. The control relay is a SPDT type fully enclosed in a dust-proof nylon cover. The contacts are limited to 200 ma due to internal RF protective filters. The walk-test light is a light-emitting diode (LED) with unlimited life. Operating frequencies are: Type 1, 20.5-21.5 kHz; Type 2, 23.0-24.0 kHz; Type 3, 28.0-29.0 kHz. The unit measures 10.5 inches by 3 inches by 3 inches.

To install the unit, remove the bottom cover held in place by two screws. Check the power switch (see Fig. 6-14) and make sure it is off. The battery may be discharged with the power switch on before installation.

Turn walk light switch to on. Set the range control to the desired area to be protected; refer to Fig. 6-14. A higher range than necessary should not be used because it makes the unit extremely sensitive near the transducers which results in nuisance alarms. Connect the wires from the 24-volt AC transformer (T-24V) to the terminals as shown. Turn the power switch on.

Movement in front of the unit will cause an alarm condition and cause the red "walk light" on the front panel to light. The walk light will remain off in the alarm condition if the walk light switch is off. Allow the unit to run at least one hour and, if possible, overnight before testing for sensitivity to insure a full charge of the battery and to enable the unit to stabilize.

Test the "norm open" and "norm closed" contacts of the terminal with an ohmmeter before connecting the relay wires. Note: The "norm open" and "norm closed" at the terminal strip means with power on and the unit in non-alarm condition. While testing the "norm closed" relay contact, the tamper screw must be turned in to engage the tamper switch and a definite click will be heard. Do not turn the screw in too far or the switch may be damaged. There will be about 30 ohms between the "relay com" and "norm closed" terminals, which accounts for the RF filters in series with all outputs. In the alarm condition, there should also be about 30 ohms between "norm open" and "relay com" terminals due to the RF filters.

Relay wires may now be connected to the "norm open" or "norm closed" and "relay com" terminals according to the system used. Replace the cover plate with the original captive

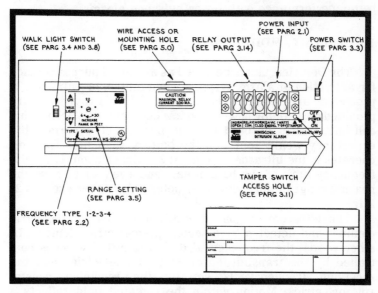

Fig. 6-14. Bottom view of the Morse MS-200FM ultrasonic system.

screws only, since the tamper switch may be defeated or damaged with others.

Any of the following actions will cause an alarm condition:

(a) Movement within the protected area.

(b) Turning the power switch to the off position.

(c) Removal of one of the terminal cover plate screws.

(d) Complete discharge of the built-in standby battery.

If the line power is disconnected, the walk light will not function, but with the standby battery will take over all other functions. The unit must never be left on without AC power or the standby battery will be discharged completely. Replace the terminal cover plate with both screws, since one engages the tamper switch. The AC outlet used for plugging in transformer T-24V must be live at all times; otherwise, the standby battery will be discharged and possibly damaged.

If more than one unit is required in the same area, be sure different frequencies are used. Use different **type numbers** for each; this designates the frequency of the unit as explained in specifications. The type number is always marked on the bottom panel.

Position the unit away from areas of large drafts or high volume heating or air conditioning vents. The MS-200FM detects any movement within its protected area. Drapes, hanging fixtures, doors, etc., when set in motion, will trigger an alarm. Careful consideration of these factors will result in better performance with fewer nuisance alarms.

DELTALERT, MODEL 10412

The DeltAlert unit is designed as a general purpose device for activation of alarm systems when motion or entry into a protected area takes place (Fig. 6-15). Provisions are provided for standby power, and low current levels permit dry cell batteries to be used for this purpose. The normal life expectancy would approach the battery shelf life. The unit operates in the ultrasonic range at 35 kHz, or about twice the frequency limit of the human ear, and even well above the hearing range of dogs and other pets, which never exceeds 25 kHz.

The ultrasonic signal is emitted by one piezoelectric element and detected by a second piezoelectric element. In other words, the frequency of the transmitted wave is controlled by the transmitting crystal (piezoelectric) and the receiving frequency is set by the receiving crystal (piezoelectric). Motion within the radiated field reflects a signal that differs somewhat in frequency from that of the transmitted signal. This change resulting from the movement of an intruder is detected and amplified to activate an internal relay.

A selective frequency amplifier is employed which requires motion to take place at specific rates and with minimum time durations of 0.4 of a second. The unit has an adjustable timing control to allow the device to remain on or activated from 10 seconds to 3 minutes. After this preset period, it resets automatically. Since the unit would be actuated when first turned on, an electronic delay is used to allow the operator to move out of the covered area. The delay is operated by the switch on the back panel. If remote switching is used, the switch must be beyond the detection range of the unit or connected to the input and battery common. If no standby battery is used, the delay will operate as soon as the input power is supplied. A single pole, double throw relay is utilized, and all three contacts are available for wiring into a normally closed circuit or normally open circuit.

The system is solid state throughout and, according to the manufacturer has the capability to completely reject noise signals from any source, and line voltage transients, power interruptions and high level RF signals will not trigger the system. No bi-metallic elements or similar devices are used; all timing is electronic and the amplifier selectivity is sharp enough to avoid the usual nuisance signals while peaking those resulting from intrusion.

A primary advantage offered by the ultrasonic system is the field directivity. Simple reflectors or barriers of absorbent material enable unusual shaping for all types of premises. Basically, a motion sensor, the movement of surfaces confining the field, such as walls, windows, doors and metal blinds, may trigger the unit if allowed to vibrate. The trouble-free installation requires careful planning and consideration.

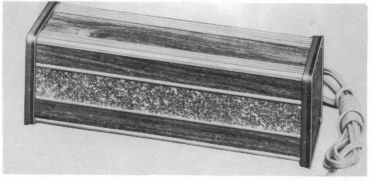

Fig. 6-15. DeltAlert ultrasonic alarm. (Courtesy Delta Products, Inc.)

The side facing the street and the amount of traffic is involved, as well as the hours of activity, aircraft overhead, vibration caused by heavy vehicles, trains, etc.; all such factors must be evaluated.

Most installations in either homes or places of business require coverage only of specific areas and the type of surfaces in the vicinity will strongly affect the total coverage. Smooth hard surfaces like concrete, wood, glass and vinyl are good reflectors and tend to increase the coverage, but draperies or carpets have little effect on range. Glass windows are subject to vibration from winds or trucks; therefore, the ultrasonic unit should be positioned in such a way as to avoid reflecting the ultrasonic waves off the glass area. The unit must not be positioned in front of such areas; a corner would be far better in this case. The controls on the back panel are adjusted in the following manner, starting with the sensitivity control to adjust the output from the Doppler frequency amplifier and determine the range at which the unit may be tripped. Sensitivity at maximum allows triggering in excess of 20 feet, but mid-point reduces the range to about 10 to 14 ft. The remote horn unit is pictured in Fig. 6-16.

The time interval control adjusts the length of time the unit remains in the activated mode after tripping. The

Fig. 6-16. DeltAlert remote horn.

minimum setting allows less than 15 seconds and the maximum setting provides about three minutes. At any setting, the unit constantly recycles whenever motion occurs and will not turn off even at the minimum setting if motion is continuous.

The persistence control adjusts the time constant of a second integrator with a memory. Primary use is to eliminate false alarms resulting from short term shock and vibration, lightning strikes and insects. When the control setting is minimum, a single motion lasting one-half second will cause an alarm condition. At the maximum setting, motion must continue for approximately two seconds before an alarm condition prevails. Continuous motion is not really required, but at least three separate motions of one-half second each must occur for the alarm to trip.

The following procedure is recommended for setting the controls:

1. Set the sensitivity to maximum, the time interval and persistence to minimum.

2. With the unit properly located and power applied, turn the switch to on and wait 20 seconds. Walk in front of the unit at the maximum range desired and listen for the relay to click on and off. Reduce the sensitivity slowly until the unit fails to activate when walking at the maximum range desired. Increase the sensitivity approximately 10 percent for the final setting (rotate the control 30 degrees toward higher sensitivity).

3. Set the persistence control to mid-range and reset the time interval to maximum.

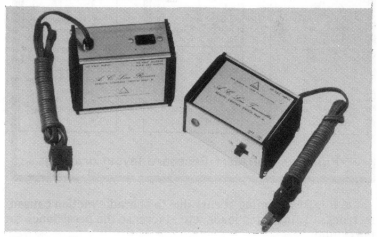

Fig. 6-17. Remote control switching units (transmitter and receiver), DeltAlert system.

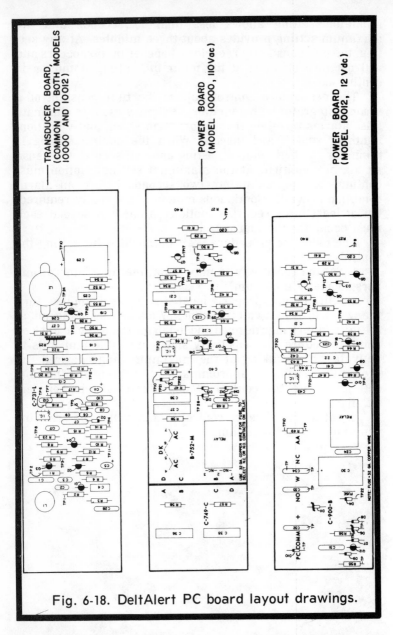

Fig. 6-18. DeltAlert PC board layout drawings.

4. If false alarming occurs due to sporadic motion caused by trucks, trains, wind loads, etc., increase the persistence to maximum.

The remote control switching units are pictured in Fig. 6-17.

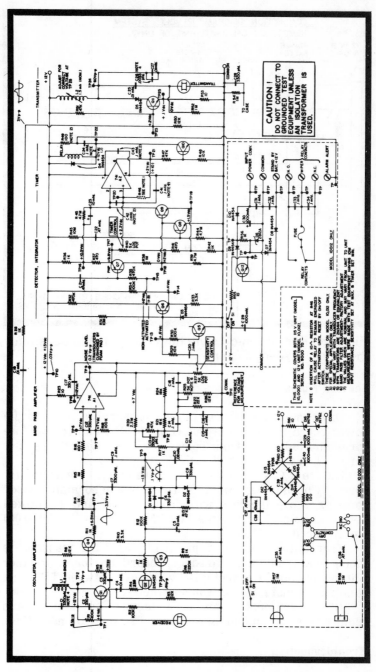

Fig. 6-19. Schematic diagram of the Delta Model 10412 ultrasonic alarm.

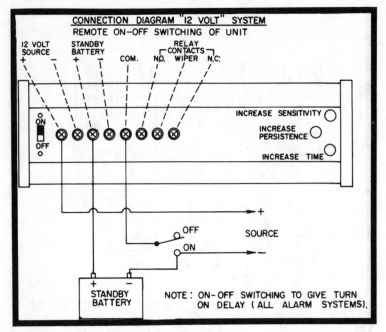

Fig. 6-20. Remote on-off switching connection diagram for the 12v DeltAlert system.

Service Notes

Dry contact conversion (Model 10000 only), refer to the power board PC board layout (Fig. 6-18). Remove two fuse wires marked "AC" from holes 4-5 and 6-7. Insert one fuse wire in holes 5-6, marked "DK."

N.O. to N.C. conversion: Units are factory connected for normally open (N.O.) contacts. To change to normally closed contacts, move the fuse wire from holes 1 and 2, marked "NO," to holes 2 and 3, marked "NC," on the Model 10000 power board.

Transmitter current adjustment: With the transducers facing down, lay the transducer board on foam or other suitable padding. Connect a DC voltmeter between TP25 and common; adjust L2 for 0.1 volt on a meter.

R25 adjustment: This is a factory adjustment and requires special equipment for correct setting. **Do not adjust.**

Troubleshooting

Listen for the relay click on activation. If the click is heard, the trouble may be a blown fuse wire. Replace with No.

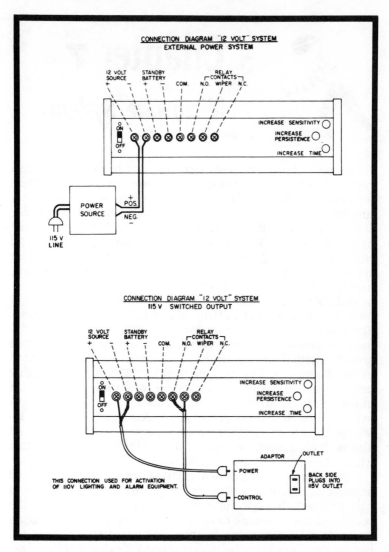

Fig. 6-21. External power system connection diagrams for the 12v (left) and the 115v DeltAlert systems.

32 copper wire. Refer to the schematic diagram in Fig. 6-19.

In case of poor sensitivity, check for the oscillation signal at TP4. If no signal is present, check the oscillator components. If the unit is dead, check the DC levels at TP1, TP4, TP9, TP21 and TP22. The connection diagrams for remote on-off switching and other external arrangements are covered in Figs. 6-20 and 6-21.

Chapter 7

Microwave Systems

Microwave alarm systems, also referred to as radar alarm systems, are used to protect areas more limited than those regularly handled by the ultrasonic detection method. Most current systems are completely solid-state Doppler type radar devices utilizing RF carriers in the UHF or microwave frequency bands. The systems afford complete wall-to-wall and floor-to-ceiling coverage, with a capability of handling areas in excess of 30,000 cubic feet per unit. The microwave field as generated by the transmitter will penetrate most non-metallic structures such as plaster, plywood, or other types of walls and, to a smaller extent, concrete and similar surfaces. The waves are reflected by metallic objects and the equipment responds to any movement by a human in the covered area, but with the use of filters, the system may be unaffected by small animals. Any movement within 25 feet of the sensing unit will cause the first alarm stage to be triggered almost immediately. If further movement does not occur, the alarm will reset itself after a preset time. A movement by the intruder in the area covered, however, could trigger the second alarm stage, a condition which could be maintained for quite a while, depending on the adjustment.

Once an alarm condition exists as produced by a stated amount of movement within a given period of time, the system will proceed through its regular cycle regardless of the position of the switching device. Turning the system off during its cycle only eliminates further movement from detection, but the cycle could not be interrupted as it existed at the time. Any tampering with the off-on switch would normally result in triggering of the alarm system. The remote detector, actually an antenna, relays microwaves generated by a solid-state oscillator. A 5,000 square foot area from floor to ceiling may easily be protected, and any slight human movement will change this load and at the same time the frequency. This is the well-known Doppler effect or frequency shift, and when amplified by a series of solid-state stages, the change is detected and automatically used to produce the alarm condition.

When an intruder hides on the premises during occupancy and awaits night closing to burglarize, he will be detected as soon as he moves by the radar waves saturating the protected area. There is no way out from this wall-to-wall and floor-to-ceiling radar wave coverage. Other types of systems could ignore the thief during his inside operations and only pick him up and sound the alarm after he left the premises. This is definitely too late and is a big plus with the radar system. An intruder can defeat the photoelectric beam even though invisible and pulsed by lining up the transmitter and receiver while avoiding the straight line between the two. This would enable penetration of the protected area with little effort, but the microwave system would be far too much because its waves cover every nook and crevice of the assigned area. Foil systems require regular maintenance and repair, are obvious to the observer and very easy to defeat. The radar system is easy to conceal, since its waves will penetrate any non-metallic material including plaster walls.

Installation offers no problem with most manufactured systems of this type, and in most cases the only requirement is the ability to follow simple directions, plug in, connect accessories, and turn it on. After checking operation, advise the owner or manager of the system operation and who to call in case of malfunction. Some remote types, along with necessary supplies, will necessitate a minimum of installation know how, but even these units are easily located, and with the complete step-by-step instructions usually included, no trouble should develop.

Servicing microwave detectors should prove quite simple as a result of modular type construction embodying complete solid-state circuitry. Replacement of panels is not difficult and a limited stock of the ones needed most is well within reach of a small business. Since these are mostly plug-in types, a few spares may be carried by the alarm servicing specialist for replacement of defective units by the well-proven substitution method. The defective panel or module can then be returned to the distributor or factory, as the case may be, for replacement or credit.

AMERICAN DISTRICT TELEGRAPH CO. MODEL 7130-205

The radiation of a pattern of microwave energy within an area and the reception of energy reflected back enables the ADT Model 205 to detect any intruder's movements and signal the automatic alarm. The system has the ability to compare any differences between the transmitted and received patterns, which would normally result from any movement

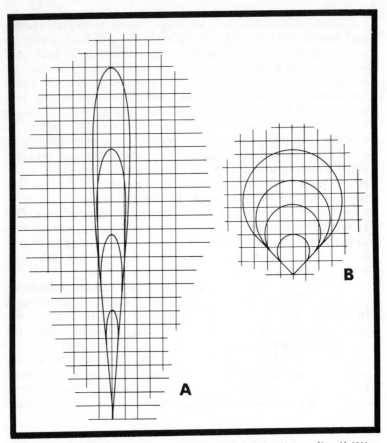

Fig. 7-1. These drawings illustrate the pattern flexibility of the American District Telegraph Co. microwave intrusion detector, from 20 by 100 feet (A) to 100 by 100 feet.

within the area covered. The fact that radio type waves are used to cover the area to be protected, rather than sound waves which depend on air for radiation, insure reliability unaffected by heating or cooling blowers, vents, ducts and changes in temperature. Vibrations and loud noises do not affect the system, and it screens out signals caused by birds, mice and other small animals. The system offers unusual flexibility in adapting to just about any shape or size of coverage. Selecting an appropriate pair of antennas from five different patterns offers positive space protection for almost any premise configuration. Patterns vary in shape from the narrowest (20 feet by 300 feet) to the widest (100 feet by 100 feet). See the sketch in Fig. 7-1, which shows the unusual flexibility mentioned.

Consisting of but two units, transceiver and plug-in transformer, the basic system bypasses many of the costly preliminaries. The transceiver contains a microwave transmitter and receiver, and multiple units may be used in the same area without interference with each other to attain the protection coverage needed. A constantly powered wall receptacle within 200 feet of the transceiver is required to plug in the transformer. The low-voltage line from its secondary connects to the transceiver through a pair of unshielded wires. Thus, only the low-voltage standards of state and local electrical codes are applicable since the transformer output is under 25 volts. In most cases, open-type wiring is permissible.

A built-in standby power supply is provided by a battery which is automatically recharged and switched in during power failure from the line. Following a power line failure, the system automatically switches back to the line as soon as it is restored. Although ideal for many installations, microwave energy is not readily contained by non-metallic or non-masonry construction and its practicability should be considered by the installation specialist. Complete coverage of a shop-office, or similar type area is shown in Fig. 7-2 with two units placed in diagonally opposite corners.

BOURNS MODEL RA-3 & SA-3 ULTRASONIC-MICROWAVE COINCIDENT ALARM SYSTEM

The Model RA-3 alarm system combines the best features of ultrasonic and UHF sensors because **both** must be triggered

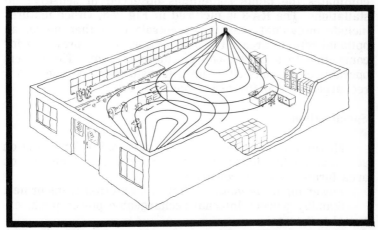

Fig. 7-2. This shop area employs two ADT Model 7130-205 microwave units. (Courtesy American District Telegraph Co.)

Fig. 7-3. Coincident microwave-ultrasonic alarm system Model RA-3. (Courtesy Bourns Security Systems)

to initiate an alarm. The ultra high frequency signal penetrates walls, windows and other solid objects and may be triggered by passing vehicles or persons; the ultrasonic will not penetrate solid objects, but may be triggered by high intensity sound waves such as air currents, large blowers, compressors and aircraft. The inherent characteristics of these two detection modes have resulted in nuisance or false alarm problems in the past, but, by requiring both types of sensors to be triggered coincidentally, the RA-3 alarm system eliminates the faults sometimes observed in sensitive installations. The RA-3 is pictured in Fig. 7-3. Other features include individual sensitivity controls for either mode, an optional remote area ultrasonic sensor, and a provision for connection to a closed-loop perimeter system. The system operates on 24 volts AC from a transformer and contains a rechargeable standby power pack.

Specifications

Maximum range: 6 to 40 feet (ultrasonic) depending on acoustics and humidity; 6 to 40 feet (microwave) depending on area furnishings and construction.

Power input: 24 volts AC from an external transformer.

Standby power: Internal rechargeable power pack, external test term.

Enclosure: Decorator wood cabinet, 11⅜" wide, 6¼" deep, 9⅝" high.

Electronics: Solid-state design.

Anti-tamper switch on the case and terminal cover.

Four different channel operating frequencies provide for multiple unit security protection in adjacent areas.

A three-position switch located on the rear panel permits the installer to adjust the range of the ultrasonic and ultrahigh frequency modes independent of each other. After adjustment of each mode, the selector is placed in the operating position for intrusion protection. Additional protection is offered by the RA-3 self-contained power pack which provides approximately four hours of operation in the event of AC line power failure. An additional set of terminals on the rear panel connect to a pair of relay contacts that may be used with a closed-loop protection system to secure doors and windows. Two other terminals on the rear panel provide for the addition of a remote ultrasonic sensor such as the SA-3 (described below) to increase the detection range in conjunction with the ultra high frequency sensor.

The SA-3 offers the same dependable, silent protection system used in banks, military installations and other high-security areas. Defeating by mirrors, reflective devices or any other means is not possible, and briefly sustained motion by intruders within the protected area will actuate the responsive device, whether it be bells, horns, lights, central station, telephone dialers, CCTV, etc. It operates from 24v AC supplied from the secondary of a 115-to-24v transformer which isolates the unit from the power line to avoid a shock hazard as well as reduce the voltage to the desired level. Internal standby power is provided by a battery which is instantly and automatically connected in case of AC power failure. The unit's range depends upon room acoustics and may be adjusted from 6 to 28 feet with a variable control on the rear panel. Reflection of the ultrasonic beam by hard surfaces will alter both the pattern and range. After initial settings, a cover protects all connections to prevent alteration and-or disconnection. Special filters and delay circuits reduce nusiance alarms caused by small animals, windblown curtains, etc., and complete shielding and filtering completely eliminates RF interference. The SA-3 is pictured in Fig. 7-4.

Specifications

Range: 6 to 28 feet, depending on room acoustics, with a range adjustment on the rear panel (knob).

Power input: 24 volts AC from an external transformer.

Standby power: Internal rechargeable battery, 4 hour minimum life with external test terminals.

Fig. 7-4. Ultrasonic alarm Model SA-3, designed to operate with the RA-3 microwave system in Fig. 7-3. (Courtesy Bourns Security Systems)

Indicator light: Indicates alarm trip for adjustment of sensitivity and beam.

Mounting: Model SW-4 swivel mount available.

Enclosure: Steel, two-tone gray wrinkle paint, 10" x 4½" x 1¾". Walnut book shelf (speaker type) cabinet available.

Electronics: Fully solid-state circuit board and transducers treated for protection against moisture and fungus. Designed to meet all requirements of UL Specification 639. Anti-tamper switch on the case and terminal cover.

A rear panel layout sketch of the SA-3 is shown in Fig. 7-5.

JOHNSON SERVICE CO. MODEL G-1 MICROWAVE MOTION DETECTOR

This intrusion detection device is designed for use in conjunction with the MPS Series monitor or any other monitor offering an alarm indication by opening or closing a relay. The G-1 unit may be mounted on a bracket or merely placed on any

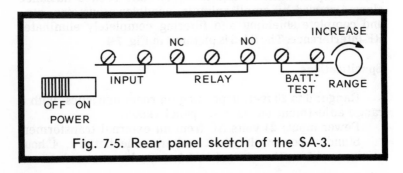

Fig. 7-5. Rear panel sketch of the SA-3.

flat surface as desired. The reflex klystron generates the microwave frequency and the remainder of the circuitry is solid state. Fail-safe circuits are incorporated to warn against tampering or component failures with alarm relays energized in the normal condition, which permits an alarm indication when de-energized. Noise, temperature changes, air currents and line voltage fluctuations from +10 percent to -15 percent have no effect on the operation of the G-1 unit. UL approved, it may be used in connection with other types of security systems. Standby power is supplied by batteries which are automatically connected when required, or connection may be made to an emergency generator for continuous operation during prolonged power failures.

Specifications

Power required: 120 volts AC (60 Hz) or standby battery pack.

Power consumption: Approximately 36 watts.

Range: Adjustable to 150 feet.

Volume of coverage: 32,000 cubic feet (maximum)

Detection capability: 3 square feet, moving 3 inches per second to 15 miles per hour.

Dimensions: 11 inches wide by 7 inches high by 10¾ inches deep.

The Doppler effect is the apparent change in frequency of a sound or electromagnetic wave caused by relative motion between the receiver and transmitter. As the two approach each other by the movement of either or both, the apparent frequency of the received energy is increased. As they separate or move away from each other, the apparent frequency of the received energy is decreased. If transmitter and receiver remain stationary with energy reflected from a moving object, as the reflected object moves toward the receiver an apparent increase in frequency of the received energy will be sensed, but the received energy will appear to decrease in frequency as the reflecting object moves away. By the same token, no frequency shift will result as long as the reflecting object remains stationary. This principle of detecting a moving object is utilized in the G-1 microwave motion detector.

A block diagram of the unit is shown in Fig. 7-6. The microwave signal is generated by an oscillator in the motion detector and transmitted through a horn type antenna. The high microwave frequency used is reflected by metal and has many of the characteristics of light. The beam from the horn antenna, in fact, simulates a beam of invisible light to protect

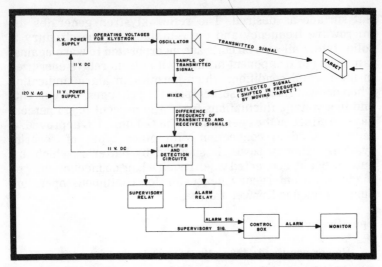

Fig. 7-6. Block diagram of the Johnson Service Co. Model G-1 motion detector.

the area with electromagnetic waves or energy. The reflected signal from the covered area is picked up by the receiving antenna located beneath the horn, and the received signal is fed to the crystal mixer located in the receiver. The signal generated by the transmitter is sampled before transmission and fed to the receiver mixer stage for comparison with signals reflected back from the protected area.

As the transmitted signal strikes an object moving away from the G-1, the signal reflected back is higher in apparent frequency. The mixer output is always equal to the difference between the transmitted and received signals, regardless of whether the received wave is higher or lower than the trans-mitted wave in frequency. If the object reflecting the signal stops moving or leaves the protected area, the output of the mixer immediately drops to a supervisory level. This crystal mixer output is amplified by the following stage (see Fig. 7-7) until it is large enough to be converted to a DC change at the alarm relay. The amplification and detection (rectification) process provides the necessary power to de-energize the normally energized alarm relay and the alarm signal is given.

The motion detector contains two power supplies; one is the highly regulated 11-volt DC source for the amplifier and detection circuits and the other the DC-to-DC converter which provides high voltage for the klystron oscillator and operates from the 11-volt output of the regulated power supply. The ripple voltage at the output of the klystron voltage source is used to modulate that tube, and the modulation is detected by

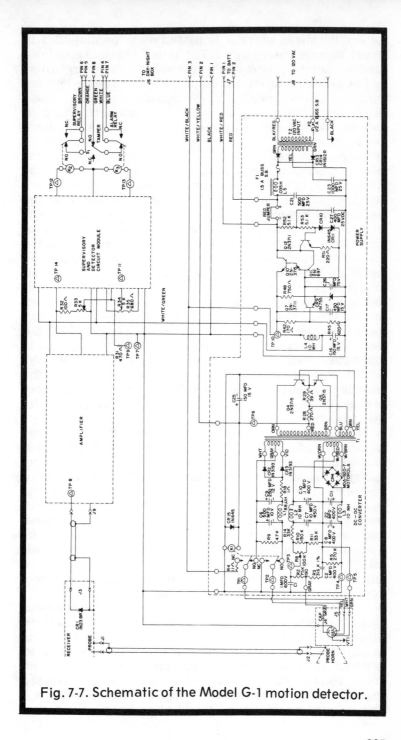

Fig. 7-7. Schematic of the Model G-1 motion detector.

the crystal mixer where it is passed on to be amplified to furnish the supervisory signal. The amplified signal goes to an auxiliary detection circuit to hold another relay energized as long as oscillator, mixer and amplifier stages are performing properly. This supervisory circuit detects any loss of supervisory signal, which may be caused by component failure, to open the supervisory relay contacts and present an alarm condition.

When used with the MPS-4 monitor, opening the alarm relay or supervisory relay results in a change in current flow through the active-standby control box as resistors are switched into the circuit. The current is produced by the monitor and any changes are sensed by the monitor circuit. The monitor is connected by a telephone-pair or any other two-wire circuit. As the active-standby box is switched to the "active" position, power from the 11-volt supply is applied to the DC-to-DC converter which in turn applies its output voltage to the klystron. In the "standby" position, the 11-volt supply is removed from the converter but applied to all other circuits as long as the unit is plugged in. The supervisory relay opens when the equipment is switched to "standby," but the alarm relay remains closed. The filament of the klystron is continuously heated, and there is a relay in the filament circuit to connect the filament to the 11-volt source in the "standby" condition. When switched to "active," the relay switches the filament to a separate 6-volt output on the DC-to-DC converter.

The klystron oscillator, shown in Fig. 7-8 with voltages required for operation, has a cathode heated by the filament which emits electrons to be focused and attracted to the anode. The anode is also a resonant cavity tuned to the operating frequency. This cavity is at the same potential as the metal envelope or shell and, for reasons of safety, operated at DC ground. In the klystron the term "resonator" is used rather than "anode" as would be the case in other tubes. Electrons are beamed from the cathode, through the resonator and out toward the repeller. Since the repeller, acting as a sort of reflector, is negative with respect to the resonator, the electrons are turned back and pass the resonator again.

When oscillating, the voltage appears across the resonator "gap," which is the region of interaction between the electron stream and the RF energy in the resonator cavity. Electrons passing through this gap are either accelerated or decelerated as the RF gap voltage changes in magnitude and polarity with time. Accelerated electrons leave the gap at increased velocity and the decelerated electrons at decreased velocity. This velocity modulation of the electron beam causes electrons leaving the gap at different times to drift together in bunches. If the bunches are in phase with the cavity, they give up energy to the resonant cavity to sustain oscillations, and if the electron passes through the gap out of phase, it takes energy from the gap and picks up speed.

The frequency of oscillation is determined primarily by the physical dimensions of the resonant cavity, but slight changes in frequency do result from changes in the applied potential. This enables the reflex klystron to be tuned electronically, and, with the resonator voltage constant, the reflector voltage may be varied to provide several oscillation peaks. Power falls off gradually on each side of these peaks until oscillation stops. The regions of oscillation are "modes" and reflector voltage is always adjusted in the G-1 to provide operation at the peak in one of the modes. A typical example of how frequency and power output are varied with reflector or repeller voltage is shown in Fig. 7-9. A small amount of residual ripple on the DC supply voltage to the klystron enables it to be slightly modulated, and this appears in the

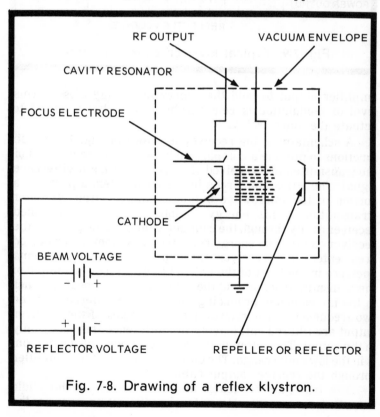

Fig. 7-8. Drawing of a reflex klystron.

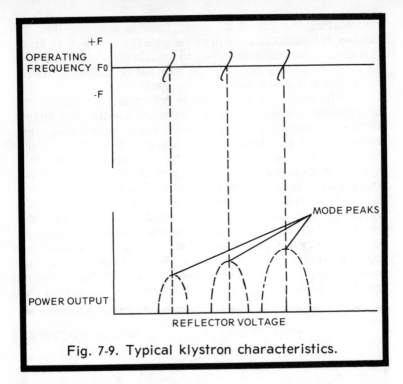

Fig. 7-9. Typical klystron characteristics.

amplifier output to hold the supervisory relay closed. This level of modulation is considerably below that required to actuate the alarm relay.

A schematic of the receiver is shown in Fig. 7-7, which functions to provide a comparison between the frequencies of the transmitted and received signals by offering a difference signal. The adjustable probe in the horn antenna picks up a portion of the microwave output of the klystron oscillator (transmitter). This energy is introduced into the tuned receiver cavity through the coupling cable and the probe in the receiver cavity. The energy reflected back from the protected area enters the receiver through the receiving antenna aperture in the front of the unit. The two signals, a sample of the transmitted signal and the reflected signal, beat together in the mixer diode, producing the sum and difference of the two frequencies. The microwave frequencies of the receiver output are filtered out, leaving the difference frequency only in the output. The output of the receiver, upon sensing motion, is in the low audio range. The output is coupled to the amplifier through the receiver output cable.

The high-gain feedback amplifier increases the audio output of the receiver to a level sufficient to operate the detector circuits. The output to the detector is taken from the center terminal (wiper) of the gain control potentiometer R33.

The audio detector de-energizes alarm relay K3 upon reception of an audio (motion) signal from the amplifier. The contacts of K3 are connected across a resistor in the active-standby box so that as the relay contacts open, the resistor is in series with the alarm line circuit. The tamper switch is connected in series with the relay contacts to provide an open-line indication when that switch is opened.

The system incorporates a fail-safe type of circuit, which is designed to present an alarm indication upon loss of the supervisory signal. In the event that the supervisory signal is lost, the circuit will de-energize relay K-2, and as the relay opens it removes a shunt from a resistor in the active-standby box, decreasing the alarm line current and causing an alarm indication. A very strong motion signal fed into the amplifier will cause the supervisory modulation to be clipped from the amplifier output to the supervisory circuit, and this causes the supervisory relay opening to give a trouble indication, in addition to the motion detection indication, as someone comes close enough to the unit for tampering.

The low-voltage power supply (Fig. 7-7) provides the operating voltage for the amplifier and detection circuits as well as the DC-to-DC converter. The full-wave type supply offers regulation provided by transistors and diodes in the output.

The converter provides voltages as required to operate the klystron. Switching transistors Q4 and Q5, connected in the primary of the high-voltage transformer, oscillate at a frequency of 2.5 kHz to convert the 11-volt DC from the low-voltage source to an AC signal which is stepped-up to the required level through a transformer. The high voltages required for klystron operation are taken from the bridge rectifier, and the 100K potentiometer (R8) controls the klystron repeller potential. Relay K-1 connects the klystron filament to the output of the 11-volt source through an 11-ohm resistor if the converter is de-energized and transfers the filament to the 6-volt output of the converter when the latter is energized. This maintains continuous filament voltage to the klystron and thus extends its useful life. The 11-volt input to the converter is controlled by the switch in the active-standby box.

The circuitry of the control box is shown in Fig. 7-10. You may notice that the active-standby switch energizes the DC-to-DC converter in the "active" position and de-energizes it in the "standby" position. The relay contacts are shown in the "active" position, with no motion being sensed by the G-1 unit.

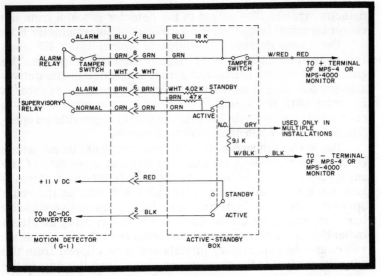

Fig. 7-10. Active-standby control box interconnections, Johnson Service Co. Model G-1 motion detector.

Resistors are switched into the line circuit by the relays to provide the alarm indications.

Any one of three positions may be selected for mounting the G-1 unit and there is a pattern of seven holes in the bottom of the case. The holes in the mount will correspond with the holes in the case in any one of the three positions only. The mount has a locking ball and socket arrangement to permit proper aiming of the unit.

The power cable plugs into the rear of the G-1 and is terminated in a NEMA 3-prong plug. If the unit is plugged into a 2-prong outlet, an adapter plug with a ground lead should be used for the safety of personnel. If the unit is to be used with a standard GS-1 standby battery pack, clip out the red jumper from the rear of the power supply circuit board. Fig. 7-11 clarifies this. Plug the battery pack output cable into the male receptacle in back of the G-1. Plug the G-1 power cable into the outlet in the side of the GS-1. Plug the cable on the active-standby control box into the rectangular outlet in back of the G-1. A schematic of the control box is shown in Fig. 7-10. If a monitor other than the MPS series is used, connections to the alarm relays can be made in the control box. Relay contacts are rated at .25 amp. If more than one G-1 unit is to be used with a single monitor, connect the control boxes as shown in Fig. 7-12, using 3-wire cable between the boxes.

When the unit is plugged in, the active-standby switch should be in the "standby" position to limit the initial surge of

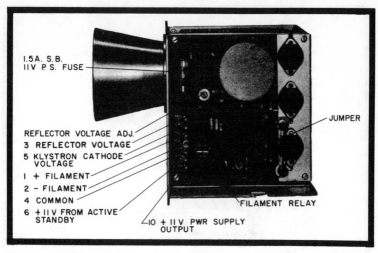

Fig. 7-11. Model G-1 motion detector with case removed.

current. After installation and checking, it should remain plugged into the AC power at all times. During daytime hours when the protected area is occupied, switch the control to "standby." The monitor switch must also be switched to "standby." Matching switches in the "standby" position disables door switches used in the system if any, and also turns off the klystron oscillator in G-1. The switches must be matched or a continuous alarm will be generated. During night hours while the area is to be protected, the active-standby switch is in the "active" position and the monitor is

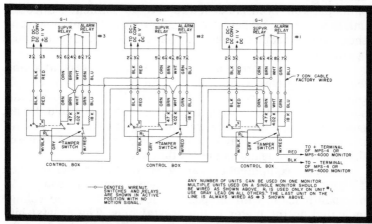

Fig. 7-12. Diagram showing interconnection of multiple G-1 units to a single monitor.

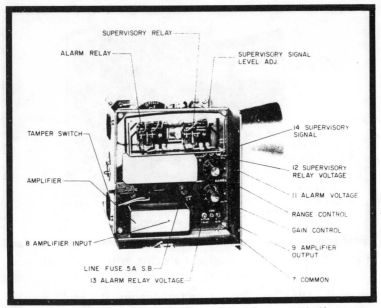

Fig. 7-13. Another view of the G-1 detector with the case removed.

also switched to "active." The monitor may not be reset and the area is completely protected.

After plugging in the unit, allow about one hour or so for warmup with the case cover on and the active-standby switch in the "active" position before making adjustments. Refer to the pictorial views in Figs. 7-11 and 7-13 for control locations and test points. The Simpson 260 or any other equivalent 20,000 ohms-per-volt VOM is needed for the adjustments. Once the unit is installed and set up properly, readjustment of controls should not be required even after several months of continuous operation.

Access to controls as well as test points is available without completely removing the unit from its cover. Simply remove the four screws at the corners of the front panel and slide the chassis forward until catches on the sides hold. Do not pull the plugs from the receptacles, and if it becomes necessary to remove cover completely, depress the catches on the sides and slide the unit out of the cover.

With the equipment operating, connect the meter between TP-8 on amplifier case and TP-7 (black, common), using a 50-microamp scale, with the positive lead to TP-8. The voltage indicated on the meter is the crystal bias. The crystal bias should be between 25 and 100 millivolts. If needed, adjust the nylon screw inside of the horn antenna to provide this range.

112

Vary the repeller voltage control (reflector) throughout its full range and two output peaks will probably be noted. These peaks are proportional to the power modes of the klystron. Crystal bias changes as the klystron output changes and operation may be on the peak of either mode, but the higher is recommended for best results overall. Be careful not to stand in front of antennas while adjusting because body reflections will affect the readings. Peak the voltage on the proper mode by adjusting the reflector voltage control. Operating on the exact mode peak is most important for stable and reliable operation of the system.

The supervisory signal level is adjusted by using common and output jacks with the meter on the 2.5-volt AC scale. (Interference should be minimized by turning off fluorescent lights.) Connect the meter between the TP14 supervisory signal and TP-7 (common). It should be 0.2 to 0.75 volts AC. If the supervisory signal level is not within this tolerance, readjust the nylon screw in the horn antenna as follows:

1. If the supervisory level is too low, adjust the nylon screw in, but do not exceed the 100 mv crystal voltage level.

2. If the supervisory signal reads too high, adjust the nylon screw out, but do not reduce the crystal voltage below 25 mv.

If these two adjustments do not permit the proper signal level to be established, replace the IN23BR crystal in the receiver cavity. Refer to the repair section instructions which follow for the proper procedure in replacing the crystal, and after replacement recheck the klystron mode to determine if it is correctly peaked. Then, readjust the crystal voltage level as suggested previously.

Switch the active-standby control to "standby" and turn the range control clockwise (right) until the alarm relay drops out. Decrease the setting 2½ small divisions on the dial; this is the maximum range setting. The alarm bias voltage should be about 1.1 to 1.2 volts DC. Later adjustment of this control will be necessary, but never use dial settings higher than this point or nuisance alarms may result.

The amplifier gain control must be set to suit the installation, since operation at higher settings than necessary is definitely not recommended. Remove the cover from the active-standby control box and disconnect the blue and white wires from the potted switch. Connect an ohmmeter across these wires from the G-1 unit. Pull out the tamper switch operating plunger at the back of the G-1 to lock the tamper switch in a closed position. Switch to "active," and the limits of the protected area can now be determined by walking in the zone to be protected while watching the meter deflections. A short circuit indication means motion detection. If a monitor can be brought to the area and connected as usual, it will offer a more convenient means of testing than using the meter.

The following table shows the approximate initial dial settings for the range and gain controls for use in adjusting the equipment. These settings will definitely vary in different environments:

Range (ft.)	Gain Control	Range Control
150	8.5 to 9.0	8.0 to 8.5
125	8.0 to 8.5	7.5 to 7.0
100	7.5 to 8.0	7.0 to 7.5
75	7.0 to 7.5	6.5 to 7.0
50	6.5 to 7.0	6.0 to 6.5
25	5.0 to 6.0	4.0 to 6.0

Begin with the setting that is close to the actual range required and adjust the gain control until the desired coverage is obtained. At ranges less than maximum, it is advisable to slightly decrease the range control setting along with the gain. The two controls do interact, since if one is lower, the other may have to be increased. It is best to adjust the controls to barely cover the required area.

Servicing

Motion detectors and monitors should be returned to the factory for major repairs, but fuses, crystals and any minor repair that can be accomplished quickly in the field should be handled on location if possible. If the G-1 fails to operate properly, the following checks will facilitate the location of trouble and the repair.

The 11-volt DC source may be measured between TP-10 (red) and TP-7 (black) and should measure about 11 volts. If there is no voltage, check the line fuse and 11-volt supply fuse.

Checking the high voltage supply (DC-to-DC converter) requires the use of **caution** because voltages are present that are dangerous to life. Be careful at all times! Position the active-standby switch to "active" and measure voltages as follows:

1. TP-3 (reflector) to TP-4 (common), -310 to -440 volts, depending on the reflector control position. TP-4 is positive (+).

2. TP-4 (common) to TP-5 (cathode), -250 volts, TP-4 is positive (+).

3. TP-1 (white, filament) to TP-2 (yellow, filament), +6.3 volts. **CAUTION:** +250 volts to ground. TP-1 is positive (+).

If voltages are close to the values given, the DC-to-DC converter is satisfactory; if voltages are zero, check the 11-volt supply fuse. Never disconnect the klystron plugs when the equipment is in the "active" condition with the klystron operating—**the klystron will be damaged!**

To check the crystal mixer, place the active-standby switch in the "standby" position and remove the amplifier plug from the amplifier. Measure the resistance across the receiver output cable with the meter on ohms X100. Reverse the meter leads and repeat. The forward resistance should be about 200 to 400 ohms and the back resistance should approximate 50K to 110K. If the readings are reasonably close to these values, the crystal has an adequate front-to-back resistance ratio and is all right as a rule, unless it is noisy. Even though the crystal checks okay on the ohmmeter, the noise problem could exist which, in turn, could lead to false alarms. If this problem appears, a known good crystal should be substituted. Where the area to be protected is large or an excessively high supervisory signal level is indicated, the crystal should be replaced. Sometimes a sluggish condition will appear, but in any event another crystal is likely to be the solution. Any time the crystal is replaced, readjustment of the G-1 controls will probably be necessary. At this time, a review of the protected area for moving or vibrating objects is in order, as fans, air conditioners, swaying fixtures, and venetian blinds could be causing a problem.

To replace the crystal, remove the phono plug from the crystal cap and unscrew the cap. Remove from the receiver shell. The crystal can be removed by lifting the ear washer with pliers or a bent paper clip. The transparent plastic insulating washer may come out with the crystal or stay in place, but be careful not to lose it. When replacing the crystal, put the insulating washer on the crystal if it came out with the old one. Then push the new crystal in gently to locate the blind socket and seat firmly. After cap and cable are replaced, recheck the resistance to make certain there are no shorts. Always keep spare crystals in their protective foil containers, and when handling crystals be sure to pick up both ends at the same time to avoid the possibility of destroying with stray electrostatic charges!

Check the crystal bias and vary the reflector voltage as explained previously. If a normal bias of 25 to 100 mv is obtained and the power modes can be peaked normally, the klystron may be assumed to be good. Re-peak the klystron output. If required voltages for the klystron are present and the crystal is good, but no bias voltage can be obtained, the klystron is probably defective.

When replacing the klystron, make sure the G-1 is turned off. Then remove the rubber plugs and four screws holding the klystron in place. Remove the old tube and install a new klystron with the 3-pin end of the tube toward the right with the serial number up. Both rubber plugs must be in place before applying power to the equipment. Readjust all controls as previously explained.

Check the maximum range potentiometer setting with the equipment in "standby" and the amplifier gain control fully clockwise (right). Increase the range by turning the control clockwise (right) until the alarm relay de-energizes; then slowly readjust to just achieve pull in. Measure the voltage from TP-11 (alarm bias) to TP-7 common, which should be about 1.1 volts DC. The fully clockwise position of the range control should be about 0.8 volts. Set the voltage to 1.1 volts, which should be approximately 8.4 on the control dial. Place the active-standby switch in the "active" position. With motion detected the voltage should drop sharply and the alarm relay should open. The relay should close again if motion stops.

If the alarm relay remains open at a setting of 1.2 volts, check the supervisory voltage level and reduce to allow proper relay action. If the alarm relay remains open at a supervisory voltage of less than 0.2 volts, there may be excessive ripple on the high-voltage power supply output. Check the adjustment of the reflector voltage, as this may be caused by the klystron operating off the mode peak. Finally, check the crystal as explained above.

If the equipment is properly adjusted and in the "active" position, the failure of the supervisory relay to pull in may indicate a problem in the amplifier or detection circuits, assuming the rest have checked out properly. It should be noted that very strong motion signals may cause the supervisory relay to drop out, as a result of amplifier saturation. As this condition is normal, it should not be considered to be a problem.

Relay contacts often require cleaning after a year or so of continuous operation. Although relay adjustment on location is not recommended, the relay contacts may be safely cleaned with a piece of smooth paper carefully drawn between them. Do not use force as they may be bent out of adjustment quite easily. The voltage from TP-13 of the alarm relay to the TP-7 common should measure about 3.0 volts DC for hold-in with no motion near the unit, while the voltage on TP-12 of the supervisory relay to TP-7 common would approximate 4.5 volts. A careful check of all adjustments is recommended before concluding that the equipment is defective.

Modification of the G-1 Microwave Motion Detector

The advantage of replacing the klystron oscillator with the AG-1001-3 solid-state oscillator is at least three-fold. The original expense incurred will be returned many times in future savings. The AG-1001-3 oscillator is installed in the G-1 unit as follows:

(a) Remove the G-1 detector from the case.

(b) Refer to Fig. 7-14 and remove connector (1) as shown. Save the mounting hardware for later reassembly.

(c) Remove and discard the klystron assembly (2) including the mounting hardware (2A). Do not return the klystron to factory (give or sell it to a radio amateur friend).

(d) Clip the gray klystron cap lead (3) at the point of origin on the PC board and discard.

(e) Install the AG-1001-3 oscillator assembly (4) on the rear of the antenna horn (5), using the mounting screws (4A).

(f) Remove the AG-1001-3 oscillator cover (4B).

(g) Connect the klystron socket (6) as shown.

(h) Replace the cover (4B) and make sure the access hole is positioned above the modulation adjustment (7).

(j) Replace the connector (1).

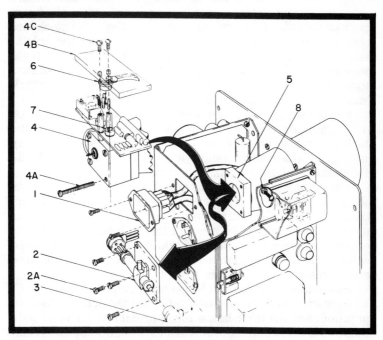

Fig. 7-14. Klystron replacement modification procedure, Johnson Service Co. Model G-1.

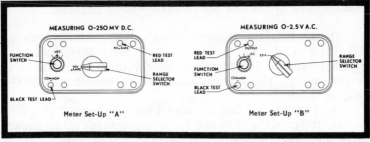

Fig. 7-15. Simpson meter function positions for setting up the G-1 after modification.

A screwdriver and the good old Simpson 260 VOM or equivalent are the only tools needed to adjust the unit. Refer to sketches of the Simpson meter in Fig. 7-15 for easy test connections and switch positions. By following instructions to the letter, possible damage to the meter will be avoided.

To adjust the crystal bias (meter set up A), apply power to G-1 in the "standby" mode and switch to the "active" mode for this check. Connect the red meter lead to test point 8 (Fig. 7-13) and the black test lead to test point 7 common. The voltage indicated on meter is the crystal bias and should measure 70 millivolts, plus or minus 10. If not, rotate the nylon screw on the side of the horn antenna (8 in Fig. 7-14) clockwise (right) to raise or counterclockwise (left) to lower the crystal bias. This adjustment may be made with the unit in the access mode (standby) and checked by placing the unit in the secure mode (active). This must be done to avoid a potential shock from the high voltage present around the AG-1001-3.

For the supervisory signal level adjustment (meter set up B), connect the red meter test lead to test point 14 and the black meter lead to test point 7. Minimize the interference by turning off fluorescent lights in the area and adjust the modulation (7) for 0.20 volts, plus or minus 0.07.

The amplifier gain and bias adjustment should be made as follows; if the MPS or BG series monitor is available, connect it to the G-1 for adjusting the system coverage. If a monitor is not available, remove the cover of the active-standby control box and disconnect the blue and white wires from the potted switch. Connect the Simpson meter and set to measure resistances across the wires from G-1.

Pull out the tamper switch operating plunger to lock the G-1 tamper switch closed and switch G-1 to the "active" mode of operation. See the table below for approximate bias and gain adjustment knob settings for various design ranges. Actual settings may be at different values due to building construction and layout. However, start with like adjustments and increase or decrease the bias and gain as needed. Make a fine-tuning adjustment with either knob and never exceed the knob setting of 8 in either adjustment.

Range Adjustment Settings

Design Range	Bias & Gain Controls
150 feet	7.5 to 8.0
125 feet	7.0 to 7.5
100 feet	6.5 to 7.0
75 feet	5.0 to 6.0
50 feet	4.0 to 5.0
25 feet	3.0 to 4.0

The limits of the protected area can be determined by walking in the area and watching the meter deflections or monitor the alarm indication. A short circuit reading on the meter indicates motion detection.

If the G-1 is to operate at less than maximum range, both the bias and gain controls should be set at lower values. The detection sensitivity of the G-1 is not affected or limited when the coverage is reduced, but never exceed a setting of 8. When all adjustments are completed, the modified G-1 is ready for operation.

JOHNSON G-7B MICROWAVE MOTION DETECTOR

The G-7B is a self-contained, solid-state microwave space alarm for indoor coverage. The unit detects movement of intruders in the protected area to generate an alarm. Three different antennas are available according to the specific area coverage desired. An approximation of coverages for the short range antenna, intermediate range antenna and long-range antenna are shown in Fig. 7-16.

Specifications

Range (adjustable): 80' x 60' with short range antenna, 100' x 40' with intermediate range antenna, 150' x 30' with long range antenna.

Detection capability: 1 ft. per second to 22 ft. per second

Transmitted frequency: 2.45 GHz (S-band).

Supply voltage: 24v AC (+10 percent, -15 percent) 50 to 60 Hz with a stepdown transformer 120 to 24v AC, TZ-5001.

Power consumption: Less than 10va.

Power output: 15 milliwatts.

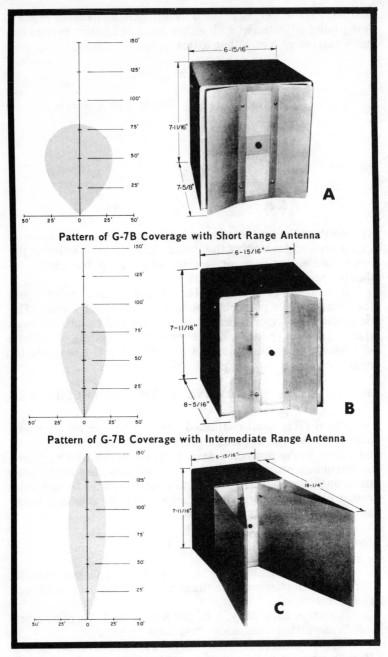

Pattern of G-7B Coverage with Short Range Antenna

Pattern of G-7B Coverage with Intermediate Range Antenna

Fig. 7-16. Johnson G-7B coverage with a short-range antenna (A), intermediate range antenna (B) and long-range antenna.

Ambient temperature limits: 32 to 120 degrees F (0 to 49 degrees C).

Accessories (optional): VQ-6001-1 or VQ-6001-2 standby power supply, EG-1001 vertical or horizontal mounting bracket, intermediate range or long range antenna.

The unit performs intruder detection by transmitting a 2.45-GHz microwave signal into the selected area and compares the frequency of the signal reflected back from that area to the original transmitted signal. As movement occurs in the protected area, the microwave signal is reflected back to the detector with an apparent frequency shift. That frequency difference is proportional to the velocity of the moving object.

The alarm circuitry in the G-7B discriminates against small moving objects so that alarms are not initiated by mice, insects or other small moving objects. The alarm circuit is non-integrating and contains a noise-gating circuit to prevent nuisance alarms from short duration transients frequently encountered in most environments. This same circuit causes the alarm to trigger quickly when a man-sized object moves in the protected area and not to trigger from a series of small mass movements. The unit detects very slow as well as very fast movements.

The G-7B detector unit is self-supervising with a patented fail-safe circuit that causes a relay to de-energize and trigger an alarm when the unit becomes incapable of detecting motion. The device is UL listed for both local and central station use and remote testing is not necessary because a walk-test light is provided on the face of the unit for testing and adjustment. Operation is stable, with no variation from changing humidity, pressure, noise and temperature. An anti-jam circuit included forces the unit into alarm if a modulated microwave source is introduced into the protected area in an effort to jam it. A case tamper switch prevents tampering with the unit.

Power is supplied by the TZ-5001 120-to-24v AC plug-in transformer, but in areas where power failures are common, or if continuous power is specified, the VQ-6001 standby power supply may be used. This consists of a charge circuit and sealed lead-dioxide rechargeable batteries. Two types are available in the VQ-6001 Model standby, 12 hours or 48 hours of standby power with no alarms resulting from power loss or restoration. The power supply circuit is specially designed to maintain operation of the unit, without standby power, in the event of momentary power outage, without alarming the unit.

The unit is normally mounted about 8 to 12 feet above the floor to a vertical or horizontal mounting bracket to provide

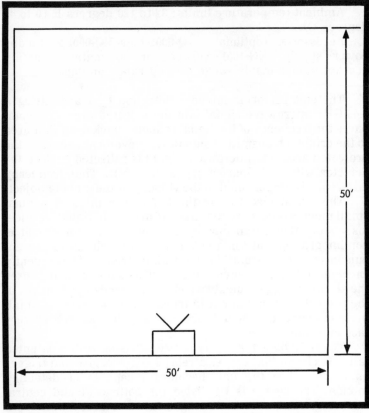

Fig. 7-17. Typical square-room installation with a short-range antenna.

the desired coverage. There are numerous ideal locations for this type of motion detection and general methods of installation suggested will provide the best possible coverage with minimum nuisance alarms. Large fixtures and obstructions in the protected area must be carefully considered for shielding effects. The G-7B units must be strategically located to provide full coverage.

A typical room 50' by 50' can easily be covered by a single unit with a short range antenna as shown in Fig. 7-17. Since the pattern shown in Fig. 7-17 is broadened by reflections from walls in this type room, total coverage is assured. Very large or odd-shaped rooms will require additional G-7B units for complete protection. The length and width of zones must be weighed when planning. The odd-shaped rooms are more easily protected by selecting the proper antenna to provide the pattern of coverage required.

In addition to effectively covering the security area, equipment must be placed to prevent nuisance alarms. Basically, this is accomplished by preventing movement of reflecting objects inside the secured area during the hours of protection and by adjusting the range to avoid detection of moving objects outside the protected area. While some objects capable of causing false alarms can be easily overlooked, the area should be carefully checked before a permanent installation is made. Potential sources of nuisance alarms are:

1. Walls, ceilings or floors that tend to flex or bow as a result of heavy normal traffic.

2. Bats or birds flying near or in front of the antenna.

3. Large animals, like dogs in the protected area.

4. Venetian blinds swinging in air currents.

5. Exposed fans or moving machinery unless enclosed in metal cases that do not vibrate.

6. Loose fitting roll-type doors.

7. Hanging fixtures, moving duct covers, etc.

The G-7B should not point directly at glass or thin wooden doors, since these materials usually allow direct waves to pass through and thus cause alarms from outside motion. The range of the unit should be adjusted for coverage of the desired area only, nothing extra. When in doubt about alarms resulting from movement outside the secured area, walk tests should be made and the range lowered to the point where such is not the case.

The bottom of a G-7B unit accepts the threaded stem of the EG-1001 vertical or horizontal mounting bracket and the bulletin included with these brackets offers detailed mounting information.

The required operating voltage may be provided by the TZ-5001 plug-in transformer operating on 120v AC 50 to 60 Hz with a 24-volt secondary to furnish power to the G-7B by connecting to terminals E and F as shown in Fig. 7-18. A

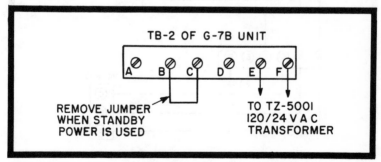

Fig. 7-18. Johnson G-7B connections without standby power.

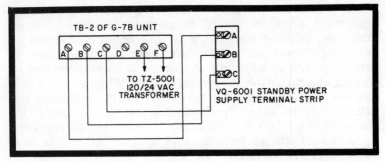

Fig. 7-19. G-7B connections with standby power.

standby power supply should also be used with the unit and mounted near the detector supplied. Fig. 7-19 shows the connections for the standby power source, the VQ-6001. The detector requires a good earth ground for best results and the connection should be made to terminal 4 of TB-1. An optional method of connecting two G-7B units to a single VQ-6001 supply is shown in Fig. 7-20. A VQ-6001-4 adaptor is required for proper operation and the 24v AC transformer secondary is connected directly to the adaptor. All power wiring must be made according to the applicable electrical code requirements.

The large number of available security monitors make the interconnection drawings too numerous for inclusion in the limited space available here, but typical connections are shown in Figs. 7-21 and 7-22. These should aid the installer in ad-libbing any variations that may be required in his work.

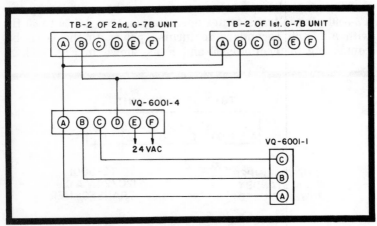

Fig. 7-20. Optional standby power wiring for two G-7B units.

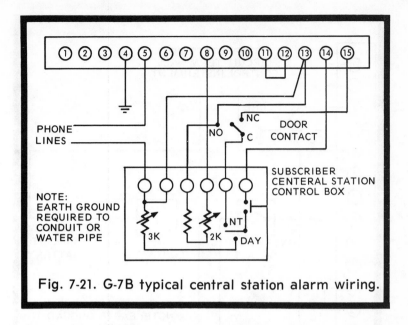

Fig. 7-21. G-7B typical central station alarm wiring.

The central station monitor wiring is typical of most double drop systems to provide constant supervision of the wiring through the G-7B unit and tamper switches. A break and cross occurs when motion is sensed by the unit, and equipment failure that causes the supervisory relay contacts to open results in a break indication. The local alarm and police connection in Fig. 7-22 offers a method which may be used for police connected alarms or local alarms. All alarm wiring must meet applicable electrical code specifications.

Adjustment for proper coverage of the protected area should be carried out by connecting a Simpson 260 VOM or equivalent to the test points as shown in Fig. 7-23. With the detector in the "active" mode of operation, connect the negative meter lead (black) to common and positive (red) lead to the 50 microamp scale. Measure the crystal bias between TP1 and ground. Do not stand in front of the antenna while making an adjustment; the meter should show 70, plus or minus 15 mv. If the voltage is outside this range, loosen the lower locknut on the coax cable fitting (coupling adjustment) on the receiver cavity to increase the crystal bias as needed. When correct bias is obtained, tighten the locknut again.

Adjust the range control to provide the coverage desired. Check with walk tests. A walk test light has been added to the G-7B unit to aid in making these tests. It has an opaque lens cover to conceal the light when the unit is in operation. As the walk test light is normally off, it is energized only when the

125

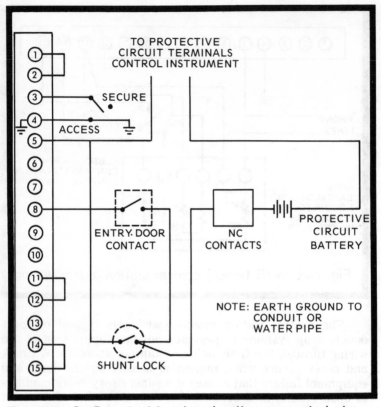

Fig. 7-22. G-7B typical local and police connected alarm wiring.

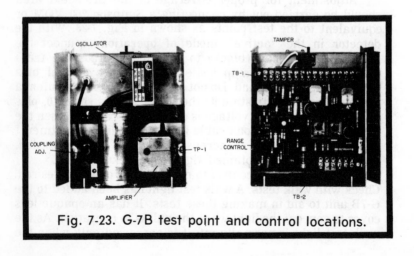

Fig. 7-23. G-7B test point and control locations.

unit detects motion. The light can be used to check an area for coverage and also periodic operational checks by the sub-scriber. It is most important that the range control be set to cover the area desired, and not more than this exact pattern. The chances of frequent nuisance alarms are considerably increased by too high a setting. Too low a setting may offer an intruder a chance to slip by undetected. Following these adjustments, the installation is ready to turn over to the customer for immediate protection. A pictorial view of an installation using an intermediate range antenna is shown in Fig. 7-24.

ALARMTRONICS ENGINEERING, "MICRO-X SPECIAL"

Designed for protection in high-level security areas, the Alarmtronics X-band microwave motion sensor offers adjustable coverage from 100 to about 8,000 square feet. This solid-state device includes features such as tamper-proof mounting for walls, built-in rechargeable batteries, integrated walk-test light with latching capability and a fail-safe continuous oscillator and monitoring circuit. The overall dimensions of the unit are 10" x 7" x 5" and the weight is only 7½ pounds. It is highly stable, according to the manufacturer, and not affected by air turbulence, noise, RF interference, line

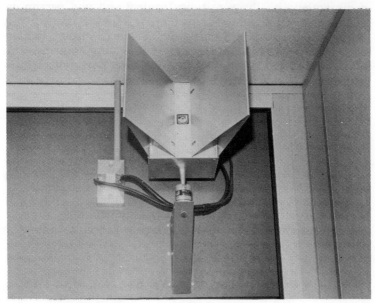

Fig. 7-24. G-7B with an intermediate range antenna. (Courtesy Johnson Service Co.)

surges, birds or insects. The "Micro-X" X-band microwave sensor is much smaller in size than the "Special," but it is said to have similar characteristics.

Specifications:

Coverage: Maximum 100 feet by 80 feet wide; minimum 15 feet with teardrop pattern.
Supply voltage: 120 volts AC, 60 Hz
Operating potential: 12 volts DC, nominal 9-15 volts
Adjustments: Range or sensitivity control.
Alarm relay: SPDT, 0.5 amps at 250 volts.
Accessories: Setup meter, rechargeable standby battery.
Power consumption: 2 watts.
Transmit power: 10 milliwatts.
Wavelength: 3 cm (10 GHz).
Mounting: Attached ball-joint bracket.
Tamper switch: SPDT.
Temperature limits: 0 to 55 degrees C.

Detectron Security Systems, Model 307

The Model 307 microwave motion detector operates on a frequency of 915 MHz with an omnidirectional radiation pattern and a variable range of a few feet to 40 feet in diameter. Adjustment may be made according to requirements by the sensitivity control and any person entering the unit's doughnut-shaped radar field will immediately be detected, which will energize the alarm circuit that includes a C form dry closure relay with 1 amp contacts. This allows the Model 307 to be included in any perimeter loop or used as a direct actuator for dialers or other responsive units. See the pictorial view in Fig. 7-25.

Specifications

Operating frequency: 915 MHz.
Antenna: Omnidirectional ground plane.
Operating range: To 40 feet in diameter (depends on environment).
Power requirements: 12 volts DC, 70 ma.
Alarm output: Relay closure, 1 amp contacts.
Interconnecting cable: 4-conductor cable, 22 gauge or heavier.
Size: 4½" x 3½" x 3".

SYSTRON-DONNER MICROWAVE SYSTEM MSA-1MA

System features include an adjustable range with a minimum radius of zero to 35 feet, an insensitiveness to currents, and the capability to detect through walls, windows, ceiling or floor with no metal or heavy structural material to reflect or absorb a microwave signal. It complies with FCC regulations covering frequency, emission amplitude and harmonic suppression. The system may be easily hidden with no protrusions to mark the location and it may be installed with an internal battery for standby operation during power failure. The IC solid-state device also includes a built-in horn and light plus tamper switches. The movement control allows one-shot events like a falling box or a big electric motor to start without triggering the alarm and 60 to 90 seconds are allowed the operator to leave the protected area after setting. Beams that may be detected are completely eliminated with this system.

The MSA-1MA microwave space alarm comprises four units—detector, control, transformer and cable. The detector unit shown in Fig. 7-26 contains a transceiver board with a 915-MHz transmitter, receiving antenna, detector, high-gain amplifier and the logic circuitry required to send an alarm signal to the control unit in order to actuate the alarm relay. The two controls under the protective dome are the range and movement controls. The former permits a variable range coverage of a 0 to 35 foot radius from the unit in all directions, unless otherwise desired, and the latter sets the number of alarm pulses the unit will allow before actuating the alarm. This control may be varied from a minimum of three to a maximum setting of 15 to allow sufficient flexibility where the

Fig. 7-25. Radar motion detector, Model 307. (Courtesy Detectron Security Systems, Inc.)

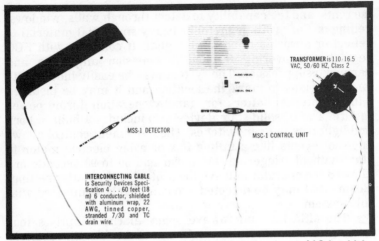

INTERCONNECTING CABLE
is Security Devices Specification 4 . . . 60 feet (18 m) 6 conductor, shielded with aluminum wrap, 22 AWG, tinned copper, stranded 7/30 and TC drain wire.

MSS-1 DETECTOR

MSC-1 CONTROL UNIT

TRANSFORMER is 110/16.5 VAC, 50/60 HZ, Class 2

Fig. 7-26. Systron-Donner microwave system MSA-1MA.

installation area requires it. A box falling over in a warehouse could provide several reflections.

The control unit contains the power supply, walk-test and alarm circuits, standby battery and trickle-charge, on-off switch, visual and-or audio alarm control. If the line power fails, the standby batteries will automatically supply power for up to 12 hours, and the 3-position switch sets the alarm mode. The off or center position disconnects power to the detector unit, but the batteries are still connected to the trickle charger. With the switch at "audio-visual," the speaker and lamp are actuated with each alarm condition, but with the switch in the "visual only" position, just the light comes on. These alarms are triggered with a single movement for walk-test aids and it is necessary to monitor the alarm relay separately since its alarm condition is set up by the movement control adjustment. During standby, the visual alarm light is inoperable.

The transformer which reduces the line power from 110 volts to 16 volts AC and operates on 50-60 Hz is known as the Model XF-16 or may be ordered in the export type (Model XF-230) for 230-volt AC lines with the same 16-volt secondary. The cable is available to interconnect the detector unit with the control unit and is a shielded 6-conductor type, 60 feet long. All wires near the detector head must be shielded completely.

The microwave space alarm operates on the frequency shift principle. Any movement within the energy field of a radio frequency signal will result in a shift in the frequency of that part of the signal being reflected by a moving object. This frequency change is detected and promptly forces the detector unit into an alarm condition. The space alarm (MSA-1MA) transmits the RF signal at a frequency of 915 MHz. Radio frequency signals are not affected by air movement which would cause false alarms. Only objects or materials capable of reflecting RF energy and on the move will offer an alarm response. This RF energy is able to penetrate most building materials to increase the capability and versatility of the microwave method of protection. While maximum coverage for a person is 35 feet, trucks or other large moving targets will cause an alarm at much greater distances, depending on the building materials involved. Reflections can result in greater coverage under favorable circumstances, and most interior walls of plywood, fiber board or even sheet rock will attenuate the microwaves only slightly. Therefore, the unit is able to provide adequate surveillance of several rooms or offices, which lowers the installation cost considerably. Under test conditions, it has been found that good penetration is possible through one or two ordinary sheet rock walls. Plywood walls afford even less attenuation, thus three or four rooms may be protected by each unit. Solid wood does absorb more of the signal, concrete is a good reflector and steel is an excellent reflector, with nothing passing through. See Fig. 7-27.

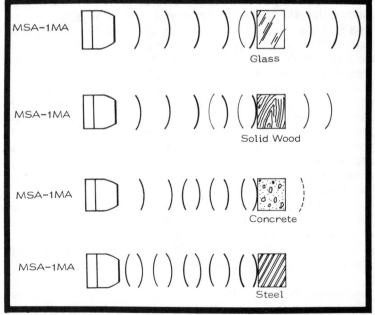

Fig. 7-27. Drawing illustrating the reflection and attenuation qualities of various building materials.

The variations in response to different materials makes the performance of walk-tests almost mandatory to actually determine the penetration in any given installation. Checks should also be carried out for penetration through glass and thin insulating materials because these offer little if any resistance to the microwave signal. Many cases will be found where the area of surveillance extends too far and does cause excessive false alarms. Attempts will be made to correct these conditions as installation procedures are covered.

The reflection pattern provided by common building materials is a factor to be carefully considered in the use of microwave protection. As a rule, materials that attenuate this energy the most will offer the most reflection. Thus, we may assume that metallic surfaces are far better reflectors than plywood, and these reflections enable the installation man to cover corners of rooms and other areas outside the normal circumference of coverage. Good coverage in most installations depends on an abundance of reflections.

Since the microwave space alarm is rated at 35 feet, an alarm may be anticipated when an average-sized person approaches within 35 feet of the detector unit. Because the radiated energy field is weaker the farther away the intruder is from the transmitter, and since the reflected energy from the intruder is correspondingly less at greater distances, it follows that the unit will alarm when small objects such as cats and dogs are moving close by the detector. It will also alarm when larger objects in the form of cars and trucks are moving outside the 35-foot radius. This is the square law effect, where the energy received at distance D from the transmitter is proportional to one over D squared. The re-radiated energy from the intruder or moving object is also subject to the same formula. Thus, the Doppler signal seen by the MSA-1MA is proportional to one over D to the fourth power. This adds up to the fact that the detector will pick up a person moving at 35 feet at the maximum setting, a moving object 16 times that cross section at 70 feet and a moving object 5 times the person cross section at 52 feet.

Conversely, a moving object one-16th the cross section of the human will be detected at 17.5 feet and very small objects in even closer proximity to the detector unit such as swaying drop cables will cause alarms. Methods of overcoming these problems are discussed in the installation section.

Installation of MSA-1MA

The detector and control units should be installed within the area to be protected by the system whenever possible in order to obtain maximum control unit security and to minimize the cable length needed to properly install the system. A 60-foot cable is provided, and if it is not possible to locate the control unit in the protected area, the case tamper switch should be connected to the alarm system. Since coverage is omnidirectional, it is largely dependent on target size.

When large objects present serious false alarm problems, the detector unit should be located where heavy building materials such as reinforced concrete in the actual line of sight will attenuate the microwave energy. (See Fig. 7-28.) Where penetration through window areas becomes a problem, the use of venetian blinds or mesh screen over the window area should provide adequate attenuation. Shadowing an area by placing a small piece of metal between the detector unit and the area to be blocked off from microwave energy often is the best answer to high windows exposed to main thorough-fares when the detector is mounted in the ceiling. Installation of the MSA-1MA on a concrete wall adjacent to a window will enable the use of such heavy building material to block off microwave energy from other than the area to be protected. The use of reflecting surfaces for shadowing certain areas will concentrate the microwave energy for extended coverage of other sections as shown in Fig. 7-29. This shows a slight lobe created by the reflector which will vary according to material and pattern desired. The walk-tests will establish the actual area coverage under conditions where reflections are involved as shown in the sketch of the 4900 square foot area in Fig. 7-30.

Elongation of coverage pattern is shown in Fig. 7-31 where reflections from walls and ceilings in a room 50 feet wide using

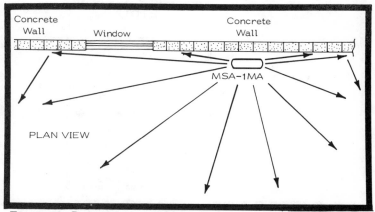

Fig. 7-28. Detector located to make use of heavy building materials to block microwave energy.

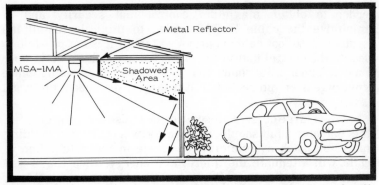

Fig. 7-29. A small piece of metal may be used to "shadow" or block off microwave energy.

a 25-foot radius adjustment stretches the length an additional 15 feet to total 65 feet in length by 50 feet wide. The ideal application of the microwave alarm is for locations where multiple room surveillance is required, since a single detector unit can penetrate walls to cover several adjacent rooms. A 20-foot setting (6 meters) may protect areas close to valuable property, such as access areas through glass doors and all doors that would provide access to valuables. Since the omnidirectional pattern extends vertically, access through roof and floor areas are fully protected. The 20-foot coverage allows freedom of movement for personnel in the rooms and people in front of the glassed door area, but large trucks passing outside

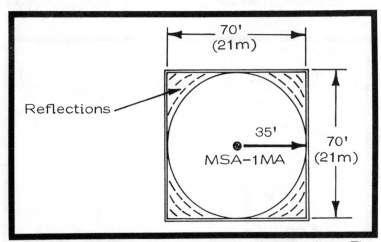

Fig. 7-30. Range control set for a 35-foot radius. The corners are covered by reflected energy.

the glass door area may result in some false alarms. Concrete exterior walls will protect other potential false response zones. A 35-foot range setting gives more complete coverage of the building as shown in Fig. 7-32, but will restrict movement in certain areas and offer a better chance of false alarms through glassed areas. Shadowing by the use of a reflector between the unit and glass doors will correct this condition and either aluminum foil or a mirror type may be utilized. A decorative touch is offered by taping the foil to the back of a painting, but naturally this area will not be protected against intruders.

The pattern of coverage is spherical and roof and cellar areas are properly covered. Any effort to intrude through the roof or cellar areas will be quickly detected. Some roofs are quite flexible and, although the MSA-1MA is not subject to air motion, wind often causes vibrations that cause alarms when near the detector unit. Birds on the roof area near the detector will sometimes result in unwanted alarms and shadowing the roof area in such cases will correct this problem. The metal reflector must not be allowed to vibrate or shift and must hide all parts of the roof from the detector which will, however, pick up the intruder as he comes through the shadowed area.

Warehouses of sizable proportions provide another ideal installation for the unit due to its lack of sensitivity to moving inventory. The "beamed" systems will not provide true volume coverage and are easily compromised by large mass blocking such as stacks of cartons or containers. When the detector is mounted high, shadowed areas of the warehouse to hide intruders are non-existent. Fig. 7-33 shows the real

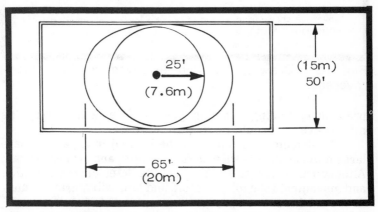

Fig. 7-31. With the range control set to cover the 25-foot width of a room, reflections may cause the length to be covered to 65 feet.

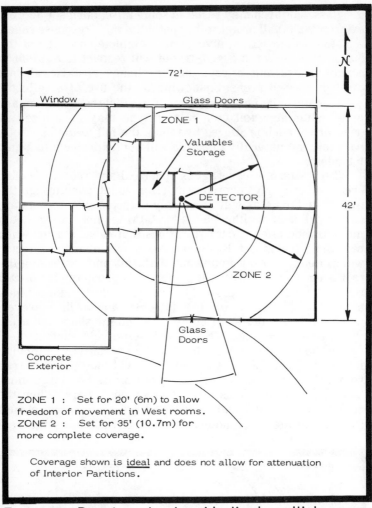

Fig. 7-32. Drawing showing idealized multiple room coverage.

problem of finding a hiding place where detection by the microwave unit could be avoided.

The detector unit must not be located in an area where large moving objects such as fans, motors and cranes prevail. Although air currents do not affect the detector, the vibration and movements of cables, motors and fans will alarm the unit. Areas outside the temperature extremes (0 to 140 degrees F) should not be selected for satisfactory installation sites. The detector should not be installed closer than 6 inches to any large metal area such as aluminum siding.

The detector may be mounted in any position desired and installation is quite simple; merely attach the unit with two screws through holes provided in its base. Care should be exercised to prevent damage to the circuit board inside the base. System operation is controlled only by the off-on switch located on the control unit. Removing AC power automatically switches the unit to battery operation. When two units are within 150 feet of each other, there is a possibility of interaction. In such cases, the factory will detune the oscillator frequencies for multiple unit installation upon request. FCC regulations (Part 15, Subpart F) require the frequency of such microwave transmitters to be held at 915 MHz plus or minus 13

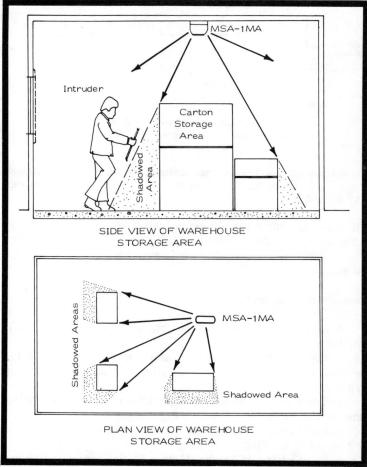

Fig. 7-33. With the detector mounted high in a warehouse, only a few shadowed areas can hide an intruder.

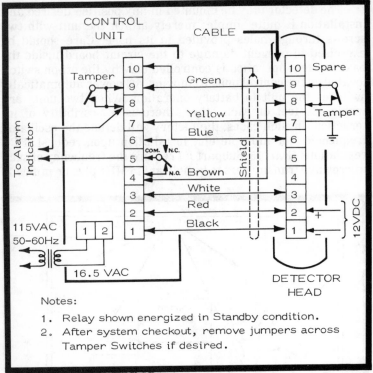

Fig. 7-34. Connection diagram for the Systron-Donner MSA-1MA.

MHz, so the unit must not be adjusted for frequency at any time except at the factory or by other authorized testing facility. **This is important to avoid penalties provided by FCC Regulations!**

Installation Sequence

1. Make sure the control unit switch is in the center (off) position.

2. Remove the cover of the control unit and install in the desired location; the distance from the AC outlet is not critical.

3. Connect the 6-conductor shielded cable to the control unit and detector as shown in Fig. 7-34.

4. Remove the cover of the detector and install the unit in the selected location.

5. Connect the 16.5-volt AC wire to the control as shown and to the transformer. **Do not connect the 115-volt AC to the control or detector units!**

6. Connect the transformer (primary) to the 115-volt AC 50-60 Hz line, or in areas where only 230-volt power is available, use XF-230 transformer.

7. Check the battery voltage using the following procedure:

(a) Disconnect the transformer from the AC line.

(b) Turn the switch to the "audio-visual" position.

(c) The battery voltage should read 12.5 to 13.7 volts DC. The full 12-hour standby capability is not available unless the voltage reading is 13.0 volts or more. Allow 24 hours for the internal charger to bring the battery to full charge.

If desired, remove the jumpers across the tamper switches as shown in Fig. 7-33 after system has been completely checked.

System Adjustments

Before applying power, check carefully to insure that both the control unit and detector are mounted and connected correctly. The control unit should have the top cover in place and securely attached, but the detector should be mounted and have the top cover removed:

1. Defeat the tamper switch if wired for tamper protection by installing the screw in the proper location to close the switch contacts under the detector unit cover.

2. Insure that the **range** and **movement** controls are fully counterclockwise (left).

3. Turn the control unit on and switch the walk-test indicator to "audio-visual." Now, wait 90 seconds before starting the walk-tests, which allows the inhibit circuit to stabilize.

4. Adjust the **range control** clockwise (right) until the desired protection area is determined. The control unit will give an audio tone and a visual light display when the range of the unit is penetrated. Following each indication of penetration, **wait at least 45 seconds before the next walk test** in order to allow the movement circuit to discharge properly. Several walk-tests should be made to insure proper range of the system and adequate alarm delay. Survey for areas of microwave leakage where trucks or other large objects may cause alarms. Check carefully for objects close to the detector head and make sure they are secure and free from vibration. Double check to make sure no wires in the ends of the 6-conductor cable are unshielded.

5. Adjustments of **movement control**: If delay of the alarm is required, adjust the control clockwise (right) from the minimum position to give the desired delay. Several walk tests should be made, **allowing 45 seconds between each walk-test for the unit to fully reset.**

6. Remove the tamper-defeat screw and re-install the cover.

7. On the control unit: Switch to the "visual" light display and the system is now ready for operation.

System Operation

Recommended procedure: To **set up** when leaving the protected area:

1. Turn the microwave control (MSC-1) to "visual" or "audio-visual" position.

2. Activate the alarm device (transmitter, local or dialer).

3. Leave the premises within one minute.

Re-entering protected area:

1. Turn off the alarm device directly or by using a shunt lock without entering the protected space.

2. Turn the microwave control (MSC-1) switch to the off position.

Repair

Whenever a product of Security Devices requires service, it should be returned to the factory at buyer's expense. No charge will be made for the repair if the conditions stated in the warranty apply. Otherwise, a minimum charge will apply.

Chapter 8
Proximity Alarm Systems

The average proximity alarm is sensitive to changes in electrical capacity between the protected object and earth ground. By connecting the object to any of several types of tuned circuits or to the gate of a silicon control rectifier, the circuit balance is upset by the intruder's approach, and even more so by his touch. The tuned circuit in simplified form is shown in Fig. 8-1 and the SCR gate sensing arrangement is illustrated in Fig. 8-2. These operate on the basis of a capacity change between the device and ground, a change which may not be avoided by the intruder. The safe or vault door being protected is actually surrounded by an electrostatic field that may not even be approached without signaling an alarm condition.

The sensitivity of such a system is independent of the size of the protected object because the circuit may be easily balanced to fit the conditions at hand. A simple capacity balancing control or padder enables the technician to adjust the system for various capacities. The change in capacity in the proximity system should be fast in order to trigger an alarm condition, and the slow changes resulting from temperature and humidity variations must be cancelled by a compensating circuit to avoid false alarms.

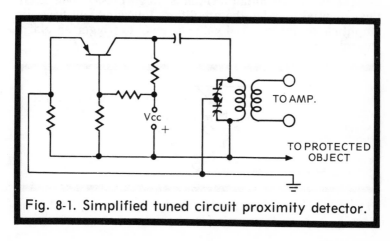

Fig. 8-1. Simplified tuned circuit proximity detector.

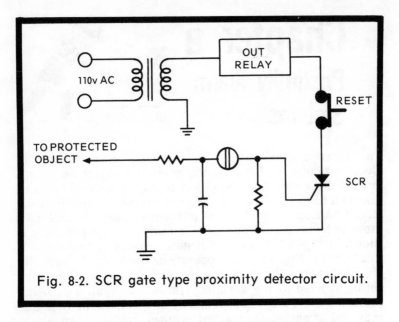

Fig. 8-2. SCR gate type proximity detector circuit.

The balanced bridge circuit offers still another form for proximity detection through capacitive changes, and a simplified detail of this arrangement is shown in Fig. 8-3 where the two resistors on one side of the bridge offer the same impedance as the capacitors on the other side to maintain balance. Applying a sine wave to the input terminals of the bridge will show zero output when precisely balanced. If capacitor "B" is changed by the shunt capacity of the protected object, as would be the case if an intruder were in its proximity, the bridge is no longer balanced and an output does exist at the bridge output terminals. Regardless of how small this potential may be, the amplifiers following will boost its amplitude to the required value or level to trigger an alarm control circuit.

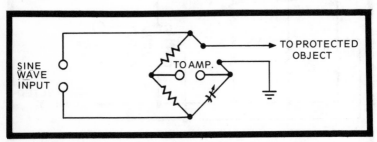

Fig. 8-3. Simple balanced bridge proximity detector circuit.

INSTALLATION

Needless to say, it is imperative with proximity detectors to keep a clean house in the area of the protected object. Even a small piece of paper could be sufficient under the correct conditions to cause a false alarm. By removing trash or other loose material from the vicinity of the safe, cabinet or other protected item, the possibility of unnecessary nuisance alarms is eliminated, if air currents should happen to come along. Wet mopping in the area is also to be avoided, as it will definitely upset the stability of the detection circuit. When properly installed and **adjusted**, the system provides an assignment that could hardly be defeated by even the most experienced.

The tuned circuit oscillator uses a padder or trimming capacitor for fine adjustment in order to peak the tuning exactly on resonance. The output of the discriminator in this arrangement provides a DC voltage to bias the amplifier and the alarm circuit, in turn, reacts to the amplifier output. Since any change in the capacitance of the object protected will detune the discriminator, which changes its voltage level as used in biasing the amplifier. After the output of the amplifier is rectified, it turns on a switching transistor to de-energize the alarm relay.

The control unit is provided with the ability to compensate for a change in capacitance from temperature, humidity and other environmental conditions, and if the lead wires are tampered with, the fail-safe circuit immediately responds with an alarm. When approached by any intruder, the resulting change in the electrostic field actually disturbs the circuit balance to cause the detection system to respond by triggering the alarm. Just a few millionths of a millionth of a farad is sufficient, in other words 5 to the -12 power or 5 picofarads (5 pf) is an ample change to signal the detection circuit and trigger the alarm condition. The sensitivity could be lowered to one-hundred times this value, however, before the signal was given. Since the intruder has no way of sensing or knowing about the protection afforded, the time must be very short until his presence is relayed to the monitoring system.

The tuned plate—tuned grid type oscillator would show minimum current at resonance in the output circuit, but adding the capacity provided in the sensing loop by the intruder, the circuit is sufficiently detuned to cause the output current to rise sharply and be detected by the triggering circuitry.

MULTI-ELMAC CO., SS-4, SS-5 PROXIMITY DETECTOR

The Model SS-4 all solid-state radio control set is specifically designed for security applications and operates in

143

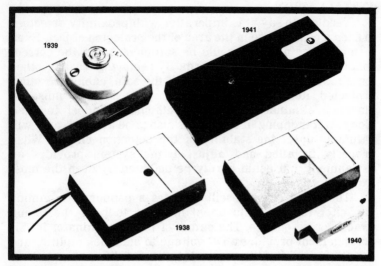

Fig. 8-4. Multi-Elmac proximity detector transmitters.

the frequency range of 220 MHz to 320 MHz. The precision modulation technique is designed to virtually eliminate spurious operation. No transmitting license is required in this application.

The coded signal is composed of the RF carrier modulated by a piezoelectric mechanical filter operating at a frequency in the audio range and selective and stable to better than 0.35 percent in spite of several variables. The matching mechanical filters used in both transmitters and receivers provide exceptional selectivity, which provides a greater potential of different frequencies or channels than would otherwise be possible. A time delay requires the received signal to be held for approximately one second. The modulation frequency may be changed by simply replacing a plug-in module, which certainly requires no electronic skill or special equipment. The SS-4 radio control link will normally operate over a distance of 100 to 200 feet, but the range capability will vary for some equipment locations.

Specifications

RF carrier tuning ranges: 220 to 285 MHz and 280 to 320 MHz.

Standard channel frequencies: 220 MHz, 230 MHz, 250 MHz, 260 MHz, 290 MHz, 300 MHz, 310 MHz and 320 MHz.

AF modulation frequency range: 300 to 1,600 Hz.

Bandwidth (average): Plus or minus 3 Hz.

Transmitter (Fig. 8-4):

Power requirements: NEDA Type 1604 dry cell battery.
Voltage: 9 volts.
Current (transmit): 3.5 milliamperes.
Standby: 5 microamperes.
Size: 2.4" by 3.5" by 0.95", cash drawer type 2.4" by 6.3" by 0.95"
Weight: 6 ounces.

Receiver (Fig. 8-5)

Power requirements: Model 1933 & 1930, 115v AC plus or minus 15 volts, 60 Hz. Power consumption: 2.5 watts. Model 1934 & 1935, 12 to 14 volts DC. Power (idle): 20 milliamperes, relay energized: 35 milliamperes.
Relay contacts: 3 A, 50v AC inductively loaded.
Antenna: 11 inches (copper or brass wire).
Size: 3.60" by 4.75" by 2.0".
Weight: 1 pound
Temperature range: -10 to 140 degrees F.
The radiated output complies with FCC regulations, Part 15.

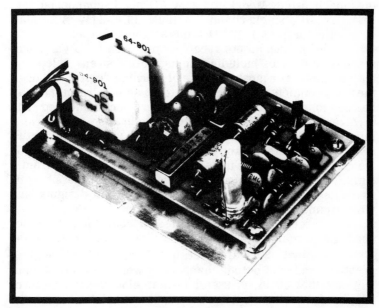

Fig. 8-5. Circuit board used in the Multi-Elmac Model 1935 receiver.

Transmitters

Five standard transmitter models are available with variations according to specific use: Model 1937, Pushbutton with spring return; 1938, 3-wire for open or closed circuits; 1939, heat sensor (135 degrees F and up); 1940, built-in reed switch (magnet operation); 1941, cash drawer in which the removal of the last bill turns it on.

The pushbutton model (1937) is for use when held in the hand, carried in a pocket, clipped to the belt or any other handy location. All models are furnished with convenient mounting hardware for various installations.

The transmitter is powered by a single standard 9-volt dry cell battery within the transmitter case, and with normal use, the battery should last about one year. No license is required for operation of the SS-4 transmitters in the United States since low-power UHF transmitters used in this manner are required to have a built-in timing circuit to restrict the duty cycle to no more than one second on and at least thirty seconds off. The SS-4 transmitters do include this timing circuit.

Receivers

The SS-4 series receivers offer a choice of input power in the models listed: Model 1933, 115v AC, single-channel output; 1934, 12v DC, single-channel output; 1930, 115v AC, dual-channel output; 1935, 12v DC, dual-channel output.

Single-channel output receivers may control a variety of responsive devices including lights, horns, sirens, telephone dialers, motors or most any type of warning device. Although the relay contacts restrict current to a 3 ampere rating, it may be used to trigger a heavier relay where such is needed. The receiver relay remains closed for the duration of the transmitted signal. Dual-channel receivers are used to control two devices independently and such operation is made possible by frequency coding of the units. Control of two functions from a single receiver without increasing size and cost is possible due to the degree of selectivity of the coding circuit designed and built around a precision mechanical filter.

Receivers may be mounted in convenient locations near the primary alarm system or even adapted to fit the system cabinet. Special order units are available with a greater number of output channels as well as different input voltages that could be useful in matching the main power supply of the alarm system.

The Model SS-5 solid-state radio control security set operates on the 27-MHz band with crystal control and dual frequency modulation for the precise coding needed to attain the degree of performance so essential to security applications. Various transmitter models are available according to the method of activation that is desired. Although the transmitting antenna is self-contained (ferrite rod), the receiver requires an external antenna consisting of a single wire about 2 to 6 feet in length. A special antenna may be required in extreme situations. The SS-5 security set transmitter is shown in Fig. 8-6 and the receiver in Fig. 8-7, with the circuit module of the receiver pictured in Fig. 8-8. Radio control applications of the remote radio link are shown in block diagram form in Fig. 8-9.

SYSTRON-DONNER CAPACITANCE ALARM BCA-1

This system is designed to protect up to 12 file cabinets. The sensitivity is adjustable for response to a touch or approach within a few inches. The system is self-protecting with a dual fail-safe circuit to assure satisfactory performance in the event of excessive capacity drift or cut antenna wires. It is completely solid-state with temperature and humidity compensation and is acceptable for Grade "A" certification by central alarm stations. The unit may be placed on a shelf or mounted to a wall.

Fig. 8-6. Multi-Elmac Model 1621-01 transmitter.

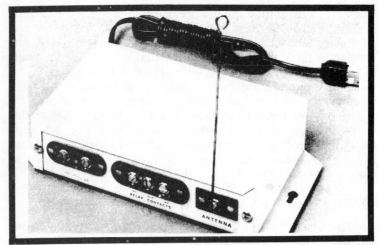

Fig. 8-7. Proximity detector receiver with antenna mounted.

The electrical capacitance between the protected objects and ground is connected to a tuned circuit with a center-tapped transformer and a choice of parallel capacitors selected to correspond to the approximate capacitance of the protected objects. The oscillator feeds the tuned circuit and has a trimmer capacitor for fine adjustment to resonate the tuned circuit. The discriminator output provides DC for biasing the amplifier and alarm circuit.

Fig. 8-8. PC board used in the receiver in Fig. 8-7.

Any change in the capacitance of the protected object will detune the discriminator and thus change the bias fed to the amplifier. The output of the amplifier is rectified and turns on the switching transistor to de-energize the alarm relay. The control unit has the capability to compensate for changes in capacitance resulting from humidity or other environmental conditions. Tampering with an object protected or its lead wires will cause the fail-safe circuit to present an alarm condition.

Specifications

Power supply: 12 volts AC supplied through XF-12, a UL listed Class 2 115v 50-60 Hz transformer. A half-wave rectifier maintains 6.5 volts DC at 14 ma. The circuit is designed to work normally with no loss in sensitivity when varied from 85 to 110 percent of its normal voltage output and at 85 percent humidity at 85 degrees F, plus or minus 3 degrees F.

Standby power: Nickel cadmium battery, trickle charged at 3.4 ma, providing a minimum of 4 hours operation.

Total capacitance: The total range of capacitance between ground and protected objects is from zero to about 1,000 pf.

Sensitivity: Senses a change of 5 pf at maximum gain.

Sensitivity is relatively independent of size of the capacity between a protected object and ground, since the circuit may be adapted by means of a selector switch which permits a change in the object-to-ground capacity from zero to 1,000 pf. The alarm is triggered only if the capacity change is fast. Those very slow changes resulting from temperature and humidity variations will not trigger the alarm. Such variations

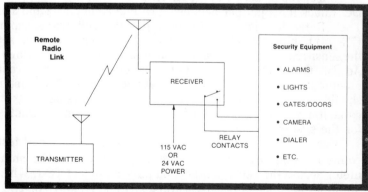

Fig. 8-9. Block diagram showing possible proximity security system applications.

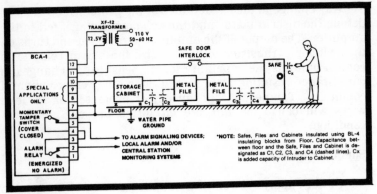

Fig. 8-10. Systron-Donner BCA-1 proximity alarm installation.

may slowly change the meter from 0.3 to 0.7 ma without affecting the alarm operation.

Relatively large changes in capacity always trigger an alarm independently of the speed with which capacity changes as a result of the internal fail-safe device. Extreme care must be taken to keep the area clear around the immediate vicinity of the objects to be protected by the system. Metal chairs, typewriters, lamps or any metal object moved toward or away from the protected area will affect the capacity to ground, as will wet mopping of wood floors or liquids spilled under or near the safe or filing cabinets protected. See Fig. 8-10 for a block diagram of a typical protected area.

Receiving Check

Check the battery voltage: normally it should be 6.6 to 7.2v DC. Check for a jumper between terminal strip pins 2 and 3 of TS-2. Refer to Fig. 8-11. Connect the 16.5-volt transformer (XF-16) to pins 6 and 7 of TS-1. Turn the power switch on, set the sensitivity control to 5 and the range selector S-3 to 1 (low). Adjust the oscillator trimmer capacitor until the front mounted meter reads mid scale (about 0.5 ma). The meter should move through 0.5 ma from 0.6 ma to 0.4 ma as the trim capacitor is turned clockwise (right). Wait several minutes for the system to set up.

Connect a VOM (20K per volt) across the relay coil test points TP1 and TP2 (use the 10-volt range), or connect an ohmmeter across the relay contacts on pins 2 and 3 of TS-1. When a jumper is added between terminal strip pins 1 and 5 of TS-2, the relay voltage should change from about 5.5 volts to about 0.2 volts, or if the ohmmeter is used, a short would be indicated on pins 2 and 3 after the jumper is added. About 15 to 30 seconds after the jumper is placed on pins 1 and 5, the voltage should return to 5.5 volts or the ohmmeter should indicate an open. After about 2 minutes, remove the jumper on pins 1 and 5 and the relay coil voltage or ohmmeter should respond in the same manner as above.

System Set Up

All objects to be protected must be made of conducting materials and be well insulated from ground. Use BL-4 insulation blocks between the protected object and the floor. In cases where non-conducting materials must be protected, it is possible to cover them with conducting material to obtain indirect protection.

The exposed total capacity of a group of protected items should be kept as small as possible. A series of file cabinets should be arranged 6 to 12 inches from the walls. In order to keep the exposed surface area small, form a block of two rows of cabinets placed side by side, with their backs touching each other. In this way, the exterior surfaces contribute to the total capacity of the block. Metal straps between cabinets are necessary to assure good electrical contact. The main capacity is usually from the floor to the bottom of the protected safe or cabinet. This capacity can be reduced by a factor of 4 if the insulating support blocks are doubled in height. All cabinets are connected in series and the ends of the loop are connected to terminals 2 and 3 of TS-2. A breaking of

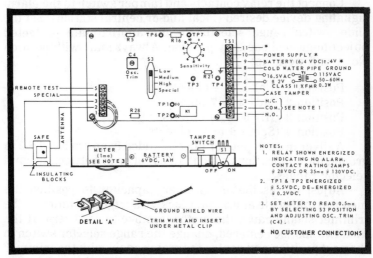

Fig. 8-11. Systron-Donner Model CA-3 capacity alarm.

the loop (often referred to as an antenna) will immediately cause a continuous alarm condition.

The control unit should be connected to a good electrical ground such as a cold water pipe or copper rod driven into the earth in a damp place if possible. If the protected object is in an area with wooden floors, carpeting or other insulating materials, a grounded plate or foil may be required for best results. This should be installed under the carpet or on the floor close to but not touching the protected objects. All wires leading from the protected objects to the alarm circuit should be secured against movement to prevent small capacity changes which could interfere with proper operation. Coaxial cables with small capacity per foot (36 pf) are suggested in cases where two or more objects are not located very close to each other. A total initial capacity of up to 1,000 pf, which corresponds to about 12 file cabinets, may be connected into the circuit loop.

The housing of the alarm may be included in the protection loop, and it can then be grounded or connected in the protected loop. In the latter case, the security against intruder tampering is increased. The grounded case is shown in the hookup diagram in Fig. 8-11. Safe door interlocks should be put in the protected loop for added protection.

The control unit can be mounted in a horizontal position (desk) or vertical position such as a wall. Placing the control unit on top of the protected cabinet is usually recommended because the housing is not accessible without causing an alarm and this also permits short antenna lead lengths.

Connect the relay contacts and tamper switch to the alarm signaling device desired (local and-or central station). Set the slide switch range selector to the approximate protected object-to-ground capacity position. Always start with position No. 1 and work up:

Position 1 (Lo) 1 to 4 objects
Position 2 (Md) 3 to 7 objects
Position 3 (Hi) 6 to 10 objects
Position 4 (Spec) 9 to 12 objects

A silver mica capacitor may be added from pin 5 of TS-2 to ground for applications which fall out of or in between normal selector ranges.

Adjust the oscillator trimmer capacitor to position the meter to mid-scale at 0.5 ma. Clockwise (right) rotation of the trimmer should cause the meter to move toward zero. If the meter cannot be centered, change the range selector switch to the next position and center the meter again with the trimmer adjustment. Wait about 2 minutes for the alarm relay to energize which is the no-alarm condition. Set the sensitivity control so that the flat palm of your hand, when separated from the safe wall by a ¼-inch thick pad of paper, will trip the alarm relay. Pause between each test for the unit to reset. Recheck the above procedure if the system does not operate correctly.

ADCOR ELECTRONICS TELEPHONE COMMUNICATOR

The Model NW222AC is a solid-state electronic device which automatically places telephone calls and gives pre-coded messages when activated by automatic sensing devices or personnel. Two independent message channels are provided, with each equipped to monitor and respond to its emergency function independently of the other. Up to four separate calls may be made on each channel with the same or different messages left at each number called. If the called number is busy or fails to answer, the NW222AC continues with the next number, and following completion of the last call, it automatically resets to await the subsequent activation to resume operation.

A memory circuit eliminates the necessity for a priority channel. With one channel in operation and the second channel tripped, the unit continues making calls on the first channel, but "remembers" that the second channel is tripped. After completion of the first, the second is activated at once so that sequential operation of both channels is accomplished with no loss of information. The unit makes use of the existing telephone service and does not require a separate leased line. Connections to the telephone line are through a coupler usually supplied by the local telephone company, but the unit is capable of being connected directly on the telephone line without the coupler.

Each channel is capable of separate programming in the field using the NWP100 programmer. The tape head has a separate built-in erase function for each channel to permit a change in one channel without erasing the second. The NW222AC also is equipped with a motor control jack to allow the programming sequence to be interrupted and started again when desired. Fig. 8-12 shows an inside view of the unit.

The device is power by the 117-volt 60-Hz line and equipped with nickel-cadium batteries to act as standby to operate the machine during power failure. The batteries are maintained full charge at all times while the NW222AC is connected to the 117-volt power line. The fully charged battery will permit the unit to monitor for a period of 20 days for most applications, or two days with NC trip circuits. The NW222AC Communicator will turn itself off in the event overuse of the battery occurs

Fig. 8-12. Adcor Electronics Model NW222AC telephone communicator.

during power failures and await restoration of power before continuing. As soon as AC power is restored, the unit automatically resets itself and operates normally upon subsequent operation. The Nicad battery will be fully recharged in 24 hours, so this feature prevents complete discharge of the battery and the risk of permanent damage to it.

Each channel contains a separate operational amplifier with feedback stabilized gain so that voltage variations and aging do not affect the operation of the unit. By boosting the signal to a high level ahead of channel selection, minimum noise and highly reliable switching characteristics are attained.

The dialing circuit employs an active filter and transistor to operate the dialing relay. A test lamp may be used in conjunction with the relay circuit to test the operation of the unit without actually dialing the telephone. This test function is selectable with a switch so that the operating condition of the unit may be completely checked without removing the cover.

An output stage with feedback provides a stable audio level into the telephone line, and the level is adjustable to compensate for telephone line length and varying input requirements. In direct telephone line installations, the line current is balanced in the output transformer for low saturation distortion.

The NW222AC uses all solid-state trip circuits that are able to operate from open-circuit or closed-circuit loops or from applied DC battery voltages, either positive or negative, from six to 12 volts. The circuits trip only upon changes in the circuit condition so that the unit will not continue to operate for more than one cycle even though the circuit remains in the condition that caused the initial operation. The trip circuits function on time constants equivalent to those for relays to ensure that they are not overly sensitive to surges from lightning, etc. Trip circuits may be deactivated by the switch on the front cover to prevent tripping in the off position. Once the circuit is tripped, moving the switch to the off position will not interfere with the placing of any emergency calls. In critical applications, a key lock is available as an option to lock the unit in the armed condition.

An adjustable delay circuit may be set to provide 0 to 60 seconds between tripping and the actual starting of the mechanism. This feature allows sufficient time to abort the call (using the hidden abort feature) in the event that the unit is inadvertently triggered by the customer.

Specifications

Controls: Exterior on-off switch, hidden "call abort" and "test," optional key-lock arming, and "remove abort capability."

Trip circuits: Any combination—open circuit, closed circuit and applied DC voltage.

Power supply: 117v, 60 Hz, fused at 0.5A. A 20v nicad battery is provided for standby. The battery is kept charged by the AC supply, and a pilot light indicator lights when the AC is turned on.

Number of channels: Two, with six minutes of tape on each. The device automatically resets after operation.

Output: Adjustable up to +6 dbm. It may be connected through a telephone alarm coupler or directly to a telephone line.

Tape drive: 12-volt DC high-torque motor driven by a voltage regulated power supply. A fly-ball governor maintains a constant speed. It uses a double belt tape drive and incorporates an anti-tape-foul device that protects against tape sticking to the rubber pinch roller.

Telephone line seizure: May be connected with an auxiliary relay to open the telephone line to "house-side" instruments.

Anti-line jam: Programmed to clear the line if someone has phoned in to try to jam the line, and this may be done on any telephone exchange equipped with "called party control" ("number 5 crossbar" and "ESS" exchanges). It is accomplished in programming the dialer and requires no extra equipment.

The terminal strip connections for the NW222AC appear in Fig. 8-13.

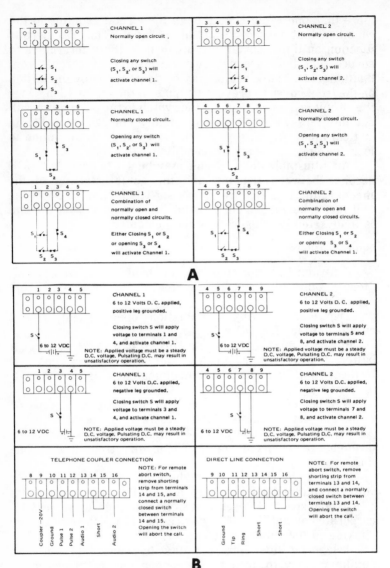

Fig. 8-13. Model NW222AC terminal strip connections.

BOURNS DIGITAL DIALER SYSTEM

The basic Model 401 system consists of two electronic units: a send unit, Type SU-401, and a display unit, Type DU-401. No magnetic tapes are used. The SU is a continuous automatic telephone dialer which is installed at each customer location and actuated by a burglar and-or fire sensor (Model

SA-3 or HS series). Up to 1,000 customer located send units may operate with a single display unit. The SU will (1) automatically dial the display unit, (2) communicate to the DU both the location and type of emergency, and (3) permit an audible verification of the disturbance by a central control operator in order to minimize false alarms. A pictorial view of the Model 401 SU and DU units is shown in Fig. 8-14.

Send Unit: SU

The automatic "dialing" microphone inputs for audible disturbances are compatible with approved telephone company couplers. The dialing number is simply set by the installer; no programming is required and there are no moving parts nor magnetic tapes to fail. It sends both the location and type of emergency and features continuous "dialing" until acknowledged. The system triggers on NO or NC contacts.

Display Unit: DU

The display unit will monitor up to 1,000 SUs and permit an audible verification of alarms by a central station operator. The device features a digital readout on a "nixie" display and is compatible with approved telephone company couplers. Visual and audible alarms can be actuated. It is pre-wired to accept a digital printer.

Specifications

Size: Send unit is 6½ inches long by 8½ inches high by 4 inches deep.
Power: 110-volt 60-Hz single phase.
Weight: Send unit, 5 pounds; display unit, 7¼ pounds.

Fig. 8-14. Bourns Security Systems digital dialer Model 401.

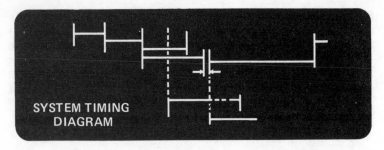

Fig. 8-15. Model 401 timing diagram.

Options: Automatic print-out display at the central alarm station with a record or coded "address" type emergency, date and time.

The system timing diagram is shown in Fig. 8-15.

DETECTRON SECURITY SYSTEM EMERGENCY COMMUNICATOR

In this solid-state automatic dialer, two channels may be programmed on a magnetic tape cartridge. A five-minute cartridge is included to allow up to four or more separate telephone numbers and messages to be programmed for each channel (A and B). Tape cartridges for longer messages to 20 minutes are available on special order. Cartridges for the dialer are pre-programmed at the factory, or the Model 1520 programmer may be used for the purpose. Either of the channels may be activated separately through contact closure or momentary application of 6 to 12 volts DC. When energized, the dialer operates automatically. It dials the programmed numbers in sequence, states the messages, hangs up, shuts itself off and resets for the next sequence. If both channels are energized simultaneously, B will precede A.

The dialer operates from the 110-volt power line and has a provision for automatic switchover to a 12-volt standby source in case of line outage. Two 6-volt 510-S Eveready batteries (or equivalent) are required. Where permissible, the dialer may be connected directly to the telephone lines or the standard coupler supplied by the telephone company may be used.

Specifications

Power requirements: 110 volts AC or 12 volts DC.
Number of channels: Two (independently energizable).
Triggering: Dry closure on each channel or momentary wet closure on each (6 to 12 volts).

Programming: Available at factory or a Detectron Programmer Model 1520 may be used.

Size: 10" high, 10" wide, 7" deep.

Weight: 13 pounds, less batteries.

Construction: 16 gauge steel cabinet, vertical mount, key lock.

LECTRO SYSTEMS, INC., MODEL 2001 TELEPHONE DIALER

This system is all solid-state with no moving parts. It will recycle until a shutdown command is received; therefore, a dial tone delay is unimportant, a busy signal only means repeat, and a telephone company caused wrong number causes no problem. An IC circuit dialing pulse is used, along with on-line tone data transmission, and it is easily programmed by trained personnel.

Specifications

Power: 115v AC primary, 18v DC NiCad standby.

Input: Three sensing circuits (each NC and-or NO and momentary).

Fig. 8-16. Automatic telephone dialer, Mark 2000, made by National Alarm Products Co., Inc.

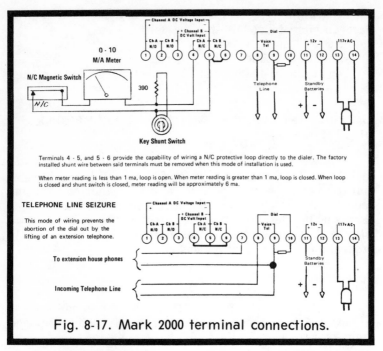

Terminals 4 - 5, and 5 - 6 provide the capability of wiring a N/C protective loop directly to the dialer. The factory installed shunt wire between said terminals must be removed when this mode of installation is used.

When meter reading is less than 1 ma, loop is open. When meter reading is greater than 1 ma, loop is closed. When loop is closed and shunt switch is closed, meter reading will be approximately 6 ma.

TELEPHONE LINE SEIZURE

This mode of wiring prevents the abortion of the dial out by the lifting of an extension telephone.

To extension house phones

Incoming Telephone Line

Fig. 8-17. Mark 2000 terminal connections.

Output: Pulse dialing to 11 digits, 3 message channels, tone data report, local alarm dry closure with a 1 amp capacity.

Report timing: Activation, 10 seconds; pulsing cycle, 20 seconds; 10-second pause; message data, 10 seconds; listen period, 5 seconds (for shut-down tone); hang-up.

Command function: Constant recycle of dialing and data reporting until a shut-down command signal is received from command central.

Monitoring lights: Circuit activation and respective reporting, channel indicators, closed-circuit (burglar) continuity when switch keyed to triangle, and a pilot to indicate that AC is present.

Keyed switch: Nite position, all sensing circuits on; day position—same as nite, except the Channel 1 NC circuit and local alarm are off; triangle position; abort alarm; reset unit; check the Channel 1 NC circuit.

Physical: Cabinet, 18 guage steel. Dimensions are 12¼" by 9¼" by 3¼". The weight is 12½ pounds.

Companion Readout Receiver, Model 2002, Features

115v AC power.
Numitron sequential digits.

Instant operator alert, but alarm data storage.

Signal control (command) of all associated dialers.

Reads tape dialer voice message.

NATIONAL ALARM PRODUCTS CO. AUTOMATIC TELEPHONE DIALER

The Mark 2000 features 2-channel capacity with priority over-ride and up to four messages per channel, with 20

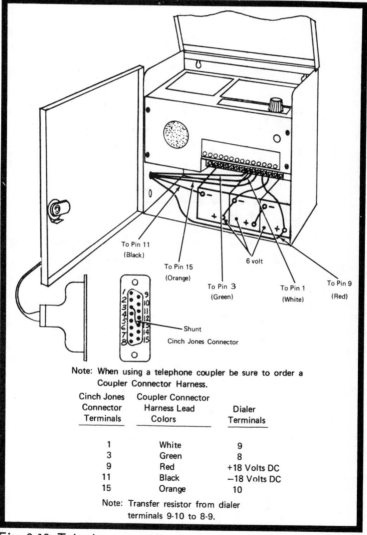

Note: When using a telephone coupler be sure to order a Coupler Connector Harness.

Cinch Jones Connector Terminals	Coupler Connector Harness Lead Colors	Dialer Terminals
1	White	9
3	Green	8
9	Red	+18 Volts DC
11	Black	−18 Volts DC
15	Orange	10

Note: Transfer resistor from dialer terminals 9-10 to 8-9.

Fig. 8-18. Telephone coupler connections to the Mark 2000.

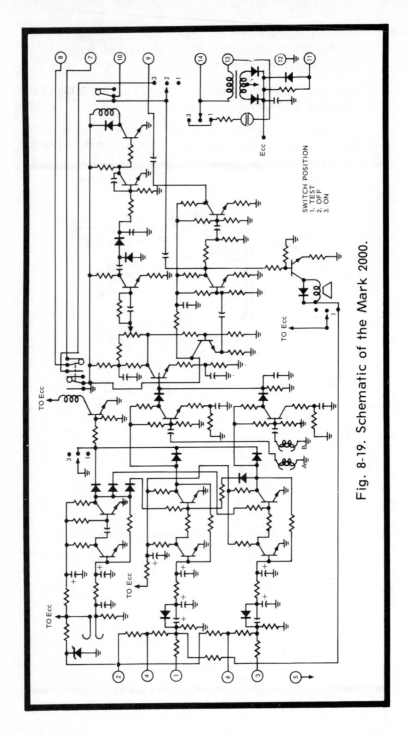

Fig. 8-19. Schematic of the Mark 2000.

SWITCH POSITION
1. TEST
2. OFF
3. ON

minutes program time available on special order. The equipment operates on AC, but it houses a DC standby power system in which the battery supply is maintained by floating charge. A test speaker is built-in for monitoring the taped program. Line release, a programming option, prevents incoming calls from interfering with an emergency dial-out. The activating inputs on both channels requires 3 to 5 volts DC and includes both normally open and normally closed circuitry.

A telephone line may be connected directly to the Mark 2000, or a telephone coupler may be used. The battery compartment holds three 6-volt batteries, supplying 18 volts for a telephone coupler. An automatic stop feature enables the Mark 2000 to stop automatically after a complete execution of the program, then reset itself for emergency readiness. Line seizure, an optional feature at no cost, prevents interruption of an emergency dial-out by the lifting of an extension telephone. The voice-tuned output ensures that emergency messages are transmitted clearly at the proper volume.

The device uses all solid-state active components mounted on a mil standard epoxy glass printed-circuit board, paladium cross-bar contact relays, lubricated mylar tape, stainless steel and precision bronze bearings and special hyperbolic playback head. Idling power consumption is 18 milliwatts. The input impedance is 2,000 ohms.

Dimensions: Height, 9 inches; width 9¾ inches; depth 6½ inches.

Weight: 14 pounds.

A pictorial view of the Mark 2000 appears in Fig. 8-16. The terminal connections are shown in Fig. 8-17, and the telephone coupler hookup in Fig. 8-18. The schematic diagram is shown in Fig. 8-19.

Chapter 9
Audio & Visual Alarms

By canceling out ambient noise, most audio detection systems will provide an alarm condition in response to any additional sounds. The internal space in any selected area may be monitored with low-voltage wiring circuits through PA speakers used as sound detectors, as well as by regular audio sensors. Since sensing circuits are normally adjustable over an extremely wide range and in conjunction with sound cancellation plus time-delay circuits, most sources of false alarms are eliminated. The selective response of multiple detection networks ensures the required information being picked up from protected areas where variations in sound levels exist to a greater degree. Heavy machinery operating intermittently will cause excessive fluctuations in sound levels, and carpeted areas often result in the opposite extreme. In such cases, the audio detection approach would be useless without numerous assists, such as sound filters, time delay, sound cancellation and other selective factors. Where external noise is excessive, a sound balancing arrangement could be useful by coupling internal and external transducers to the usual discriminator to require the inside level of sound to equal or exceed the outside level during a particular time segment.

ALARMTRONICS ENGINEERING MODEL AE-1

The Model AE-1 electronic audio detection system provides an early warning whether forced entry is attempted through walls, roof, door or window. It will also sense the presence of "stay-behinds" as it contains transistorized circuitry with emergency power and tamper-proof features. The system monitors all internal space or selected sections. It is designed to use existing PA and paging speakers and-or its own sensors and may be programmed to screen out normal background noises. The device can be connected to a central station, dialers, an answering service, etc. The system is designed to protect against intruders by operating bells, sirens, lights, etc. Supplementary sensors may be added for fire, smoke, flood, freeze, etc., and it may be used to protect safes, cabinets, racks, and fences by adding vibration type sensors. The system is activated by a pick-proof key switch and-or a time clock and it carries UL approval. The dimensions are 15⅝" wide, 15⅝" high, 3¼" deep.

Performance Specifications

The sound detection sensitivity of the audio circuit can be adjusted by a control. Sound detection is provided by special microphones or by a tie-in to an all-call bus or a public address system, or both, wired into the main detection input to the unit. Each special microphone contains a rheostat for individual sensitivity control. A control adjusts the sensitivity of the cancellation circuit. Cancellation of the "spectral frequency" of normal building sounds is provided without a loss of overall detection sensitivity by the use of special microphones wired into the cancellation input of the unit.

A control adjusts the number of sounds required to trigger an alarm; that is, the sounds occurring within 30 seconds of time. The number of sounds is adjustable from 3 to 10, with a minimum half-second between sound pulses. Another control adjusts the time that an alarm is triggered and then automatically reset. The timer will vary the alarm from one second to two minutes. There is a control to balance the microphone line impedance so that an alarm will be triggered if the line is cut.

Provided is an input for auxiliary sensors, such as thermostats, hold-up switches and door contacts, which will also trigger an alarm. There is a supervised input for the alarm system detector unit for arming and disarming by remote key switch or time clock. A tamper switch inside the cabinet housing automatically triggers the alarm when the cabinet is opened.

A self-contained 6-volt dry cell battery provides standby power, which becomes operative during a power outage. The standby supply will permit continuous operation for a week or more and is automatically switched in at the time of AC line failure and remains in operation until the line is restored. A built-in test board with a meter helps determine the status of all major unit functions. A supervised single pole, double throw (STDT) output relay is utilized to trigger an alarm. The input from the sound detector to the detection unit audio amplifier is electrically balanced. The sketch in Fig. 9-1 shows the placement of the various units.

SYSTRON-DONNER, MODELS VA-2, VA-3 & VA-4 VAULT ALARM

Features include solid-state circuitry, UL listing, internal sensitivity adjustment, a temperature range of 32 to 140

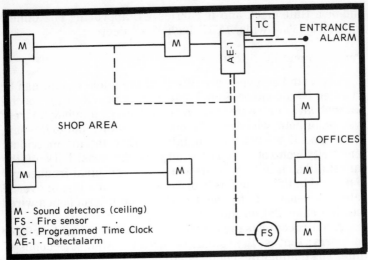

Fig. 9-1. Diagram of a typical Alarmtronics Model AE-1 installation.

Within the diagram:
TC
ENTRANCE
ALARM
M
M
AE-1
M
SHOP AREA
OFFICES
M
M
M
M
M - Sound detectors (ceiling)
FS - Fire sensor
TC - Programmed Time Clock
AE-1 - Detectalarm
FS
M

degrees F or 0 to 60 degrees C, fail-safe circuit, cabinet tamper protection, noise pulse counter to discriminate against transient signals, noise burst counter with three time durations, vibration and sound sensors with built-in tamper circuit, ion detector with built-in tamper circuit, optional locked enclosure, central station interrogation and 16.5-volt AC operation with a 36-hour standby power reserve from a lead acid battery (72 hours optional).

This system is designed to operate on 115 volts AC, 50-60 Hz. Other line conditions require special transformers, but for standard line conditions, an Underwriter's Lab approved Class 2 transformer is provided (10 to 16.5v AC). Power consumption is ¼ watt. The output relay is an isolated SPST type with 2 ampere contacts.

Audio vibration sensors have a frequency response of 200 Hz to 8 kHz, and the system capacity is 1 to 5 sensors (with increased capacity available) connected by a 4-conductor cable with a built-in tamper loop. Fire detection is possible with optional ionized products of combustion detectors. The enclosure measures 11⅛" by 7½" by 3½" and weighs 7 pounds; a lock with built-in tamper switch is optional. A test feature included provides remote interrogation on the supervised line. VA-2 is designed to be interrogated by DWP-6. VA-2 connects to the alarm signal device on the premises, VA-3 connects directly to ADT (or similar) central station equipment and VA-4 connects directly to Potter (or similar) central station equipment.

As mentioned previously, as many as five sensors may be attached to the inside wall of the protected enclosure. The number needed is determined by the size and reverberatory properties of the protected enclosure. A vault containing stacks of papers or racks of furs, for example, would be classified as nonreverberating and would require additional sensors. A block diagram of the vault alarm system is shown in Fig. 9-2.

The sensors are parallel connected, and signals from the sensors are amplified and fed to the pulse counter. Noise bursts, such as caused by an intruder's attack, have high pulse counts. Short duration transients, usually with lower pulse counts, are rejected. As the noise burst signal is fed to a wave shaper, it triggers a fixed duration signal. This signal charges a 2-step integrator circuit with selectable discharge rates which controls the frequency of occurrence of the noise bursts. When the integrator circuit receives two signals within a given discharge time, it reaches a trip level to drop out the normally energized alarm relay.

A continuous noise, as caused by a drill with a duration exceeding four seconds, will reset the pulse counter automatically and send a second signal to the integrator to trip the relay circuit. The ion detector, when used with the system, will trip the relay circuit with the presence of an ionized product of combustion such as generated by fire.

A tamper circuit is incorporated in the system to protect the sensors, ion detector, and control unit while the vault or safe is open during working hours. The on-off switch located on the side of the control shunts the signals from the sensors so

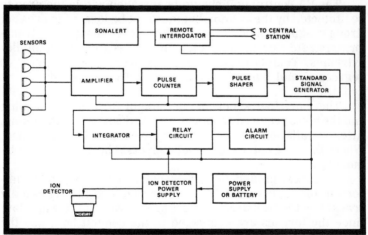

Fig. 9-2. Block diagram of the Systron-Donner vault alarm system.

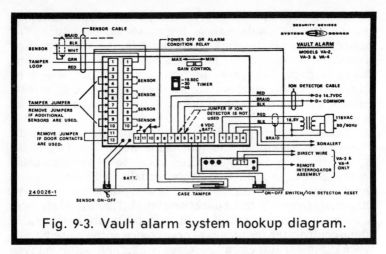

Fig. 9-3. Vault alarm system hookup diagram.

the alarm relay with tamper circuit is still in operation. The standard system is available with 36-hour standby battery; a 72-hour standby is available at additional cost. The Model VA-2 is the basic vault alarm system with no provision for remote interrogation. Relay contacts are available for connection to commercial alarm signaling devices. Model VA-3 and VA-4 are equipped with remote interrogation modules. The former may be used with ADT and the latter with Potter central station equipment.

Installation & Checkout

The VA control unit should be installed within the area to be protected by the system, but must not be located in areas of strong magnetic fields created by motors, generators, transformers, etc., or be subjected to temperature or humidity extremes. Temperatures above 120 degrees F or below 30 degrees F and humidity in excess of 95 percent should be avoided.

There are four knockouts in the unit for conduit coupling and the holes required should be knocked out before mounting. After installation, the conduit may be connected as needed. Where they are not used, ⅞-inch universal bushings should be mounted.

A conduit ground for the transformer is extremely important for suppressing RF interference, and the right-angle bracket on the transformer must be screwed to the wall-plate since the threads are connected to the conduit box; see the hookup diagram in Fig. 9-3. Make sure that the outlet selected is grounded. The XF-16 transformer has a 3-prong plug. Do not remove the third prong (ground) since it must be grounded.

An audio vibration sensor is shipped with the system; additional sensors are optional. The sensor has a 30-foot cable with a built-in tamper loop. A typical vault installation is shown in Fig. 9-4. Notice the connection of the VA-3 to a central station as shown in Fig. 9-5.

Operating Instructions

A. Before operating, be sure that the tamper jumpers are in the terminals where sensors are not connected (Fig. 9-3).

B. The power switch in the off position will remove power from the unit; however, the charging voltage remains on the battery.

C. Tape down the case tamper switch when operating and testing the unit with the cover off.

D. Select one of the three discharge periods for the integrator. In a typical installation, the 15-second time period is used, but period selection depends on the geographic location of the installation. Consideration should be given to conditions such as thunder in a storm or a whistle from a passing train.

E. Set the gain control high enough for the unit to respond to a light tapping noise on the wall and not to respond to ambient noise of the enclosure.

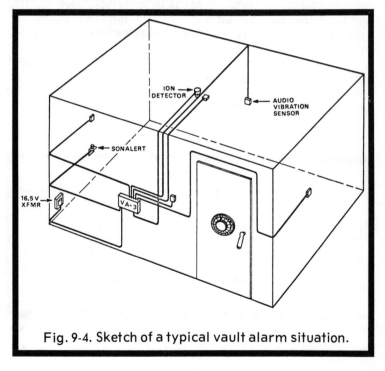

Fig. 9-4. Sketch of a typical vault alarm situation.

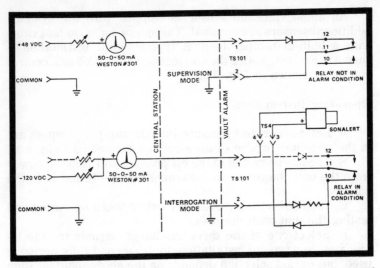

Fig. 9-5. Diagram of vault alarm system VA-3 connected to a central station.

F. Alarm condition: Two bursts of noise or a continuous noise with a duration of four seconds or longer will trip the relay circuit momentarily. A break in the tamper loop will trip and latch the relay circuit until the loop is closed again. The presence of fire will trip and latch the relay circuit until reset by turning the power off in the unit.

G. Remote interrogation assembly: A test of the vault alarm can be performed in the vault or remotely from the central station (see Figs. 9-6 and 9-7). Model VA-2 should be hooked up as shown in Fig. 9-5. To connect the Model VA-3, refer to Fig. 9-6.

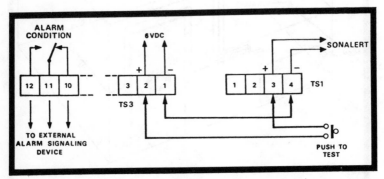

Fig. 9-6. Vault alarm system connected for local interrogation.

For central station supervision, apply the positive (+) terminal of a 48-volt DC supply to terminal No. 1 of TS101 and the negative (-) to terminal No. 2. Apply the voltage to the central station side of the lines. Adjust the line current for 10 ma.

To test the vault alarm from the central station, reverse the polarity of a 120-volt DC supply to TS101 with -120 volts DC to terminal 1. Adjust the line current for 5 ma to energize the Sonalert. Energize the Sonalert for 4 seconds or longer and the unit will go into alarm; the current will be approximately 10 ma. This indicates an alarm condition in the VA-3 and the relay contacts are open. This test simulates drilling and two short bursts within the time selected will also trip the alarm.

For central station supervision of the VA-4 (refer to Fig. 9-7), apply the positive (+) terminal of a 130-volt DC supply to terminal No. 1 of TS101 and the negative (-) to terminal No. 2. Apply the voltage from the central station side of the lines. Adjust the line current for 15 ma. Keep the ring switch at position A during supervision.

To test the vault alarm from the central station, set the "ring" switch to position B for approximately 3 seconds. Return the switch to position A and the current reading on the meter will drop from 15 ma to 0. This indicates an alarm condition in the VA-4 and the relay contacts are open. The relay will reset in approximately 1 second and the meter will again show 15 ma.

BOGEN AUDIO ALARM SYSTEM

The Bogen Model CA-20 and -21 systems utilize existing two-way school sound systems to reduce installation costs, and protect the entire building with lock-in or stay-behind detection along with break-in detection. Normal building

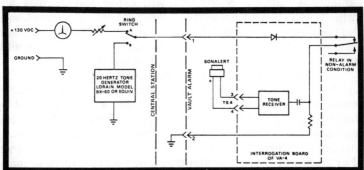

Fig. 9-7. Vault alarm system connected for central station interrogation.

sounds and outside noises are screened out to prevent false alarms. The system consists of detector components in the building and alarm components located at the police station or central security office or even a telephone answering service. The CA-20 or CA-21 intrusion detector is usually installed in the school system console and the existing speakers plus any additional sensors required connect to the detector panel. Abnormal sounds such as breaking glass are picked up by the speakers and fed to the detector unit which transmits the alarm. The normal building sounds made by clocks, compressors and outside noises are filtered out by a computer circuit to prevent them from triggering a nuisance alarm.

Whether the alarm is sounded locally or at a remote station, the basic components required at the remote station (police or security) are the CA-22 audio monitor and 132 alarm cabinet with appropriate horn and alarm modules. The alarm signal also may be used to operate a telephone dialer to pass on a pre-recorded message to the proper authorities. The use of solid-state (silicon) circuitry with stabilized amplifiers makes the system immune to line changes or interference of an electrical nature. Standby battery capability provides protection against line outages or tampering.

The usual loud speakers in the school or similar system act as microphones or sound sensors to pick up any sounds that may be originating in the vicinity. Any parts of the building not covered by speakers are protected by adding microphones to act as audio sensors. Cancel microphones or transducers are also added when required to detect and screen out normal building sounds. Doors and windows may be easily protected with magnetic type switches, and when closing the building at night, a simple turn of a key renders the CA-20 or CA-21 capable of sensing any intrusion or unauthorized activity within the premises. Entering the building, opening file cabinets or moving equipment will cause sounds that are immediately picked up by the loudspeakers or microphones and fed through the switch banks in the console to the intrusion detector. Opening a door or window equipped with a magnetic switch would also pass a signal to the detector.

Intrusion sounds are sharp and sudden as a rule and fall within the 1,000 to 5,000-Hz frequency range, but ambient sounds fall outside this frequency segment and are ignored by the detector. Ordinary building noises within the frequency limit are blocked out by canceling circuits, and those that pass through are stored in a memory circuit requiring three sounds of appropriate sharpness and frequency within thirty seconds to close the alarm relay.

Several choices are available when the relay closes. It may sound an alarm at the school or building being protected to frighten off the intruder, or actuate an automatic telephone dialer to call the police or even to signal a central station or answering service to initiate immediate action. An alarm receiver unit at a remote station can monitor up to nine schools and indicate an alarm condition on the appropriate alarm module.

Triggering of the alarm by the intrusion detector in the protected area causes the polarity of the DC on the telephone line to be reversed, which sets off the Model 131 horn module in the alarm cabinet and turns on the pilot light of the Model 130 alarm module for that specific school. The horn is silenced by a reset button on the alarm module. The observer checks the alarm meter at the remote station to find out which school is involved and if the trouble is in the telephone line or if an actual alarm condition exists. A monitor selector and volume control at the CA-22 alarm monitor permits listening in to the school building directly to detect sounds which may be caused by someone on the premises.

The intrusion detector in the console is connected to the 120-volt AC line and turned on when the alarm system is set up after regular school hours. An optional fail-safe feature automatically switches operation to a standby battery if the normal AC should fail or be cut off.

The CA-20 intrusion detector is sound operated with an alarm triggering capability, which is normally installed in a school sound system console or a similar type separate cabinet. The detector system is designed to function with regular school system loudspeakers serving as microphones to pick up sounds in the vicinity and provision is made to transfer all speakers to the alarm system when the sound system is turned off. The unit also may pick up audio information from the microphone sensors and electrical inputs from the magnetic door and window switches.

Not only does the detector respond to only sound frequencies in the 1,000 to 5,000 Hz range, but an additional requirement is a fast attack time. The unit counts each sound once, regardless of amplitude or duration, and when three are counted within 30 seconds the alarm condition exists. Random sounds over an extended period leak off without effect. The audio output line is biased 12 volts negative to ground in the normal condition and 12 volts positive ($+$) to ground when the alarm is set off. A zero level audio output at 500 or 600 ohms is provided for monitoring from a remote area.

The unit is equipped with a speaker-microphone and test switch to check its operation, with the pulse count and alarm condition indicators located on the front panel, plus a key-operated on-off-test switch. The adjustment controls and fuses are in a locked compartment behind the front panel to avoid tampering by unauthorized personnel.

The CA-21 parallels the CA-20, except that a canceling channel is included to detect and count sounds generated by the cancel microphones which are placed as close as possible to the normal noise sources. The cancel channel responds in the same manner as the regular channel, except that a pulse generated in the cancel channel is coupled to an impede circuit to neutralize the pulse generated in the main channel from the same source, if they occur simultaneously.

The CA-22 audio monitor is a self-contained monitor and power supply unit which is incorporated in the alarm receiver at a remote point. The primary function of the unit is as a control station for listening to sounds transmitted from any one of as many as nine protected areas. It also receives the alarm signal from any of the schools to which it is connected and passes the information along to the horn module and appropriate alarm module in the alarm receiver.

The monitor selector switch permits a choice of the building to be monitored and the monitored sound may be heard in the front panel speaker. The monitor volume control and power-on pilot light are also located on the front panel. The WMT-1 transformer furnished with the CA-22 permits separating the input DC and audio signal from the telephone line while providing a 500 or 600 ohm input for monitoring one school building. Additional WMT-1 transformers are required for each school building connected to the alarm receiver.

The Model 132 alarm cabinet is used with the CA-22 in the alarm receiver, and the pre-wired cabinet houses the horn and alarm modules which function to sound the alarm and indicate the nature and location of the trouble. Although the cabinet may be mounted or placed on the table, for convenience, it is usually mounted immediately above the CA-22. The cabinet holds up to five modules and in the basic system one is the horn module and the others are alarm modules for each of four different schools. When one cabinet fills, another may be stacked on the first to afford space for five more alarm modules.

The Model 131 horn module is an alarm buzzer housed in the alarm cabinet, and when an alarm is triggered at any of the schools carried and connected to the alarm receiver, the horn starts to sound off. At the same instant, a pilot light goes on in the proper alarm module. The horn continues to operate until the horn reset is pressed on the alarm module.

The Model 130 alarm module provides a visual indication of an alarm condition at the point monitored or a problem in the wiring to that point, but has the ability to distinguish between the actual alarm and an open or short in the telephone line. The answer is indicated by the meter which reads "normal," "trouble" or "alarm." A pilot light on the alarm module goes on when there is an alarm or trouble on the telephone line and the alarm buzzer goes off. A reset button on the module will turn off the horn, but the light remains on until the telephone line has been repaired or the alarm detector resets itself. The alarm module then resets automatically and is set for another alarm.

Model WMT-1 is a line-matching transformer designed to match either inputs or outputs to a 500 or 600-ohm line and used in the alarm receiver to provide an audio input to the CA-22 audio monitor for monitoring sounds in the protected area. One transformer is required for each telephone line input to the alarm receiver. A block diagram of a typical sound intrusion alarm system is shown in Fig. 9-8, using the various Bogen units described above.

MULTRA-GUARD, INC., SONIC-2

This DC supervised sonic, perimeter and holdup alarm monitoring unit is designed for connection between four protected premises and a central station over four separate leased telephone lines with DC continuity between terminal equipment. The Multra-Fone (MS2MF) is a solid-state, miniature, preamplified sound detector and alarm discriminator. It preamplifies to 300 times the normal pickup sensitivity with an effective surveillance capability said to

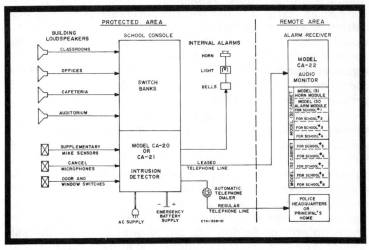

Fig. 9-8. Block diagram of a typical Bogen alarm detector system.

exceed 2,500 square feet. While measuring 2½" by 3¾", it has the appearance of an ordinary thermostat and may be mounted in the ceiling or overhead, as well as wall mounted. It is not necessary to conceal the unit, which operates at the same high level regardless of mode of entry—through a door, window, skylight or a hole in the ceiling. Even an intruder hiding until after closing time sets off the alarm as soon as he attempts to work on the area under surveillance. The detector not only transmits alarm information, but enables the central monitor to listen in on the activity throughout the protected area just as though he were there in person. The circuit remains active until reset by the operator on duty at the central station and each sonic circuit in the system may be carefully adjusted to respond to exceptionally loud noises in a noisy location or to lesser noises in a quiet area.

The control unit at the protected premises operates on 117v AC, 60 Hz, or a 12-volt battery which is maintained in a charged condition for standby power. The cabinet is 10" by 10" by 4" with a tamper switch and a protective circuit sensitive to resistance substitution. The day-night switch gives a visual indication at the central station when it is in the night position and the test switch offers a continuity test of the night protective circuit before switching from day to night. The day circuit is supervised at all times unless the system is off. The day-night switch does not disable the tamper in any position and a reset switch is provided to return the circuit to normal following a holdup indication. Any act which introduces a change in the perimeter resistance greater than 50 percent will give an alarm, as will a polarity reversal on line. Shorting, cutting or grounding both sides of the telephone line gives a trouble indication with an audible signal at central. Grounding one side of the telephone line does not interfere with normal logic and interruption of the 117v AC does not alter normal operation if the 12v standby is used and normal power is resumed before battery power drops appreciably.

Since the signal voltage source is at the subscriber's control unit, shorting the telephone line cannot give a false normal indication. Instead, a shorted line will show a trouble indication. The monitor modules at the central station use 12 volts DC at 50 milliamperes per module and four operate from a 250 ma 12-volt supply. A common Sonalert is required for each four units or less, and there are audible and visual signals for trouble, holdup and perimeter trouble. A continuous alarm on holdup will sound until reset by the subscriber. The half brilliance holdup alarm light stays on until the operator resets, and there is an audible signal even when the subscriber's signal is no longer on the line. The night signal switch breaks the line to provide a visual signal back to the subscriber.

The trend away from local alarm systems in which a bell or siren announces a break-in outside the building has reached a new high recently, since this action has offered little if any deterrent to such crimes. The general public has grown so accustomed to these alarms in central city areas especially that they are either ignored or purposely overlooked in the overriding decision not to get involved.

More than ever before, such characteristics enhance the central station approach to security system protection as the only complete solution to a frustrating situation. Since police, firemen and all other available public servants are taxed far beyond their capacity, it would be inconceivable to assume or expect an instantaneous response to an alarm or warning device without any confirmation or even authentication from a reliable source. This also rules out the performance of central station simulated duties by the police department personnel without any monitoring assistance from the establishment or business expecting such cooperation.

Although considerable assistance along these lines may be rendered by an answering service at a cost lower than most central station services would have to charge, such could barely meet the basic requirements of around-the-clock surveillance. So many times, the answering service is unable, due to insufficient information and technically oriented personnel, to evaluate whether or not the signal received at their switchboard is authentic or just another false alarm. Rather than guess the wrong way, most of these operators have been instructed to call the police on all alarms and this does result in numerous nuisance calls for the police. So, at best a temporary service may be rendered by such a service until the proper central station type is available and arranged. Needless to say, the response that could be anticipated from the latter could never be more than a mere fraction of the time required for any other type.

Confidence in requests from central station operators, from an experience standpoint, enables instant dispatching of police mobile units to the scene. The ability to check out the alarm line and even to "listen in" at the source of the intrusion makes the central station report positive in each and every case. With expertly trained operators to handle each individual subscriber, a 24-hour monitoring service, the means to check lines and systems, repair and-or maintenance, plus instant action when the emergency is indicated, the decision makers of any successful business must eventually demand this type of a security system for their company. The

```
          Hilton Central Station

              Break-In Report
Sadowski's Music Store
King Street
Hampton, Virginia

10:31 P.M. our monitor heard someone breaking through the
rear door of Sadowski's Music Store. He immediately
contacted the Hampton Police Dept., who arrived on the
scene at 10:33 P.M. The police informed the vandals that
the place was surrounded and to give themselves up. There
was no answer from the vandals who were trapped inside, so
the police informed them that they would send the police dogs
in if they did not come out. This is when the vandals
surrendered. There were three vandals apprehended, two (2)
adults and one (1) juvenile.

One of the vandals was caught with drug paraphenalia in
his possession. They were taken to Hampton Police
Headquarters and charged with breaking and entering, plus
one was charged with the possession of narcotics. Our
monitor, at the request of the Hampton police, went down
to the police station and made a statement as to what he
had heard.

After the business was secure again, Mrs. Sadowski called
and thanked us for doing a fine job. She also informed us
that ten or twelve police cars were on the scene when she
arrived.

                         Jesse R. Kersey
                         Jesse R. Kersey
                         Multra-Guard of Virginia
```

Fig. 9-9. Copy of an actual report using a sound security system.

letter in Fig. 9-9 is ample testimony to the effectiveness of such systems.

Lectro Systems, Inc., LSI, Model 500A Alarm Control Panel

This combination fire and burglar alarm control panel has sensing circuits that cannot be armed until all sensors and detectors are ready for arming. The panel features six monitoring lights which indicate the status of the system, armed or disarmed, etc. Monitoring can be linked to remotes, too. Many options are offered such as a bell no-bell switch, delay logic to permit authorized exit and entrance, and a connector for either dialer or leased line reporting. The system operates on 117v 50-60 Hz AC, from which an internal transformer provides filtered 12v DC for the operating voltage. Standby power is furnished by a NEDA no. 922 battery.

Fire supervision is provided on a 24-hour basis; the emergency (panic) is a 24-hour open circuit. The burglar alarm will accept open, closed or both open and closed circuits. Separate closures are provided for automatic dialers and leased line, and there is a terminal position to supply continuous 12 volts DC for smoke sensors. The cabinet measures 11⅞ by 15¼ by 3½ inches. Three conduit knockouts facilitate installation, along with keyed holes for wall mounting. There is a locking door on a full length hinge. It weighs 17 pounds without a battery.

VISUAL ALARM SYSTEMS

The visual system, or closed-circuit television (CCTV) as it is often described, possesses many features for overcoming the limitations of sound and other types of security systems. Although the average cost figure would exceed many other arrangements, the reliability and flexibility of the video method offers at least two major points for consideration when such features may be almost mandatory. The closed-circuit television camera-monitor loop does require continuous vigil, but this disadvantage may be easily eliminated by the addition of detection devices to signal the precise time that attention is warranted. Even though the closed-circuit TV camera may be easily spotted by the subject to be watched, this is frequently a deterrent to the thief, and decoy cameras often "operate" on this assumption.

Motion detection to augment visual systems provides valuable information while relieving the need for continuous observation of the monitor screen. The use of a memory circuit permits a comparison of changes in the scanned area to indicate that significant motion has occurred. Samples taken at selected intervals, as well as numerous other modifications, offer much in the way of concrete information that could hardly be obtained in any other manner.

GBC CLOSED CIRCUIT TV CORP., MODEL CTC-5000 VIDEO CAMERA

Six operating modes are available: (1) internal sync random interlace, line lock; (2) external sync, EIA horizontal and vertical drive pulses from an external sync generator; (3) internal sync, crystal-controlled horizontal oscillator, random interlace, line lock (with the optional CTP5-71); (4) internal sync, 2:1 interlace, line lock (with the optional SG-101A module); (5) internal sync, 2:1 interlace, crystal-controlled (with the optional SG-102A module); (6) RF output, tunable on Channels 2 through 6 (with the optional CTP5-81 module).

The camera is designed for continuous duty operation. The power required is 100 to 120v AC, 50-60 Hz, at 18 watts. A 3AG slo blow fuse prevents overload or damage to the camera in the event of component failure. Focus current, picture size, contrast and resolution are held constant within 5 percent for line variations between 100 and 120 volts. The image tube is a 7735A type. The horizontal sweep rate is 525 lines per frame, random interlaced, crystal controlled (optional), with 2:1 binary sync (optional) or extended drive. The vertical sweep rate is 50 or 60 Hz, locked to the line. Automatic light compensation will accommodate a 5,000-to-1 change in light level with less than a 25 percent change in the video output level. The signal-to-noise ratio is 50 db (weighted). Usable pictures are attainable with a faceplate illumination as low as 0.1 footcandle. The manufacturer also says that all 10 shades of gray scale are discernible on a standard EIA test chart with 10 footcandles of scene brightness. The output impedance is 75 ohms.

Both composite and noncomposite video outputs are provided. The composite is 1.4v p-p and the non-composite is 1.0v p-p (switchable). The optional RF output is 50 mv, tunable to Channels 2, 3, 4, 5 or 6. Horizontal resolution is claimed to be at least 650 TV lines in the center and the vertical resolution at least 350 TV lines. The video bandwidth is 8.5 MHz, plus or minus 3 db. Rear panel controls include external-internal sync, composite-non-composite video output switch, power on and off and focus; internal controls are target, focus and beam. A picture of the camera appears in Fig. 9-10. A view of the control panel is shown in Fig. 9-11. The camera is 4" high' 5¾" wide, 11" long and weighs 7¼ pounds.

Video Monitor

The 9-inch solid-state (IC) video monitor in Fig. 9-12 is used to monitor the picture picked up by the camera in Fig. 9-10. It contains a 230ADB4 picture tube and will accept a 1.4v p-p black negative composite video signal. The input impedance is 75 ohms nominal or a high impedance through a switchable bridge. The scanning rate is 15.75 kHz horizontal, 60 Hz line lock vertical, and horizontal resolution is said to be more than 500 lines at the center. The manufacturer says the signal-to-noise ratio exceeds 32 db, the video amplifier gain is at least 30 db, and the frequency response is 5 MHz. It operates on 100 to 120v AC, 60 Hz, drawing approximately 20 watts. Overall dimensions are 8⅝" wide, 9¼" high, 9" deep. The weight is approximately 13 pounds. Front panel controls include the off-on switch, pilot light, horizontal hold, vertical hold, contrast and brightness controls in that order. The rear panel provides access to the horizontal frequency, focus and height controls. Video is applied through connectors and a terminating switch.

JOHNSON SERVICE CO., MPS-4 ALARM MONITOR

The monitor unit offers visual and audio alarm indications as well as alarm supervision for the G-1 motion detection and other security devices. The degree of alarm supervision is adjustable from plus or minus 2 to plus or minus 25 percent. Sixteen variations of the unit are available from the manufacturer with or without an alarm current meter, standby power supply and auxiliary alarm relay. Either a piezoelectric or a speaker type tone generator is available, along with any combinations of previously mentioned options to meet the needs of individual customers. The solid-state unit is designed for 120 volts AC, 60 Hz, operation at a power consumption of 10 watts (approximate). The supervisory line current is 400 microamperes. Dimensions are 8 3 32 inches wide by 5½ inches high by 6¾ inches deep. The standby battery capability is 9 hours without the auxiliary alarm relay. Relay contacts are rated at 5 A at 24v DC and 3A at 115v AC (resistive load) or 2A at 24v DC and 1A at 115v AC (inductive load).

The complete schematic diagram of the MPS-4 is shown in Fig. 9-13, which shows both types of tone circuits, optional standby battery power supply and line current meter. The auxiliary alarm relay and associated components are also included in the diagram. On models without the line current meter, only the meter and two diodes which shunt it are not

Fig. 9-10. CCTV camera, Model CTC5000.

Fig. 9-11. Control panel of the GBC CTC5000 camera.

Fig. 9-12. GBC video monitor, Model MV-900. (Courtesy GBC Closed-Circuit TV Corp.)

included. Models without the standby battery supply have batteries and associated charging and regulating circuits omitted. The jumper shown in the power supply is installed instead. The auxiliary alarm relay, relay socket and transistor and diode controlling relay are furnished only on models with the relay option. Operation of all MPS-4 monitors is essentially the same, regardless of the optional features selected.

The monitor unit senses a change in the supervisory line circuit resistance caused by action of the relays in the motion detector, the tamper switches, the active-standby switch, tampering with the line or line malfunction (shorted or open line), and gives an alarm for any of these indications.

A 400 microamp supervisory current is produced by the regulated power supply in the monitor unit. This current flows through the resistors in the active-standby control box as shown in Fig. 9-14. Resistors are switched into the line circuit to provide the various indications. When the alarm relay in the motion detector opens, the 18K resistor is switched into the circuit, which reduces the line current to 250 microamperes. Dropout of the supervisory relay in the motion detector reduces the line current to 150 microamperes by inserting the 47K resistor. An open line or blown fuse will drop the line current to zero. Open door switches have the same effect, except the MDS-100 door switch inserts a value of resistance to indicate a 285 microampere line current. If a tamper switch in the motion detector is open, the current will drop to zero, but will go to 250 microamperes if the alarm relay opens.

The amount of current change required to cause the monitor to go into alarm is adjustable by means of the 1K

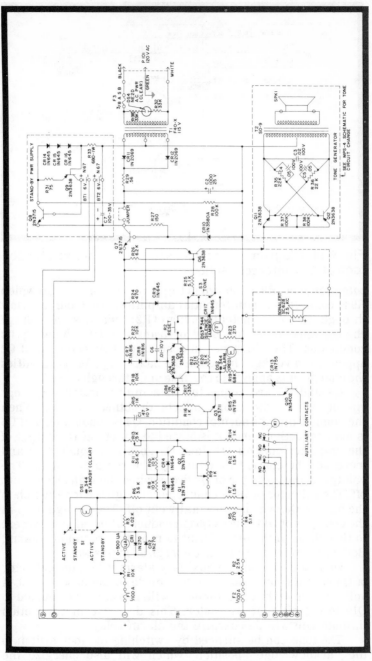

Fig. 9-13. Schematic of the Johnson Service Co. MPS-4 monitor.

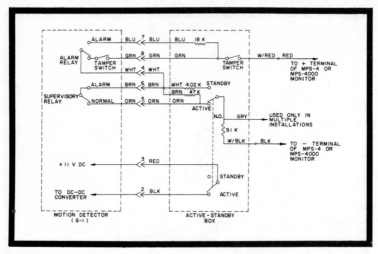

Fig. 9-14. Diagram of the Johnson system active-standby control box interconnections.

potentiometer, R9, as shown in Fig. 9-13. The circuit into which R9 is connected is a differential amplifier. When current flow through the 2.5K potentiometer (R2) changes, a voltage change appears at the base of transistor Q1, changing its conduction. The difference in conduction between Q1 and Q2 appears as a voltage change on the base of Q3. As Q3 amplifies the change, it is applied to the base of Q4 through CR6.

Q4 and Q5 are connected in a multivibrator (flip-flop) circuit. As one transistor conducts, the other is cut off. When the monitor is in the normal condition, Q4 is conducting and Q5 is not conducting, since it is biased to cut off. If the output of the amplifier cuts off Q4, then Q5 goes into conduction and increases the current flow through the red alarm light. The voltage at the collector of Q4 drops when the transistor is cut off. The collector of Q4 is connected through the tone switch to the base of Q6, which is normally cut off. The voltage drop at the collector of Q14 causes Q6 to conduct, which allows current to flow through the tone circuit to produce an audible alarm. Both types of tone circuits are energized in this way.

On models having an auxiliary alarm relay, the collector of Q4 is also connected through a diode to the base of Q10. A voltage drop at the collector of Q4 will, therefore, be coupled to Q10 to cut off that transistor. This decrease in conduction through Q10 will de-energize the alarm relay.

The tone can be silenced by switching the tone switch to the "acknowledge" position, which will also energize the "silence" light. The monitor may be reset with the tone switch in the "acknowledge" position only. Depressing the reset button places a positive voltage on the base of Q5, cutting it off. Q4 now conducts and causes Q6 and Q10 to conduct. Q6 is cut off and the tone is silenced when the tone switch is returned to the tone position. This avoids having the tone advertently remain in the turned off position when the monitor is reset. Failure to match the active-standby switches in the active-standby control box and monitor gives an alarm by changing the line current to either 350 or 470 microamps.

With both switches in the "active" position, a resistor in the monitor is switched in series with the line circuit. If the active-standby switch in the control box is put in the "standby" position, a resistor in the control box is also in series with the circuit, reducing the line current to 350 microamperes. Putting the active-standby switch in the monitor in the "standby" position shunts the resistor in the monitor to return the current to the 400 microamp level. If the active-standby switch in the monitor is in the "standby" position and the switch in the control box is in the "active" position, the resistor in the control box is bypassed, increasing the line current to 470 microamps. Matching the switches returns the line current to the normal 400 microamperes.

On installations where multiple motion detector units are connected to a single monitor, the control boxes are wired as shown in Fig. 9-15. Operation is similar to that of a monitor connected to a single control box. Load resistor RL is not used on any control box other than the first one on the line. Three control boxes are shown in Fig. 9-15, and any door switches used with a control box are inactivated when that control box

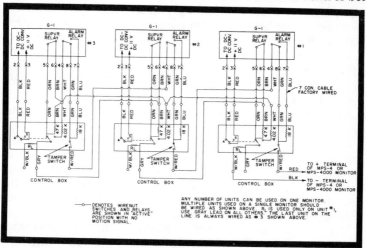

Fig. 9-15. Diagram showing the interconnection of multiple G-1 units to a single monitor.

is in the "standby" position. On monitors with built-in standby batteries, the batteries are kept charged by the power supply when the unit is plugged in. The batteries supply power upon a loss of the AC line power.

Installation & Adjustment

Remove the four screws in the corners of the front panel and carefully pull the front panel and chassis away from the case. Insert the wires from the active-standby control box through the rubber grommet near the bottom center of the back panel. Connect the wire from the black and white wire in the active-standby control box to terminal 2 on the terminal strip. Connect the wire from the red and white wire in the active-standby control box to terminal 1. Wires for the auxiliary relay contacts are brought into the monitor through the rubber grommet in the back panel.

If retransmission of the alarm signal to another (remote) MPS-4 is required, install resistors across the terminals on the terminal strip and connect the remote monitor as shown in Fig. 9-16. The remote monitor will give a 250 microampere meter reading on alarm, either supervisory or motion detection. However, the same degree of alarm line supervision is maintained by the remote monitor as a monitor directly connected to an active-standby control box.

The MPS-4 relay contacts are adequate to handle most alarm horns and bells from a current standpoint, but the manufacturer's specifications on the particular horn to be used must be taken into account prior to installation of the equipment to assure reliable performance.

Notice that both an alarm horn and a remote monitor can be connected to the same MPS-4, as shown in Fig. 9-16. Two remote monitors or two alarm horns may be used on the same MPS-4 unit by wiring both sets of relay contacts to accommodate a horn or remote monitor. More than one low-current horn can be connected in parallel to operate from the same contacts if the total current needed does not exceed the contact rating of the relay.

On some installations where the alarm line runs close or parallel to AC power lines or other electrical noise sources, interference can be greatly reduced by the addition of a 0.5-mfd, 400-volt capacitor between each side of the alarm line and ground. Shielded wire will also be quite helpful where conditions require such measures.

Some installations require the use of the MDS-100 switches, and any number of door switches can be connected into the circuit at the active-standby control box. Simply connect the switches in series with the normally closed contact of the

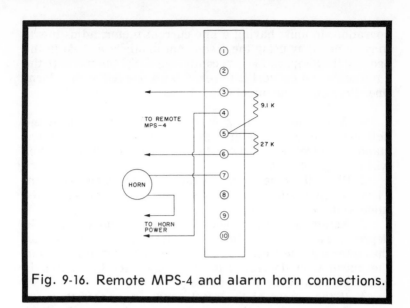

Fig. 9-16. Remote MPS-4 and alarm horn connections.

supervisory relay as shown in Fig. 9-17. The monitor will show a 300 microampere current reading if the door is opened or if an external magnet (tampering) is applied. When using a type switch other than the one shown, the hookup is essentially the same. A good, balanced magnetic switch should be used and the resistor must be included inside the door switch case by connecting it to available screw terminals or soldering. If the unit has a standby battery, connect terminals 9 and 10 together by using the jumper supplied. This connects the battery for operation when needed, but if the monitor is taken out of service for any reason, the jumper must be removed to prevent discharging the batteries. Plug the power cord into any 117-volt AC outlet, but if a 2-prong outlet is used, a 3-prong adapter with a good ground lead is recommended for best and safest results.

Adjustment of the 10K and 2.5K potentiometers located on the rear of the chassis prepares the monitor for proper

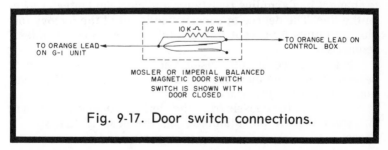

Fig. 9-17. Door switch connections.

operation. In units having a line current meter, adjustments may be made by using the meter, but in others a VOM in the order of the Simpson 260 is recommended. Set the meter to the 1 ma scale and connect it in series with one leg of the alarm line. Perform adjustments as follows:

1. When the system is wired and energized, place the active-standby switches of both the monitor and the active-standby control box in the "standby" position. The monitor will now go into alarm.

2. Place the tone switch in the "acknowledge" position. The tone will be silenced. Adjust the 10K potentiometer for 400 microamperes of line current.

3. Rotate the 10K potentiometer back and forth while depressing and releasing the reset button. Notice the points on the meter scale between which the tone continues to sound and the alarm light decreases in brilliance after the button is released. This is the reset range.

4. If the center of the reset range is greater than 400 microamperes, rotate the 2.5K potentiometer slightly counterclockwise (left). If the center of the reset range is less than 400 microamps, rotate the 2.5K potentiometer slightly clockwise (right). Repeat Step 3 to determine the location of the reset range.

5. Repeat Step 4 until the center of the reset range is 400 microamps. Reset the monitor and place the tone switch in the "tone" position. After replacing the chassis, the unit is ready for service.

When long lengths of alarm line are required, extending to several miles, the degree of supervision may be increased to fill the need. The resistance of the very long lines will vary enough with temperature to cause the line current to vary more than five percent. This often results in excessive false or nuisance alarms. In most cases, 5 percent supervision will be satisfactory for lines up to 5 miles in length, but greater distances may need as much as 10 percent or more, according to changes in alarm line resistance and electrical interference on the line. The degree of supervision is set at the factory for plus or minus 5 percent and should not be adjusted unless required.

If the degree of supervision required is greater than 5 percent, it may be increased by adjustment of the 1K potentiometer on the rear of the chassis as follows:

1. Remove the chassis from the case and the locking acorn nut from the 1K potentiometer on the rear of the MPS-4 chassis.

2. With the equipment energized, place the active-standby switches on both the monitor and active-standby control box in the "standby" position. Put the tone switch in the "acknowledge" position to silence the tone.

3. Turn the 1K control slightly clockwise (right).

4. Rotate the 10K potentiometer back and forth while depressing and releasing the reset button. Notice the width of the reset range.

5. Repeat Steps 3 and 4 until the required width of the reset range is attained.

6. Replace the acorn locking nut and readjust the unit as previously described.

Operation Procedure

The controls and indicators located on the front of the monitor unit (Fig. 9-18) are said to function as described:

1. Clear "standby" light: Indicates the monitor is in the "standby" mode of operation.

2. Red alarm light: Goes to full brilliance when an alarm is given. The light is normally at one-fourth brilliance.

3. Amber "silence" light: Indicates the tone switch is in the "acknowledge" position.

4. Reset button: Resets the monitor when normal conditions are restored after an alarm or in changing modes of operation. The tone switch must be placed in the "acknowledge" position to reset.

5. Active-standby switch: Switches the monitor to the "active" or "standby" mode of operation.

6. Tone switch: Silences the tone after the alarm is given. (It must be in the tone position after the system is reset or the tone will sound continuously.)

7. Clear AC power light: Indicates that the AC power is on. (If the light is not on, the AC power is off and the monitor is operating on the internal battery in units so equipped.)

Fig. 9-18. Front panel view of the Johnson Service Co. MPS-4 monitor.

8. Line current meter: This is optional and it indicates the type of alarm given by the amount of current flowing in the alarm line.

9. Tone sounder: Sounds an audio alarm which may be silenced with the tone switch after the alarm is given.

During daytime hours, or when the area being protected is occupied, the active-standby switch on the control box should be in the "standby" position. The active-standby switch in the monitor unit should also be in the "standby" position to keep the alarm line current at its normal 400 microamperes and remove the door switches from the circuit. Merely "acknowledge" the alarm and press the reset button to reset the alarm circuit.

During the night or away-from-the-premises periods, the system is set up by switching the active-standby switch on the control box to the "active" state and the active-standby switch on the monitor to "active." "Acknowledge" the alarm and push the reset button to reset the monitor. The system is now armed to detect any movement in the protected area and an alarm will be generated as the person switching the active-standby control box to the "active" position leaves the area to be protected. This verifies the proper operating alarm condition. Then, simply reset the monitor. When an alarm is given, the red alarm light is at full brilliance and the tone sounds. Silence the tone by turning the tone switch to the "acknowledge" position.

On units equipped with the line current meter, the meter deflection actually provides the information as to the type of alarm generated and its indications may be interpreted as follows:

1. Zero means an open door switch or an open alarm line. The open alarm line can result from an open tamper switch or a blown line fuse in the monitor. The G-1 unit will continue to detect motion with the tamper switch open and the current will move to 250 microamperes when motion is detected.

2. 155 microamperes indicates an open supervisory relay. Check the condition of the G-1 unit.

3. 250 microamperes shows motion detection by the G-1 unit (the actual meter reading may be fluctuating).

4. 250 microamperes in the "standby" condition indicates a power failure at the G-1 unit.

5. 125 microamperes (steady) indicates a power failure or possible blown fuses in the G-1 unit.

6. 350 or 470 microamperes indicates a mismatch of the active-standby switches in the monitor and control box, usually caused by going from one condition to another ("standby" to

"active" or vice versa). While the G-1 unit is in "standby" and the monitor "active," a reading of 350 will be shown; reversing this condition, i.e., G-1 in "active" and the monitor in "standby," the meter would indicate 470.

7. 285 microamperes shows an open MDS-100 door switch and would be applicable only when this type door switch is used.

8. 500+ microamperes indicates tampering with the MDS-100 door switch.

Maintenance

Minor repairs or the replacement of fuses, indicator lamps, loose connections and shorted or defective switches may be easily performed in the field and the following checks should aid in determining the extent of problems. The monitor chassis is easily removed from its case after taking out the four screws from the front panel.

Alarm line fuses should be checked by measuring the voltage across each fuse with a VOM on the 10-volt scale. A good fuse offers little or no resistance to current flow and, therefore, would show no voltage across it unless defective. Avoid using the ohmmeter to check fuses with the power on. The fuse may be blown by the meter or the meter may be damaged! Use the voltage scale in all cases where the VOM is used with the power on; this protects your voltohmmeter and the circuit being tested as well. Fuses in the alarm line should be replaced only with Buss AGX one-100th A instrument fuses. Power supply troubles are probable when all indicating lamps are out, in which case the power supply fuse in the back should be checked first.

The tone circuit may be checked for proper operation with the monitor in the reset condition by switching the tone switch to "acknowledge." The tone should sound. If it does not and the power supply voltage is present, trouble in the tone or alarm circuitry is indicated. A squeaky tone or unusual sound normally indicates a power supply problem on units having speaker-type tone generators.

Indicator bulbs may be easily replaced following burn out by unscrewing the lens cap and pulling the bulb out of the back of the lens cap. Type 344 lamps are used and under average conditions should last for several years.

The operation of relays may be checked by purposely mismatching the active-standby switches in the monitor and control box. The relay should transfer when the switches are mismatched, and when rematched the relay will return to its normal position as soon as the reset button is depressed with the tone switch in "acknowledge."

Current-sensing and alarm circuits may be checked by increasing the line current with the 10K potentiometer. The unit should go into an alarm condition at the upper edge of the reset range and the relay should transfer on units so equipped. Adjust the line current to 400 microamperes, reset the alarm circuit by switching the tone switch to "acknowledge" and depress the reset button. Decreasing the line current should force the unit into alarm at the bottom edge of the reset range.

Operation of the unit in this manner confirms satisfactory operation. Readjust the line current to 400 microamperes by a volt-ohmmeter (VOM) on the one milliampere scale (1,000 microamperes) on units with no line current meter by connecting the meter in series with one side of the alarm line for the purpose of checking.

AUTOMATIC McCULLOH RECEIVER

The Systron-Donner Model MCAR-135A features circuit condition readout lamps, telephone line current monitoring jacks, standard ½-inch register tape, lock tape reel, simple pen change, tape over-travel adjustment, plus automatic and maintenance free operation, according to the manufacturer. Solid-state design eliminates the need for mechanical limit switches. The motor is a continuous duty type without a temperature rise. The starting current is 100 ma and the normal running current is 50 to 60 ma. The specifications say the line current regulation is 5 to 10 ma from a short circuit to 20K telephone line resistance. The unit incorporates a battery standby supply using a Globe Union "Gel Cell" series-connected float charge battery, permitting a 100-hour standby under normal conditions. Abnormal line conditions are met with a delay of 2 to 5 seconds from normal to abnormal and instant return to normal condition. Operating temperatures range from 32 to 120 degrees F (0 to 48 degrees C).

Installation & Operation

1. Install the pens as shown in Fig. 9-19.
2. Make all connections shown in the hookup diagram in Fig. 9-20.
3. Check the DC supply, which for best results should be -35 volts DC, plus or minus 10 percent. Be sure that the positive side is connected to the earth ground.
4. Connect the MCAR unit to the external telephone line (20K maximum). The following table illustrates the allowable length of the circuit in miles:

LOOP MILES

AWG	(For 20K line)
20	200
22	125
24	80
26	50

An internal current-limiting circuit permits the use of shorter lines, even zero ohms, without any manual adjustment required.

5. To test the unit any any time after installation, insert an open telephone plug into either the in or out line jacks on the front of the MCAR. Both pens should pulse, the tape drive motor will run, and the white lamp will light as long as the plug is inserted.

OPERATION OF THE PEN RECEIVER

A normal line condition is maintained when continuity exists through the entire telephone loop. The 135-volt power supply sends current through:

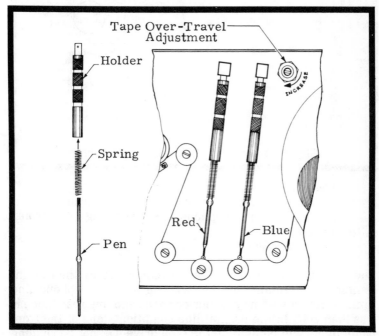

Fig. 9-19. Systron-Donner Model MCAR-135A McCulloh receiver pen installation drawing.

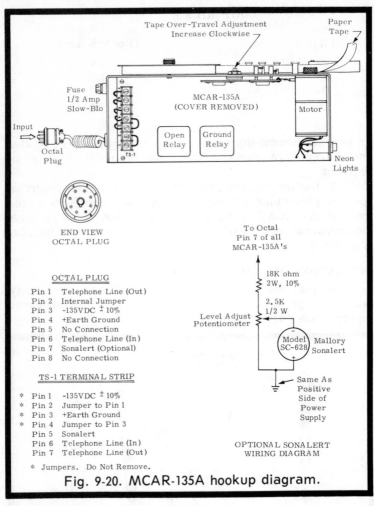

Fig. 9-20. MCAR-135A hookup diagram.

1. The current regulating circuit.

2. The sensing coil of the blue pen switching circuit.

3. The loop of the telephone line (including each transmitter code contact).

4. The red pen switching circuit to ground.

The line current (5 to 10 milliamps, controlled by the current limiter) will remain constant as long as the telephone line remains intact with no grounds or opens and line resistance is less than 20K. In the normal line condition, none of the front panel lights will be lighted, the tape drive will not be running and neither pen will be deflected (pulsed) unless a transmitter is activated.

Signal transmission: When one of the coded transmitters located on the McCulloh loop sends signals, it completes the following operations in sequence:

1. The telephone line is grounded when the code wheel first touches the switch arm.
2. The telephone line is ungrounded and opened when the switch arm rides on the top of the code wheel tooth.
3. The telephone line is closed when the arm is between code teeth.

This sequence is repeated as the code wheel rotates. Normally, three revolutions of the code wheel are programmed by the motor control for an alarm condition. The code is determined by the number and spacing of the code teeth.

Abnormal telephone lines: As previously stated, the normal operation of the transmitter and receiver depends on the continuous sending and receiving of 5 to 10 milliamperes. Any interruption of this signal for longer than three seconds is considered an abnormal condition and results in a visual indication at the central station.

1. Line Open (See Fig. 9-21). A burglar or a fallen tree can cut a telephone line at a specific transmitter, causing the loop current to drop to zero. The following then occurs at the receiver:

a. Both pens make one pulse at the time the line is opened.
b. The tape motor starts.

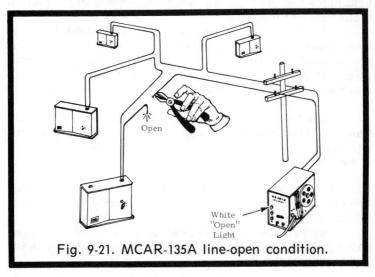

Fig. 9-21. MCAR-135A line-open condition.

195

c. The white "open lamp" on the front of the receiver lights up and remains lit for as long as the line is opened.

d. The tape motor stops 10 to 25 seconds after the pens were pulsed.

e. Three to five seconds after the line is opened, the normal ground side of the telephone line is connected to the negative power supply through the second current limiter.

f. The red pen will print out any transmitter code if the transmitter is located between the open point and the receivers' pin 1.

g. The blue pen will print out for all transmitters between the open point and the receivers' pin 6. These code pulses are sent by the transmitters grounding the open line.

Note: In a high-security system, the telephone lines in and out of a transmitter installation are located on different sides of the building and utilize different telephone poles. This makes locating and tampering with both the in and out telephone lines very difficult.

2. Line grounded (see Fig. 9-22): If any point along the telephone line is accidentally or intentionally grounded, current through the red pen switching circuit drops to zero, causing:

a. The red pen to pulse.

b. The tape motor to run.

c. The **amber** "ground-open" light to light momentarily.

d. After 3 to 5 seconds the amber light turns off, the **red** light lights and the negative voltage is applied to the normal ground side of the telephone line.

e. The receiver is now automatically conditioned to receive the open pulses from transmitters on either side of the ground fault. The red pen will receive the open pulses from transmitters on one side of the fault and the blue pen will receive open pulses from transmitters on the other side.

3. Combined ground and open line fault (see Fig. 9-23). This condition can occur when a fallen tree breaks the telephone line and one wire touches ground. Two possibilities of this fault are:

a. Ground-open (**amber** light). Caused by a ground on the line cut side of the line and simultaneous open on the line in side of the line.

b. Open-ground (**white** and **red** lights). Caused by an open on the line out side of the line and simultaneous ground on the line in side of the line.

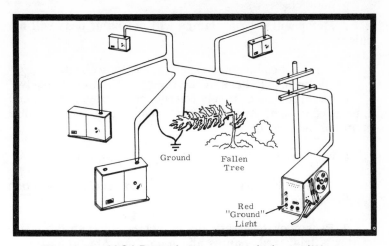

Fig. 9-22. MCAR-135A line-grounded condition.

In both cases, after a short delay, negative voltage is automatically applied to the line in side of the line through a current limiter. Only one pen will operate when a code is received, depending on which side of the fault the transmitter is on.

Field Service and Troubleshooting Procedure

Before following this procedure, the receiver should be visually checked internally to insure that relays are properly seated and no foreign matter exists.

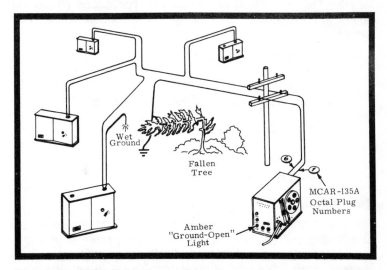

Fig. 9-23. MCAR-135A combined ground and open fault.

1. Motor will not run, lamps will not light, pens will not pulse:

a. Incorrect connections; see Fig. 9-20 for a check.
b. Blown fuse in back of the receiver (½ amp, slo-blow).
c. Incorrect power supply voltage, pins 3, negative (-), and 4, positive (+), of the octal socket should read 135 volts, plus or minus 10 percent.

2. White, red or amber lamps stay lit continuously:

a. Line fault exists, refer to the pen receiver operation section above.

3. Pens operate erratically or not at all when the transmitter is triggered. Lamps and motor operate properly:

a. Ball pens and holders installed incorrectly.
b. Positive side of the power supply not connected to an earth ground.
c. Transmitter not connected to an earth ground.
d. Poor grade telephone line.
e. Excessive line capacitance to ground.
f. Excessive telephone line length; measure the telephone line resistance. Unplug the receiver from the octal socket and measure between pins 1 and 6 of the female socket with an ohmmeter. It should indicate 0 to 20K, depending on line length: The maximum allowable line resistance equals the power supply voltage divided by the McCulloh line current minus 3K.

4. Line current below 5 ma:

a. Line resistance above 20K.
b. Power supply voltage below 115 volts.

5. Red **and** amber lamps on continuously:

a. Line current below 5 ma.
b. Partial ground on telephone line.

MOTOROLA CCTV CAMERAS

The CCTV camera by Motorola in Fig. 9-24 is an example of a wall-mounted unit that observes all people entering or leaving the garage elevators. Building security problems become more acute during nighttime hours, so admittance is controlled very carefully at this time.

The camera with the capability to pan, tilt, and zoom in for closeups gives it the necessary flexibility to cover a greater area than the usual fixed-position, fixed-lens cameras. Businesses employing women maintain 24-hour operations and those under the watchful eye of the unit pictured in Fig. 9-25 really do feel that they have someone to count on if problems develop.

The Motorola S-70 low light level camera offers protection to people and property around-the-clock without expensive lighting systems. Unlike other cameras, the S-70 is said to see in almost total darkness without added artificial illumination. Built with the latest state-of-the-art optics and electronics, it's like having two cameras in one. You get a sharp picture in sunlight as well as in moonlight, and in addition, it does this automatically. The motorized 10-to-1 zoom lens permits close observation or "zoom out" for wide area surveillance. The S-70 is self-contained in its own all-weather housing. These units provide the guard with a clear view of what's going on from bright daylight through darkness, and adjust automatically to such changes.

DETECTOR INDUSTRIES, SENTRY III VISUAL ALARM SYSTEMS

Another completely self-contained operating unit with solid-state circuitry provides store or plant surveillance. The dual RF or video output permits the use of a home receiver or

Fig. 9-24. Motorola CCTV camera installed to observe persons entering a garage elevator.

Fig. 9-25. Motorola CCTV camera with pan, tilt and zoom capabilities. (Courtesy Motorola Communications and Electronics, Inc.)

a video monitor. The Sentry III Model STVC camera uses a Model STC-1, 7735A vidicon tube. Other features include random interlace scanning, a horizontal frequency of 15.75 kHz, and a vertical frequency of 50 to 60 Hz (line sync). The output signal is composite video, the output load impedance is 75 ohms, and the output level is 1.5 volts (p-p, composite). Required illumination is 500 lux, standard; minimum, 20 lux. It operates on 117v AC, 50-60 Hz, consuming 12.5va, and is adaptable to ambient temperatures of 32 to 104 degrees F. The lens is an F1.4 25mm C mount. The camera measures 6 inches wide by 12 inches deep by 4 inches high and weighs 6½ pounds.

Film Camera, Model STFC

This security camera uses easy loading 26 mm film to achieve surveillance photography at available light conditions. The system is completely automatic with a preset

WARNING!!!

The above is an unretouched photograph taken by a Sentry III Camera the night of Tuesday, November 17, 1970, during an actual robbery. The individual with the gun in hand is now wanted by the Dallas Police Department for felony theft.

Any information to her whereabouts should be reported to Detective Richards, Homicide Division, Dallas Police Dept., AC 214 — 748-9711.

Detector Industries, Inc.

The Seco Company • 3018 Commerce • Houston, Texas 77003

Fig. 9-26. Robbery photo snapped by a surveillance camera. (Courtesy Detector Industries, Inc.)

time delay. Line current activation and automatic shutter and exposure settings included. It offers deterrent to hold-ups, burglary and other pilferage attempts. May be used alone or with other cameras. Fig. 9-26 shows an actual robbery in progress as detected by the Sentry III film camera.

Chapter 10
Seismic, Vibration & Stress Intrusion Systems

These specialized electromechanical systems are useful in certain areas of intrusion protection, which we consider here.

TELEDYNE GEOTECH SEISMIC INTRUSION DETECTORS

The IS-100 intrusion signature detector is designed for outdoor surveillance of areas and perimeters. This passive seismic detector is designed for direct burial which facilitates total concealment. The system detects generated seismic energy caused by intrusion while rejecting seismic energy generated by rain, wind, earthquakes and aircraft. This model is ideal for unattended use where no permissible cultural activity is expected to occur on the ground within its range.

Adjustable sensitivity provides for operation in a number of environments and flexible circuitry insures optimum performance even as ambient conditions change. A calculated MTBF of over seven years minimizes the likelihood of failure, while modular circuit design maximizes repair problems should failure occur. A current drain of only 1.5 ma affords continuous operation for 6 months with internal battery power.

Activation of the intrusion alarm detector results in an output pulse suitable for transmission over telephone lines or other wire links for application to an annunciator, or for transmission via a radio data link. Data-link management capability is available by selecting optional alarm-transmission line-integrity circuitry.

The IS-100 accepts inputs from between one and six subminiature reflection geophones connected in series. The number of geophones that may be used for best performance in a given installation varies, depending on the natural and cultural environment in which the unit is installed. The output of the IS-100 is a 9-volt pulse suitable for activiating a transmitter, encoder, local alarm, or other type of annunciator. The unit is shipped with a 5-foot input-output cable. Subminiature geophones and output cable assemblies are available as accessories, along with data-link management circuitry, data transmission components, and data reception-display components.

The input is designed to accept the output of one or more subminiature reflection geophones. The input has a natural frequency of 14 Hz and an impedance of 3.3K. In the nonalarm state, the output is 0.0 to +0.5v DC; in the alarm state it is +9v DC. A variable sensitivity control provides a range adequate to obtain optimum adaptive operation over a broad spectrum of environments. Operating power requirement is 9 volts DC at a current of 1.5 ma maximum, using a C size alkaline or magnesium internal battery. Maximum detection range for 1 to 4 personnel is 25 to 200 feet; for 4 or more, 50 to 250 feet, and for vehicles the maximum 300 to 1,500 feet. The unit is 4 inches in diameter and 20 inches long without a connector, a volume of 251 cubic inches. Weight is 6 pounds excluding batteries and geophone.

The IS-200 has similar operating characteristics, except the power requirement is 11 to 14 volts DC at 250 microamperes maximum. It measures 4¼ inches in diameter by 8½ inches long and weighs 2¾ pounds including internal batteries. The maximum detection range of personnel is 50 to 200 feet. While the IS-100 is designed to detect either intruding personnel or vehicles, the IS-200 is designed for detection of intruding personnel only, which permits screening out other possible sources of false alarms. Proven to be false alarm-free in outdoor industrial security applications, according to the manufacturer, the unit offers peak performance over a wide range of changing environments.

As activity takes place on the ground (walking, motor vehicles, wind moving trees), seismic energy is coupled into the soil or man-made surface. This energy or vibration is propagated in all directions like ripples caused by a stone tossed into a pond. The detailed form of the seismic energy is controlled mainly by the source, and the dependency of the seismic waveform on the source mechanism makes possible the accurate identification of energy. These seismic intrusion detectors are designed to exploit the differences in seismic waveform characteristics, responding only to that seismic energy generated by sources of interest. In this regard, the design of the IS-100 provides detection of either vehicles or personnel while the IS-200 recognizes only personnel generated seismic energy.

Typically, the seismic type of intrusion detection system uses the following group of components:

(a) Transducer: Subminiature geophone (IS-406) which detects seismic energy in the soil or man-made surface to which it is coupled.

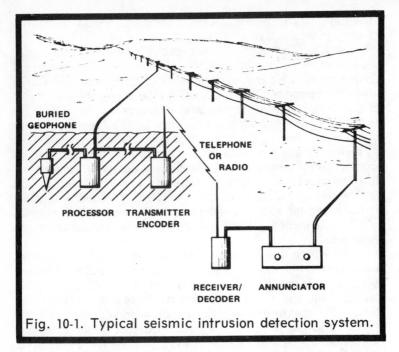

Fig. 10-1. Typical seismic intrusion detection system.

(b) Processor: The signal conditioning and recognition circuitry as the IS-100 or IS-200.

(c) Alarm transmission link: A wire line or radio link for transmission of the alarm intelligence to a central monitoring site.

(d) Annunciator-display: The central monitoring display unit, such as a central station panel, map display, etc.

The sketch in Fig. 10-1 illustrates the layout of a typical system where the signal from the buried geophone is amplified and then conditioned by the processor unit which "rejects" signals generated by non-intruder sources such as wind, rain and small animals, but "accepts" intruder-generated signals. Satisfaction of the processing logic results in the generation of an alarm pulse by the processor. The alarm signal is transmitted to the annunciator-display via the alarm transmission link and is appropriately displayed. Optional alarm encoding techniques make possible the transmission of alarm signals from several sensors over a single transmission link for decoding and display at the central monitoring site.

Normally, the area of sensitivity for a single IS-400 transducer is circular and ranges from a radius of 25 to 200 feet for personnel or to 1,500 feet for vehicles. The area of sensitivity will vary from one location to another and is dependent upon soil and geologic conditions as well as the level of noise or non-intrusion generated seismic signals from natural and man-made sources at the given location. Geologic and soil conditions control the degree of coupling of seismic energy and the propagation characteristic between that energy source and the geophone transducer. (See Fig. 10-2.)

Seismic noise affects the detection range by reducing the sensitivity at which the processor circuitry can operate, since the IS-100 and IS-200 are self-adapting to optimize the sensitivity in all environments. As the noise level increases, the sensitivity is decreased along with the detection range because larger intrusion generated signals are needed to override the noise.

Since the IS-100 is designed for situations involving both personnel and vehicular intrusion, the sensitivity is manually adjustable during initial installation to provide for use over a broad spectrum of environments and then automatically adjust to normal variations in the background noise level. Since the IS-100 responds to vehicles and personnel, it is most effective in remote or semi-remote areas.

The most common intruder in most industrial or commercial facilities is by personnel and a moderate level of permissible vehicular traffic is frequently present. Thus, the IS-200 is ideal for operation in such areas and has proven quite effective in this type of application. The device is completely self-adaptive while operating at the maximum useful sensitivity level to enhance and detect footstep-generated signals whether running or walking.

Fig. 10-2. The dashed circle shows the area sensitivity for a single IS-406 geophone transducer.

Area surveillance can be accomplished by using a single geophone transducer or several geophone transducers providing input signals to the IS-100 or IS-200. Perimeter surveillance may be provided by spacing geophones at intervals with about 25 percent overlap of coverage.

Installation

Under most conditions, more than one IS-406 transducer input can be supplied to each processor; the maximum number is controlled only by the level of seismic noise which varies from location to location. "Zoning" of areas or perimeters must be based on the processor rather than the transducer because the processor circuitry does not distinguish between the geophone transducers of multiple input installations.

IS-406 geophones are buried to a shallow depth of 4 to 8 inches in order to provide good coupling to the soil, to shield them from direct contact with noise generating environmental sources, and to conceal them. Similarly, the interconnecting cables and the processor are buried. After geophones have been located, but before they are buried, walk-tests should be made to assure that desired coverage is obtained and the tests should be repeated after burial for confirmation. Waterproof cases and connectors or a splice sealant are provided with the units to make installation easy and hook-up possible. Interface circuitry is available to connect with existing annunciation-display equipment and to provide compatibility with local alarms and other existing equipment.

The available accessories include alarm transmission line, management circuitry, Models IS-101 and IS-201, annunciators IS-400 and IS-401, transmitter-encoder IS-402, receiver-decoder IS-403, map displays, printer displays, AC power supplies, and interface circuitry for standard alarm and central station equipment. Pictures of the Teledyne Geotech units are shown in Fig. 10-3 (IS-100 intrusion signature detector), Fig. 10-4 (IS-200 seismic personnel intrusion detector) and Fig. 10-5 (IS-400 annunciator).

The loop vehicle detector (Models IS-300 and IS-301) provide reliable vehicular detection, with no loop tuning necessary, and total concealment. While unaffected by changing environmental conditions, the detector has proven false alarm-free for both outdoor and indoor surveillance. The passive magnetic detector is designed for direct burial in the earth, parking lot, or other surface for total concealment. The buried loop permits coverage of a few feet to over 400 feet with a single unit.

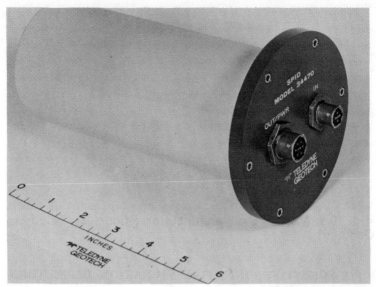

Fig. 10-3. Personnel intrusion detector, IS-200. (Courtesy Teledyne Geotech)

The detector provides detection of moving ferrous objects passing over or through the concealed loop or coil. The IS-300 dual loop detects intrusions in either a single direction or in an omnidirectional mode; the single loop IS-301 detects in the omnidirectional mode only. Signal recognition circuitry with adjustable sensitivity allows detection of targets ranging from small magnets and bicycles to motorcycles, automobiles, snowmobiles, and other vehicles. Modular analog circuitry processes the intrusion signal and generates an alarm pulse suitable for energizing a local alarm or other type link to activate an annunciator. Applications are shown in Fig. 10-6.

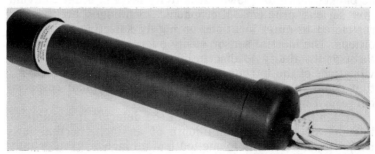

Fig. 10-4. Model IS-100 intrusion signature detector. (Courtesy Teledyne Geotech)

Fig. 10-5. Model IS-400 annunciator. (Courtesy Teledyne Geotech)

POLY-SCIENTIFIC INERTIAL VIBRATION DETECTORS
4062, 63, 67, 68, 69

The intruder must cause vibration at some level in order to enter by force, and with sufficient sensitivity in the detector, this sensing cannot be defeated by even the most professional party. By placing the sensors on the perimeter of the protected area, maximum warning time is provided before the intruder is actually at work. If the alarm response is audible or otherwise made obvious to the intruder, a reasonable deterrent to continued effort is provided. This factor alone may be responsible for a considerable saving of potential damage and inconvenience that would otherwise be unavoidable.

Some vibration sensing devices achieve high sensitivity at the expense of high nuisance alarm rates and actually have to be backed down to a lower sensitivity level in order to avoid this serious problem. Microphonic techniques are usually restricted to quiet locations or highly selective audio conditions. The inertial sensor easily overcomes such problems through its ability to discriminate between high-frequency vibrations of the intruder type and the usual area vibrations that could result in false alarms. See the typical response curve in Fig. 10-7.

Even though the sensitivity of the detector is capable of intruder detection to a millionth of an inch, normal low-frequency movements to one-tenth of an inch or greater may be ignored. As an example, attempted breaking into a car or cabinet may be detected before significant damage is done, and yet severe rocking of the car will be ignored by the same sensor. In case of more difficult false alarm situations, the slightly damped inertial detector is completely insensitive to severe movements with only a slight reduction in sensitivity to intruder shocks. Although high winds have no effect on the sensor protecting a chain link fence, any attempt to climb or cut through the fence is immediately detected.

The sensors act like switches, changing from short circuit to open circuit or vice versa for a very short time during an alarm condition. A high-speed circuit may monitor practically any number of sensors connected in series. This same circuitry can also be used to modify false alarm rejection characteristics to suit the circumstances of the installation without requiring special skills or maintenance. The number of sensors connected in the loop with a single electronic control

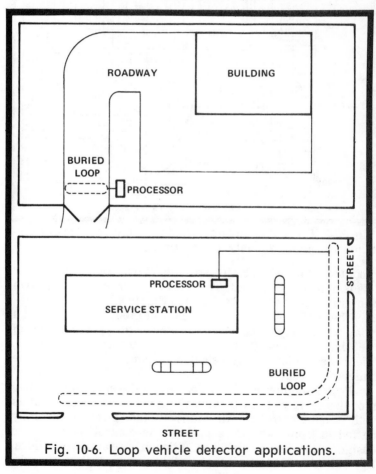

Fig. 10-6. Loop vehicle detector applications.

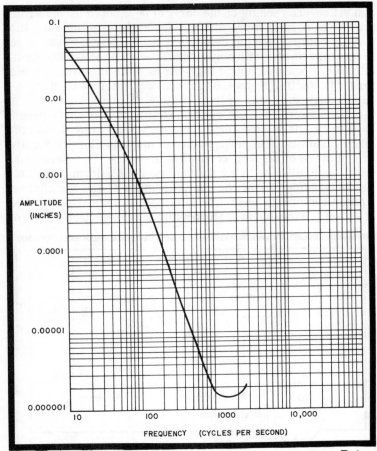

Fig. 10-7. Typical frequency-displacement response, Poly-Scientific inertial disturbance detector.

module is limited only by specific alarm requirements or levels of sensing desired. This may be avoided by using two sensor types in one loop as shown in Fig. 10-8.

The output of an electronic control module is normally a relay which may be chosen according to the specific needs of the alarm system. Bell, buzzer, radio transmitter, flasher, telephone circuit or any selected responsive action may be triggered by the relay.

Power supplies are provided within the electronic control modules by 12-volt dry batteries or power line operated units with standby batteries. Alternatively, the 12-volt source may be fed in from external supplies. The control modules are designed to go into an alarm condition in case of power failure. Dry batteries of reasonable size offer a one month life in self-contained "fail-safe" units, or about six months life without the "fail-safe" capability. Most of the power drain in the "fail-safe" results from the relay being normally energized in that mode.

The inertia sensor is tamper proof because of its high sensitivity and the electronic units are fitted internally with inertia sensors to insure protection. Any interference with inter-unit wiring will usually cause an alarm condition, and in cases where tampering is likely, a modified electronic circuit

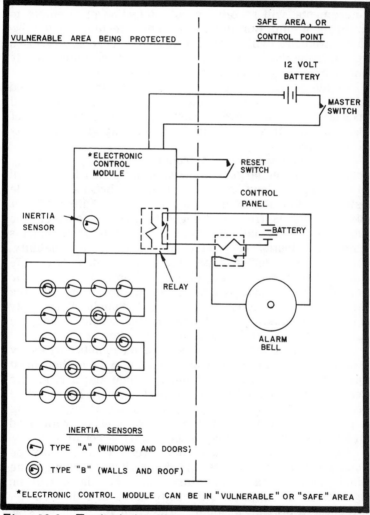

Fig. 10-8. Typical inertia sensor system installation diagram.

is used to detect looping out, insertion of instruments and other gadgets. Sensors with not only a "circuit break mode," but also a "circuit make mode" are available for additional protection where top security is required. Probably the simplest and most effective protection to wiring is conduit or a hard sheathed cable connected physically to inertia sensors at intervals of 20 feet or so. These will provide immediate detection of attempts to gain access to wiring.

Fences in the open, made of chain link, wood or concrete, with sensors at ten to 50-foot intervals according to requirements, will readily provide detection of attempts to climb, cut or chip. Burning may also be detected, and no false alarm problems will arise if reasonable care is exercised regarding overhanging trees or loose, rattling gates. Windy conditions or heavy traffic present no problem.

Building structures of brick, concrete, cinder block and lighter materials may be protected with sensors against all types of forced entry, even a Thermic Lance, without fear of false alarms. All roofing materials including glass skylights are protected.

Doors, windows and shopfronts with sensors discretely mounted (one per large window or multi-paned frame) will detect tapping long before the glass breaks. Suitable positioning will detect the action of a glass cutter without nuisance alarms from building vibrations. The electronic control unit may be set against deliberate false alarms without a reduction of genuine attack detection capability. Mounting the sensor near the edge of the window leaves the window completely clear visually. Doors may also be protected with sensitivities selected according to the frequency of use or necessary access to the public. Where only an intruder or guard is able to gain access, sensitivity may be high enough to detect the use of the correct key.

Vaults, safes, metal boxes, desks and cabinets may easily be protected with inertia sensors, which may be at their most sensitive positions with minimum nuisance alarm risk. The system may be armed during normal business hours, while there is traffic of authorized personnel in the vicinity. As long as protected objects are not moved or touched with hard implements, free movement of personnel is permissible.

High security and other commercial vehicles may be protected along with private cars. Even violent rocking of the vehicle will not cause an alarm, but the alarm will be triggered at the slightest attempt to break into the vehicle. Two sensors provide adequate protection for most cars or small vans. Setting the sensitivity at peak levels usually scares the thief away before appreciable damage is done.

Jacking up a car to steal a wheel will result in an immediate alarm before the wheel can be lifted off the ground.

Very little skill is required for installation and sensors have a fixed sensitivity level with appropriate choices available according to requirements as selected by the system surveyor based on easily gained experience. Choices may be readily verified by the use of a simple test "bleeper." This test unit will determine the best position for the anti-false alarm control in the electronic control unit. Sensors may be attached by screws or adhesive and versions are available for standard conduit mounting as well.

Connections and wiring are simple and straight-forward, with terminations inside tamper-proof electronic control modules or at sensors where appropriate protection to the wiring may be desirable in high security cases. In many cases, the sensors may be completely hidden from view, and in no event will they be obvious to "snoopers" as is often the case with other types of detection.

Maintenance is negligible, since the inertial sensor is not affected by temperature, humidity, dust or other adverse conditions. Reliability is normally much higher than the system wiring and power source.

The high-sensitivity sensor 4063 is color-coded red. Sensor 4067 is damped for difficult false alarm conditions and is coded white. Switches must be mounted vertically with the contacts at the bottom; use no. 2 wood screws in the two slots provided. When window mounted, a sensor may be secured directly to glass with any suitable adhesive. Minimum sensitivity is realized with the sensor in a vertical position; to increase the sensitivity, loosen the screws and rotate in either direction. It operates on 12 volts DC, has 100 normally closed microampere

Fig. 10-9. Type 4067 sensor. (Courtesy Poly-Scientific Litton Systems, Inc.)

contacts, but it is an open circuit in an alarm condition. See Fig. 10-9.

High-sensitivity sensor 4068 is color-coded blue. Sensor 4069 is damped for difficult false alarm conditions and is black. The switch must be mounted vertically with the contacts at the bottom. Designed for conduit mounting, the switch can also be secured by clips or adhesive. The nonadjustable 12-volt DC 100 microampere contacts are normally closed, then open in the alarm condition. See the pictorial view in Fig. 10-10.

High-sensitivity Sensor 4062 is color-coded red. The switch must be mounted vertically with the contacts at the bottom. The device is suitable for installations where space is limited and maximum concealment is required. It can be used in conduit, clips or adhesive. The relay contacts are rated at 12 volts DC, 100 microamperes, normally closed. The circuit is open in the alarm condition. Solder the leads to any two terminals; the third lead may be connected to either of the other two.

Sensors 409-1, 409-2 and 409-3 are combined inertia and proximity types. They sense attempted forced entry, a door movement of only one centimeter, and are foolproof against magnetic interference. No wiring is required to the moving member (door). Characteristics include:

409-1 (2 wires) normally open, brief circuit closures during an alarm condition (vibration), circuit closed (door ajar-open).

409-2 (2 wires) normally closed (highly sensitive), briefly open during an alarm (vibration), circuit open (door ajar-open).

409-3 (3 wires) black-red, normally open, brief closed (door ajar); green-black normally closed (highly sensitive), brief open (vibration), open (door ajar or open). The contacts are rated at 12 volts DC, 100 microamperes non-inductive.

Module 422 is designed for maximum sensitivity only. It emits a "bleeper" high-pitched warning note when activated. A type 406 or 409 door sensor is incorporated to activate the alarm. External connections are made via a 2-pole, 5 amp plug and socket connector provided with a miniature mike jack plug. A banana plug breaks the alarm circuit. Current consumption is 35 ma in a passive condition, 80 ma in alarm condition from a self-contained 9-volt battery. See Fig. 10-11.

Module 423 is an anti-false alarm circuit which permits a selection of the rejection level required. The "bleeper" output gives a high-pitched warning tone when activated; the visual outputs are a green "safe" light and a red "alarm" light. The

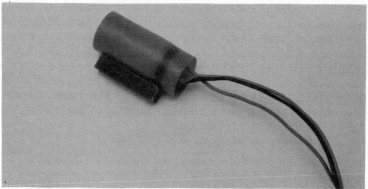

Fig. 10-10. Type 4069 sensor. (Courtesy Poly-Scientific Litton Systems, Inc.)

12-volt battery is self-contained and a type 406 or 409 door sensor is incorporated to activate the alarm. Connections vary between a 2-pole, 5 amp or a 3-pole, 5 amp plug and socket connector. It draws 35 ma in the passive or 80 ma in the alarm condition; a reset pushbutton and on-off switch are provided.

Modules 4250 and 4260 are anti-false alarm circuits that permit a selection of the rejection level required. It offers normally open contacts (500 ma at 50 volts non-inductive), with normally closed contacts or an SPDT switch as options. The "bleeper" gives a high-pitched warning tone when the system is activated. Power is supplied by a 12-volt battery (remote). As a fail-safe measure, in the event of power or battery failure, an available option allows the device to go into the alarm condition (the optional feature causes a slight increase in power drain). A type 406 sensor or 409 door switch is incorporated to activate the alarm. Connections are made via

Fig. 10-11. Module Type 422. (Courtesy Poly-Scientific Litton Systems Inc.)

a ¾-inch cable gland or conduit entry. Internally, there are terminal block screw terminations with a maximum nominal wire size of three-32nds. Several outputs are available on the 4250 and 4260 modules. Suffix letters added to the model number indicate the output; i.e., 4260A indicates a bleeper output. B an on-off relay (N.O.), C an SPDT relay, D an on-off relay (N.C.) and fail-safe, and E an SPDT relay and fail-safe. If additional outputs are included, letters to indicate each will be added to the model number.

Connections to modules 4250 and 4260:

Terminals 1 and 3: to the sensors in the alarm system.

Terminal 2: positive (+) 12 volts (external supply).

Terminal 3: negative (-) 12 volts (ground, external supply).

Terminal 4: relay common.

Terminal 5: normally closed relay contact.

Terminal 6: Normally open relay contact.

These alarm sensors incorporate the latest in the field of "g" sensitive devices, consisting of a seismic mass which is retained in a set position until disturbed by the vibration. On sensing a movement of the required threshold level, the sensor causes a momentary open circuit and then automatically resets. They are sensitive to high-frequency oscillations which are characteristic of inadvertent movement and intrusion. One millionth of an inch (.000001 inches) can be detected and since the inertial switch is quite different than linear transducers in response characteristics, the low-frequency oscillations which often cause false alarms in the latter have no effect on the inertia devices.

Low-cost modules are available for detecting an open sensor within the loop securing a given area. A special anti-false alarm circuit is among the options available for use in troublesome locations. The severe environments to which the sensors may be exposed without faulting are among the plus features offered with this type of detector. Also adding to their reliability are the gold-plated contacts used along with ultrasonic cleaning, assembly and sealing in clean, approved environments. The modular approach simplifies the specification and installation of the control systems. The standard module contains an electronic discriminator connection to the sensor loop and a built-in sensor for module security. Various options may be added as follows: external power supply contacts, battery, output to an external alarm or warning circuit, built-in alarm, special anti-false alarm circuit, choice of input and output connections, and short term or permanent installation.

SYSTRON-DONNER STRESS ALARM

This type alarm may be used to advantage for detecting intruders on floors, walls, stair cases, roofs and even fire escapes. Attempted vandalism may also be effectively detected, and any effort to remove paintings from walls or garments from racks as well as objects from shelves will cause an alarm condition as the sensor attached to a support of the protected object bends slightly. This bending results in an electrical change in resistance which is detected by the alarm system, and the alarm is then initiated. See Fig. 10-12.

The unit is completely solid-state with internal calibrated sensitivity controls permitting adjustments as required. The unit is not affected by temperature, humidity or structure type drift changes. Frequencies having rates of change greater than one Hz per second or less than three Hz per minute are filtered out of the system. An internal "fail safe" circuit and cabinet tamper protection are included. Cabinet dimensions are 11 inches by 7½ inches by 3½ inches. It operates on 16.5 volts AC with standby power provided for a minimum of 24 hours through a continuously charged 6-volt battery. The sensors are 1,000-ohm piezoresistive strain gauges mounted on 3-inch by ¼-inch strips, furnished with natural color vinyl sponge protective backings and channel metal protective covers.

The units are designed to detect structural dimensional changes due to mechanical stress. The system measures the

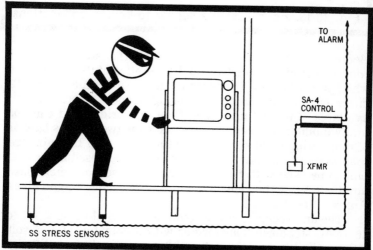

Fig. 10-12. Diagram of a simplified stress alarm system installation.

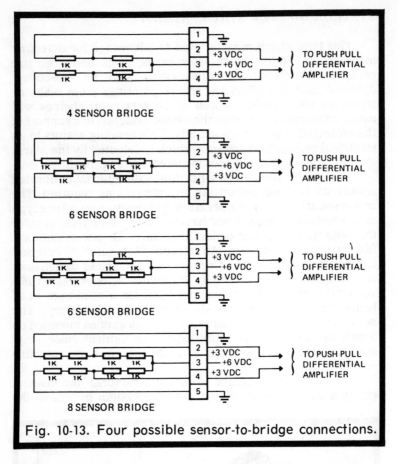

Fig. 10-13. Four possible sensor-to-bridge connections.

electrical change in resistance when the strain gauge is compressed or extended due to deformation of the structure to which it is attached. The three models (SA-4, SA-8 and SA-12) differ only in the number of bridges and sensors that are available. The SA-4 unit consists of one bridge and can normally monitor four sensors. The SA-8 has two bridges capable of monitoring eight sensors, and the SA-12 with three bridges may normally monitor 12 sensors. It is also possible for each unit to be used with twice the "normal" sensors mentioned, and the SA-8 is the replacement for the earlier Bagno Stress Alarm, Model BSA-1.

The unit receives energy from an external Class 2, 117-to-16.5v AC stepdown transformer with a potential of 16.5 volts AC supplied to terminals 1 and 2, which is then rectified to provide direct current to the circuits and also the trickle charge for the standby battery.

218

The sensor resistance changes under stress and is connected to either of three separate terminal strips, providing signals to the three identical amplifiers. As mentioned previously, each bridge will normally have four sensors connected to its terminals, and up to eight may be connected. Fig. 10-13 shows four possible ways that sensors can be connected to a single bridge. If a different number of sensors from the four, six and eight shown are to be used, fixed 1K resistors must be placed in the configuration to make up four, six or eight combined sensors plus resistors. Caution: Stress sensors used with the stress alarm are very fragile! Bending or blows on the sensor before it is mounted will destroy it. Carefully read the manufacturer's instructions with the sensor kits.

The circuit is designed to automatically reset if the imbalance of the sensor bridge output is maintained for a certain period of time. The unit is also fail-safe because it will alarm if a sensor is broken or disconnected electrically from the input terminals.

Since the amplifier circuits are identical, only one is described (Fig. 10-14). The SA-4 has only one amplifier, the SA-8 has two amplifiers and the SA-12 requires three. The signal from the sensor bridge feeds the base circuits of the first push-pull amplification stage through a bandpass filter. The filter rejects slow temperature drift and DC imbalances in the bridge. High pickup noise frequencies are rejected and intrusion voltages that correspond to frequencies from 3 Hz per minute to 1 Hz per second are passed through the filter. The intrusion signal unbalances the bases of the push-pull

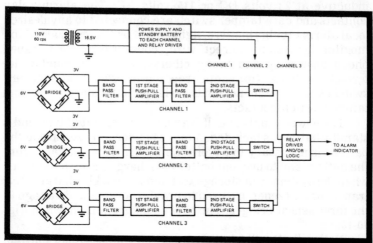

Fig. 10-14. Block diagram of the Systron-Donner SA Series stress alarm system.

amplifier, and if a bridge sensor is broken or a wire cut or broken in the bridge, the resulting 3-volt DC imbalance of the bridge will force the filter-shunting diodes to conduct and unbalance the first stage. The first stage gain is varied by a potentiometer which couples the emitters together (maximum gain clockwise at a setting of 10). The first stage differential output signal appears between the collectors. The output is nulled by a balanced potentiometer. Imbalance is primarily due to the always existing bridge imbalance and the filter capacitor leakage.

The first stage output signal is passed through a second bandpass filter similar to the first bandpass filter. Signals passing through the filter are fed to the bases of the second push-pull amplifier, and this stage is the same as the first, except that the gain is fixed and not variable. The second stage drives a pair of transistor switches. Normally, during a no-alarm condition, neither switching transistor is conducting and the output voltage is zero. During an alarm, the second stage will drive one transistor switch base positive with respect to the other. The transistor switch with the most positive base will conduct and develop about 0.7 volts across the output load resistor. This voltage turns on a relay logic transistor (one of three which control the relay driver transistor). These three transistors and the relay driver are an OR logic circuit. If any one of the three transistors is turned on, the base of the relay driver reduces its current and de-energizes relay K1. A de-energized relay is an alarm condition. The alarm relay contacts are rated for 2 amps non-inductive at 28 volts DC or 115 volts AC. The alarm relay contacts and case tamper switch are connected to any desired local alarms (bells, buzzers, lights, etc.) or to a central station monitoring system (direct wire, code transmitters, taped phone answering and many others). Door and window interlock switches (magnetic reed, microswitches, mercury switches) may be connected in series with the alarm relay and tamper switch contacts.

The power supply is half-wave, zener regulated type and a standby battery is included. A diode between the zener and the battery is necessary to absorb the higher zener voltage from the battery and to prevent battery discharge through the zener when the system is in storage (off and not trickle charging). A transistor and zener are used to provide a regulated voltage to the three sensor bridges. The hookup diagram is shown in Fig. 10-15.

Notice that radio interference may cause false alarms, but grounding the chassis (terminal 3) to a good water pipe ground will prevent them. A phone jack is available on the front of the chassis to connect an alarm test device (ATD). This device is also used with ultrasonic controls and has been used as an inside local alarm with its 2.5-kHz penetrating sound. A voltmeter can also be connected to test the relay coil voltage.

Handling Sensors

1. Remove the sensor from the packing by unwrapping the wires without touching the sensor.

2. By holding the wire, pull the sensor out to the side. If the sensor is pulled up and it sticks, it can bend and be destroyed.

3. Check the sensor with an ohmmeter; it should read 1,000 ohms, plus or minus 20 percent.

Cementing the Sensor

1. Clean the surface where the sensor is to be installed. Scrape the paint or oxidized surface to provide a smooth, flat area.

2. Mix the quick-drying cement (follow the instructions on package). Very gently apply a thick layer to the smooth surface of the sensor. **Do not bend the sensor!**

3. Install the sensor on the desired surface by applying a light even pressure with an end-to-end motion until a firm even mounting is formed.

4. A strip of masking tape lightly across each end of the sensor may be necessary to hold the sensor in place after cementing. Fig. 10-16.

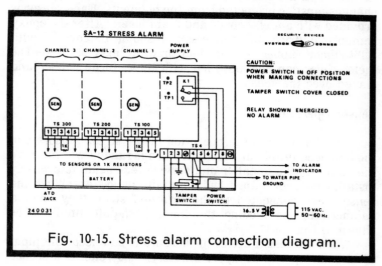

Fig. 10-15. Stress alarm connection diagram.

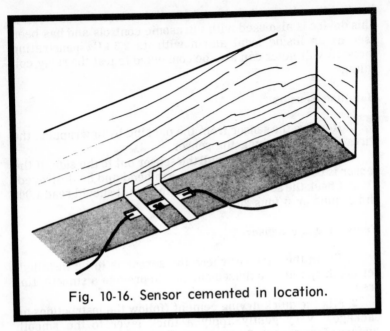

Fig. 10-16. Sensor cemented in location.

5. After the epoxy cement has dried, carefully remove the tape and check the sensor again with an ohmmeter. It still should read about 1,000 ohms.

Weather-Proofing Sensors

Any sensor exposed to the weather and wide temperature changes must be protected from the elements. Each sensor is provided with a metal cover and foam insert. After the epoxy cement has dried, the entire sensor should be covered with RTV silicon rubber; either clear or white may be used. The metal cover can now be filled with RTV silicon rubber and placed over the sensor.

Sensor Operation

Familiarity with the operation of the stress sensors and the balanced bridge in which they are arranged will improve the ability of the installer and service technician to properly install, check out, adjust and maintain the system. When the sensors are connected to the terminal strip, they form a balanced bridge feeding the input push-pull amplifier as shown in Fig. 10-17.

When the resistance of the sensors is balanced, the input from each leg will be approximately +3.0 volts. If a sensor changes resistance, the +3.0 volts changes also. The amplifier is tuned to detect a rate of change between 3 Hz per minute and 1 Hz per second, so all other frequencies are rejected. The sensors change in resistive value due to two reasons. First, the sensor detects a stress or strain which gives a proportional change in its resistive value. Normally, a sensor has a resistive value of approximately 1,000 ohms. When the sensor is placed under a force (stress or strain) its resistive value changes:

R   Resulting resistance

r   Initial resistance

Ar   Change in resistance due to stress

(+) or strain (-)

For best sensitivity, the sensors should be cemented to the region in the structural part where the disturbance to be detected will cause the greatest change in stress or strain (usually centered between the supports of a beam, as shown in Fig. 10-18).

Sensors also change in resistive value due to changes in temperature. The rate of change in the resistive value due to temperature is normally slower than 1 Hz per minute, so the amplifier rejects a signal caused by such a slow change. But if two sensors on the same leg of a balanced bridge are located in different temperature extremes (such as one sensor under a back porch and the other in the basement near the furnace), the total resistance change between the two sensors can be several hundred ohms. This condition causes a fail-safe circuit (for open or disconnected sensors) to operate, causing an alarm. Sensor A has decreased in value, since it is located

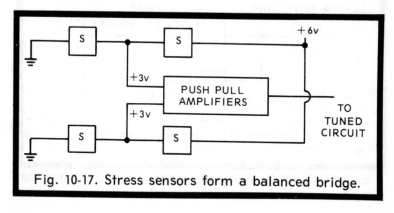

Fig. 10-17. Stress sensors form a balanced bridge.

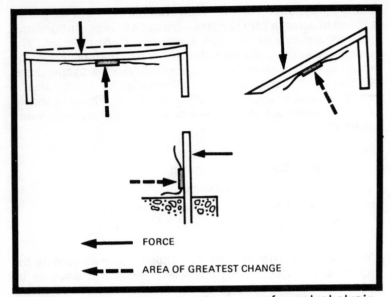

FORCE

AREA OF GREATEST CHANGE

Fig. 10-18. Drawings showing the areas of greatest strain.

outside in freezing weather, while sensor B increased in value, since it is inside near the furnace as shown in Fig. 10-19. If sensor B were located in the same environment as A, their resistive values would change equally and the bridge would not be out of balance. If sensors are located in areas that have 35 degree F difference between them, installation must be on the same side of the bridge to avoid this problem.

Normally, four sensors are connected in each bridge, but eight may be safely used. Sensors can be connected to the

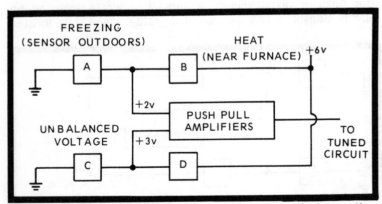

Fig. 10-19. Opposite temperature extremes unbalance the system.

bridge terminal strip in any one of the four arrangements shown in Fig. 10-13. If the number needed is not four, six or eight, the 1K resistors must be used for the open sensor position.

Floor installations have produced excellent results with sensors mounted under the floor on the beam supporting the floorboards where the intruder must step, in doorways, halls, under windows and steps which may offer access to the area being protected. Sensors mounted on large supporting beams, even 4 by 8 inches, are easily sensitive enough to pick up any intruder without fail. Mounting on the point of greatest stress, which would be the center of the beam, would cover the area of support. Locating the sensor under a door would offer even better protection where that mode of entry was used by an intruder. The use of eight sensors makes it possible to adequately protect the home by affording emphasis on the areas of major interest to the thief, such as television sets, jewelry and other valuables. As previously suggested, careful consideration must be given to temperature differences in such wide-spread arrangements; any sensors differing widely in ambient temperature must be located on the same side of the bridge.

Stairways require consideration as one of the most likely points of stress, and locating a sensor under an individual tread could miss the intruder if every other step was used. Where a common brace or support for the stairs is available, a sensor mounted near its center point serves very well. In other cases, it may be necessary to mount the sensor to the landing. Fire escapes may be protected in the same way as stairs, except the surface area where the sensor is to be mounted must be scraped with a wire brush. After the surface is clean and smooth, mount the sensor and provide the usual weather protection.

Roofs may be covered properly by installing sensors under main beams, at or near the point of greatest stress. Skylights, trapdoors and other types of possible entry may be easily protected against forced entry. Shelves and racks simply need a sensor cemented in the center of each. Where a large number is required, installation of one or two sensors under the floor where the intruder would stand to remove articles would be more economical and probably serve as well. Make sure to locate the sensors where the greatest strain must be placed.

Sensors connected to one bridge should not be applied to structures having major flexibility differences. If the sensor covers a 2 by 4 beam, for example, a sensor applied to a 4 by 8 beam may not be used in the same bridge; it must be connected to a different bridge. Since each bridge has only one sensitivity adjustment potentiometer, the proper adjustment for the 2 by 4 beam would be considerably lower than that required for a 4 by 8 beam.

Test Equipment

An alarm test device (ATD-1 and ATD-2) is available to provide a visual or audio signal when the control unit is in the alarm condition. The phone jack on the side of the control unit affords connection for the test device. The ATD does not function during battery operation and may be most useful for monitoring the system. It may be installed wherever convenient, and is ideal when making walk tests for sensitivity control adjustments.

The audio signal provided by the ATD-2 is quite handy when making walk tests where the control unit is not visible. An extension cord of any length desired may be attached to the phone plug of the alarm test device.

Voltage Measurement Locations

The following list identifies voltage measurement locations shown in Fig. 10-20:
1. Rectified voltage to ground
2. Zener voltage to ground
3. Battery voltage to ground
4. Vcc voltage to ground
18. 12K resistor (Channel 1)
19. 12K resistor (Channel 2)
20. 12K resistor (Channel 3)
21. TP1 to TP2 relay coil
22. Relay contact

Troubleshooting

If there is no rectified voltage from point 1 to ground (normally 18 to 23 volts DC), check for the presence of AC to the control. It could be a defective rectifier or filter capacitor. Refer to Fig. 10-20.

With no battery voltage between point 2 to ground (normally 6 to 7.2 volts DC), suspect a defective zener or protective diode, a dead battery or a loose terminal.

No Vcc voltage from point 3 to ground (normally 6 to 7.2 volts DC) could mean the power switch is off or defective.

If there is no bridge voltage between TS100 pin 3 to pin 1 ground (normally 5 to 6 volts DC), the regulated supply may have failed, or a short between pins 3 and 1 could exist.

Incorrect stress sensor voltages between TS100 pin 2 to pin 1, TS200 pin 2 to pin 1, TS300 pin 2 to pin 1 (each normally 2.3 to 3 volts DC) may mean a sensor has failed. If the voltage is zero, the sensor or wires to pins 2 and 3 could be open; if it is 5.5 volts, the sensor or the wires on pins 3 and 4 may be open.

Incorrect stress sensor voltages between TS100 pin 4 to pin 1, TS200 pin 4 to pin 1, TS300 pin 4 to pin 1 (each should be 2.3 to 3 volts DC) could indicate a defective sensor. If the voltage is zero, the sensor or wires to pin 3 and 4 may be open; if it is 5.5 volts, the sensor or the wires on pins 4 and 5 may be open.

First amplifier voltages:

TP101 to TP2 and TP102 to TP2: 3 to 4v DC
TP201 to TP2 and TP202 to TP2: 3 to 4v DC
TP301 to TP2 and TP302 to TP2: 3 to 4v DC
Note: **TP2 is always ground**

The Channel 1, 2 or 3 bandpass filter or the first push-pull amplifier is unbalanced or damaged. Rebalance if measurements are within 1 volt of each other.

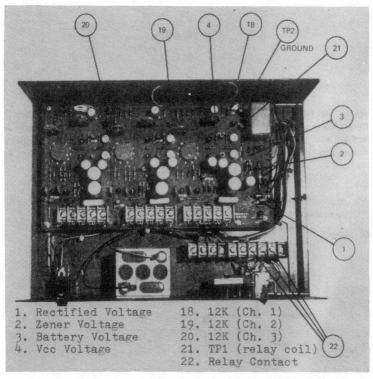

1. Rectified Voltage   18. 12K (Ch. 1)
2. Zener Voltage   19. 12K (Ch. 2)
3. Battery Voltage   20. 12K (Ch. 3)
4. Vcc Voltage   21. TP1 (relay coil)
                              22. Relay Contact

Fig. 10-20. Stress sensor voltage measurement locations.

Second amplifier voltages:

TP103 to TP104 to ground (TP2): 4.5 to 5.5v DC
TP203 to TP204 to ground: 4.5 to 5.5v DC
TP303 to TP304 to ground: 4.5 to 5.5v DC

The Channel 1, 2 or 3 second bandpass filter or push-pull amplifier is unbalanced or damaged. Rebalance if voltages are within 1 volt of each other.

If the relay coil voltage from TP1 to ground (normally 4.8 to 6 volts DC) is absent, it could be due to defective relay logic or driver failure.

Check the relay contacts with an ohmmeter at the contact terminals, then check the circuit connected.

Chapter 11
Summary of Specialized Systems

This final chapter covers those systems that do not fit into the previous categories: night viewing devices, commercial vehicular alarms and special access systems.

GTE SYLVANIA NIGHT VIEWING DEVICE

This system is available in two models—220 and 221. Both are the same, except the 221 has an adjustable "focal plane iris" for narrowing the observable field of view and eliminating bright lights from an observer's view on the outer edge of a scene. Accessories include:

1. Photographic camera adaptor that permits taking photographs through a single lens reflex type camera.

2. TV camera adaptor which attaches the NVD to any standard "C" mount type camera.

3. Biocular viewer which is connected to the NVD in place of the eyepiece lens. It permits the observer to see the magnified picture with both eyes or more than one observer can see the same scene.

4. Telephoto lens, zoom lens, or various special purpose lenses are available.

GTE Sylvania night viewing devices are electro-optic devices designed to permit the viewer to see at night as if it were daylight. Various lenses may be connected to these devices to allow near or distant viewing. Completely self-contained, they operate from two small "A" size batteries (Eveready E12N, 1.35 volts or Mallory RM-12, 1.4v). Refer to Figs. 11-1 and 11-2.

Night viewing devices operate on a light amplification principle by receiving light and amplifying it in a manner not unlike that used in sound systems. Light amplification is accomplished in a tube called an image intensifier.

An image intensifier operates as pictured in Fig. 11-3. The photons or particles of light pass through the lens and strike sharply on the photocathode of the intensifier. After several photons strike an area of the photocathode, an electron is knocked loose. Twelve kilovolts of electricity captures the electron and greatly accelerates it in the desired direction.

Fig. 11-1. Sylvania Model 220 night viewing device with 75 mm fixed focal length lens.

The electron, traveling at a tremendous velocity, smashes into a phosphor screen at the opposite end of the tube, creating a glow where it strikes. This light is about 40 times brighter than the original level striking the photocathode. It is possible to attach image intensifiers and further increase the amplification. In other words, two intensifiers in series would amplify light 40 times 40 or 1,600 times, and three intensifiers would increase the level approximately 64,000 times (40 X 40 X 40).

Lenses

The night viewing device is designed to use a standard photographic type of TV lens. Special telephoto or zoom lenses already in the owner's possession can be used with this unit. Numerous other lenses are available for long distance or close-up wide-angle viewing. Some are listed in Fig. 11-4, and

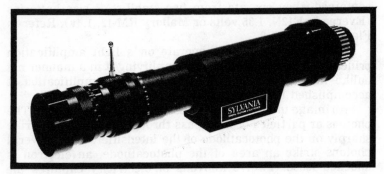

Fig. 11-2. Model 220 with a 20 to 100 mm zoom lens.

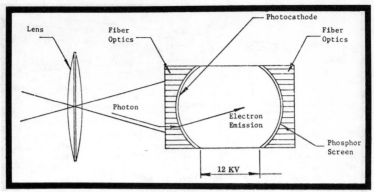

Fig. 11-3. Drawing showing the principles of an image intensifier.

are available from Sylvania or an optics supply house. Refer to Fig. 11-5 to determine the field of view and the size of the area being viewed at various observer-to-scene distances.

A 2X extender lens can be inserted between the night viewing device and the objective lens, doubling the focal length; thus, a 2X extender inserted between the device and a 75mm fixed focal length lens will change the focal length to 150mm. Unfortunately, the 2X extender doubles the f number, preventing the unit from seeing at very low light levels.

AUXILIARY LENSES		
Field of View	Lens Focal Length	f/Number
72°	12.5 MM	f/1.4
40°	25 MM	f/0.95
40°	25 MM	f/1.4
20°	50 MM	f/1.4
20°	50 MM	f/0.95
15°	75 MM	f/1.4
14°	85 MM	f/1.8
10°	100 MM	f/2
8°	135 MM	f/1.8
7°	150 MM	f/3.8
5.5°	210 MM	f/2.8
3.4°	300 MM	f/3.2
2°	500 MM	f/3.8
2X EXTENDER LENS		
40° to 10°	20 - 100 MM Zoom	f/2.5
40° to 10°	25 - 100 MM Zoom	f/1.8
45° to 9°	22.5 - 90 MM Zoom	f/1.5
62° to 7°	15 - 145 MM Zoom	f/2.5

Fig. 11-4. A listing of some available lenses.

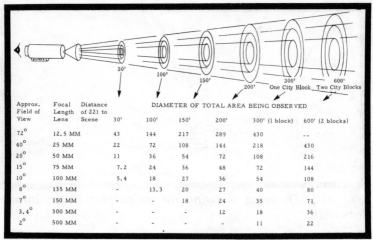

Approx. Field of View	Focal Length Lens	Distance of 221 to Scene	DIAMETER OF TOTAL AREA BEING OBSERVED					
			30'	100'	150'	200'	300' (1 block)	600' (2 blocks)
72°	12.5 MM		43	144	217	289	430	--
40°	25 MM		22	72	108	144	218	430
20°	50 MM		11	36	54	72	108	216
15°	75 MM		7.2	24	36	48	72	144
10°	100 MM		5.4	18	27	36	54	108
8°	135 MM		-	13.3	20	27	40	80
7°	150 MM		-	-	18	24	35	71
3.4°	300 MM		-	-	-	12	18	36
2°	500 MM		-	-	-	-	11	22

Fig. 11-5. Ratio of scene size to observer distance.

Selection of a lens for use with the night viewing device is the most important factor to be considered. Use the following rules to determine the optimum lens:

1. Determine the distance in feet from the location of the night viewing device to the scene to be viewed.

2. Refer to Fig. 11-5 for the ratio of the scene size to the observed distance and select the column of figures that correspond as close as possible to the distance estimated in Step 1 above.

3. Estimate the approximate area to be observed; i.e., a doorway plus 25 feet on each side or an approximate 54-foot diameter circle.

4. Go down the column labeled 150 feet (distance of 220 to the scene) until the number is found that is closest to 54. The number is 54, so a 50mm focal length lens would be optimum.

5. Determine the optimum lens to be used in looking down an alley 50 feet wide and 1 block long (300 ft). Checking the 300-foot column for the number closest to 50, we find 54. Go across the row and select the proper lens focal length, which is 100mm.

6. Select the proper lens for your application.

Focusing & Alignment

(a) Remove the night viewing device from the case and remove the plug insert from the objective lens end of the device.

(b) Select the desired lens and remove the black protective cap from the threaded end of the lens. Insert the threaded end of the lens into the end of the night viewing device and screw the lens in until the lens shoulder mates against the night viewing device.

(c) Remove the protective metal cap at the glass end of the objective lens. Make certain that the objective lens iris is at the full open position. Do not readjust the iris because the unit automatically compensates for variations in light by means of the automatic brightness control.

(d) Hold the night viewing device to your eye and turn it on by pushing down on the on-off switch located on the battery case.

(e) Adjust the objective lens focus for an optimum picture.

(f) Adjust the eyepiece lens focus for an optimum picture.

(g) If a zoom lens is used, focus should be adjusted in the narrow field of view position and it will remain in focus throughout the full zoom range.

(h) The on-off switch on the battery case has two positions:

1. Pushing the switch down turns the unit on and keeps it on until the switch is pushed back to the middle position.

2. Pushing the switch upward turns the unit on and it remains on only so long as the switch is held in the upward position. This position conserves battery life by preventing the NVD from accidentally being left on.

The NVD uses standard "A" cell batteries inserted in the polarity in which the already inserted batteries are positioned. Replacement of batteries is facilitated by inserting a coin in the metal screw on the bottom of the battery housing. Simply remove screw, push on the end corner edge of the baseplate and remove the plate. Use only Eveready E12N or Mallory RM-12 or equivalent batteries.

Fig. 11-6. Model 221 night viewing device, showing focal plane and field iris adjustments. (Courtesy GTE Sylvania)

Fig. 11-7. NVD attached to a conventional TV camera. (Courtesy GTE Sylvania)

Field Iris (Model 221 Only)

An adjustable field size control is provided on the front of the Model 221 near the objective lens (Fig. 11-6). The iris can be adjusted by the operator to block out lights on the perimeter of the field of view. This protects the unit and provides a sharper picture. It may also be utilized to adjust the size of the field of view. This focal iris should not be confused with the lens iris which adjusts the amount of light entering the lens. The automatic brightness control regulates the viewer gain, eliminating any requirement for the lens iris to be adjusted.

Optional Features

The NVD can be used to modify any daylight type camera to a low-light level TV camera by utilizing the TV adapter assembly (Fig. 11-7). When TV use is completed and the TV camera is turned off, do not forget to also turn off the night viewing device.

Use of the NVD with almost any single lens reflex-type photographic camera for night photography is possible also. The adapter assembly is required and extension tubes must be installed between the camera lens and camera body (Fig. 11-8).

The biocular viewer permits an observer to look at the NVD scene with both eyes and also allows two observers to view the scene at the same time (Fig. 11-9). Fig. 11-10 shows the night viewing device in action, apprehending a "suspect" in total darkness.

HOLOBEAM PERSONNEL ACCESS SYSTEM

The SPACS system is designed to provide entrance control to areas that must be protected from unauthorized personnel.

Fig. 11-8. NVD attached to a "still" camera. (Courtesy GTE Sylvania)

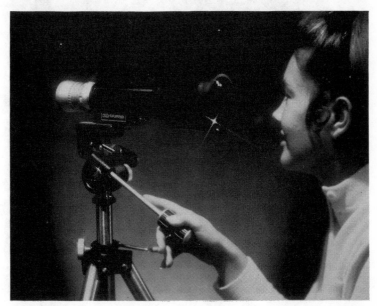

Fig. 11-9. NVD with biocular viewer attached. (Courtesy GTE Sylvania)

Fig. 11-10. NVD in action. This scene was observed in almost total darkness.

Fig. 11-11. Holobeam Model SC20 access wall unit. (Courtesy Holobeam, Inc.)

The system is operated by a card plus the dialing of the proper ID number. See Fig. 11-11, showing the wall unit Model SC20. The device may be used to determine the positive identification of authorized personnel and can monitor and control points of entry from a remote location. Each card holder has his own unique 5-digit number. An automatic siren alarm is built into the solid-state system. The polyester plastic cards will not crack or break. There are no holes in the card and it cannot be altered if subjected to a strong magnetic field.

Here's how it works:

1. Insert the card into the slot of the card reader.

2. The "Insert card" indicator light goes out and the "insert data" lamp lights.

3. The person presses his unique 5-digit number.

4. The "Insert data" indicator goes out and the "remove card" indicator lights.

5. The person removes his card.

6A. If he has accurately keyed in his number, the "go" indicator will light and a contact closure will be provided to operate an electric lock, gate or turnstile.

6B. If the individual has not accurately keyed in his number, the "insert card" indicator will light and the "entry denied" indicator lights. He must repeat Steps 1 through 5.

6C. If a card holder fails in three attempts, the "no-go" indicator and audio alarm will be activated.

Input power required is 115 volts, 50-400 Hz, 30 watts. The wall unit is 6" wide by 6⅜" deep by 9" high.

THREE-B ELECTRONICS FIRE ALARM SYSTEM

The TBE300 is a completely solid-state, self-contained, flame, smoke and heat detector with an alarm which is suitable for commercial as well as industrial use. Operating on ordinary AC current, the unit automatically switches to standby batteries in case of power line outage. RCA outlets provide a connect for a remote horn and battery operation.

The flame detector consists of five selected transistors in the Darlington configuration which affords exceptional stability against ambient temperature variations. The three photoelectric cells used in the unit were specially designed and permit operation in complete darkness without any adjustment as well as in a normally lighted area.

The smoke detector consists of a pair of transistors in a Darlington circuit, which is merely two cascaded emitter-followers having an extremely high input impedance to provide a current time-base generator. The Darlington pair is coupled to the triggering circuit commonly used by the flame detector. The lamp supplying the uniform beam to the smoke detector chamber has an average life of more than three years. The heat detector is a 135-degree F thermostat as specified by UL.

120v AC power, delayed by about 60 seconds with a 6 amp capability, is provided for turning on a sprinkling system, dialer, siren, bells and whatever responsive device is needed.

The flame detector sensitivity is 30 foot candle ambient light in the "high sensitivity." It is said to be capable of detecting the flame of a striking match up to 10 feet away or fire in a waste basket up to 30 feet away. In "low sensitivity," the flame in a waste basket would be detected 10 feet away, or in total darkness, fire will be detected 100 feet distant. Smoke detector sensitivity averages below 4 percent and is adjustable to 1 percent. The fixed temperature heat sensitivity is 135 degrees F (200 degrees F available). The power requirement is about 6 watts AC, 1.2 watts DC. The unit weighs 23 ounces and it mounts with two screws.

Optional equipment includes a police type siren with a sound interruptor, rechargeable battery (1200 ma hrs.), 12-volt battery holder, 12-volt "hot-shot" battery, replacement bulbs, remote horn, burglar alarm adaptor and instant panic alarm converter.

DETECTRON SECURITY SYSTEMS FIRE MONITOR, MODEL 210

The Model 210 fire monitor (Fig. 11-12) is a complete fire alarm system which may be used in conjunction with fixed-temperature detectors, rate of rise detectors, or smoke detectors. The monitor utilizes a fully supervised loop and provides a separate circuit to trigger a buzzer or other responsive device in the event that the fire loop is cut, broken or tampered with, plus a fire bell test button on the front panel. A control reset button, normal light and trouble light are also located on the front panel. In the alarm mode, a 12-volt DC signal is offered to the fire bell or siren. A separate relay closure is available to energize a dialer such as the Model 1500.

The monitor has its own 12-volt Gel-Cell batteries which are maintained at full charge with 1 ampere hour capacity and automatically provide power for the system during an AC line outage. The unit is powered by a low-voltage transformer at 24 volts AC. The following five sensors are available for use with the unit: Model 501 rate of rise and heat detector (136 degrees F), Model 503 fixed-temperature detector (136 degrees F), Model 504 fixed-temperature detector (200 degrees F), Model 510 heat (136 degrees F) and smoke detector.

Controls and indicators include a reset button, alarm test button, normal indicator, and circuit fault indicator. The circuit is 2-wire, fully supervised loop. Alarm bell, dialer, and trouble buzzer outputs are provided. The device measures 9½″ long, 9½″ high, 3″ deep and weighs 3¼ pounds.

DETECTION SECURITY SYSTEMS MODULAR SECURITY-FIRE CONTROL

The Model 101 security-fire system (Fig. 11-13) is constructed entirely of modular solid-state, printed circuit boards which permit it to be used in a variety of security applications. Perimeter burglar alarms, radar burglar alarms, ultrasonic burglar alarms, pulsor stress types, fire alarms, multiple station, direct telephone line and others may be readily used with this control unit.

Features include a complete burglar alarm system with first and second alarms, two C-form dry closures on the first alarm and two C-form dry closures on the second alarm plus the following:

Switch programming for exit delay (0, 30, or 60 seconds).

Switch programming first to second alarm delay (0, 30, or 60 seconds).

Switch programming for 5 minutes automatic control recycle or latch.

Uses either NO, NC or both types of detectors.

Special signal processing amplifier for pulsor detectors.

Can be used with radar or ultrasonic detectors.

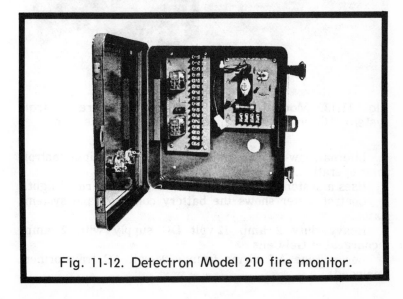

Fig. 11-12. Detectron Model 210 fire monitor.

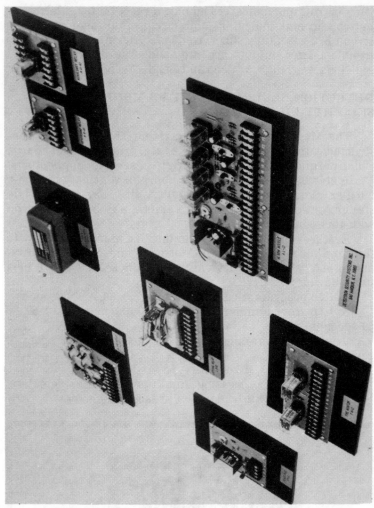

Fig. 11-13. Model 101 Detectron security-fire control system. (Courtesy Detectron Security Systems, Inc.)

Internal, low-current latching relay for multiple control point operation.

Uses a system status light, ready light and armed light.

Control meter shows the battery condition and system status.

Heavy duty 2 amp 12-volt DC supply with 2 amp rechargeable Gel-Cells.

Low-voltage AC wiring from a 24-volt AC transformer (included).

240

The 11" by 15" by 5½" unit is designed to mount on a table top or the wall with a bracket. Weight is 12 pounds.

SYSTRON-DONNER TRT-1 TRANSDUCER TESTER

This device is designed to locate faults in cable runs and transducers, plus positively indicate shorts or open circuits. It is ready for immediate use, complete with test leads, AC recharge cord and battery. The unit is self-contained with a rechargeable 6-volt battery. The 6 by 4-inch tester uses reliable solid-state component throughout.

The tester may be connected to transducer cable runs or to individual transducers, providing a tone which can be heard only from each transducer if the cable run is properly installed and the transducers are functioning. If a short or open circuit exists in the cable or if the transducer is faulty, little or no sound will be generated by the transducers connected to the tester. An experienced installer will immediately know if a short or open exists in the transducers and the transducer cables by following the field test procedure. Common causes of open and short circuits in cable runs may result from staples driven through the cable, loose cable connections at terminal strips, cables that have been pinched or pulled with too much force through conduit.

Field Test Procedure

After completely installing the transducers and transducer cable according to instructions, and before attaching the cables to the control, perform the following tests with the TRT-1:

1. Connect the transducer signal wires to the transducer tester, but do not connect the shield wire until Step 4.

2. Turn the TRT-1 switch on.

3. Each transducer should then produce an audible 3,000-Hz tone. If the tone is not produced, or if the tone is weak, a short or open circuit exists in the transducer cable or in the transducers.

4. Check for short circuits between the shield and signal wires by alternately connecting the shield wire to each post. If this causes the tone to stop, a short exists in the cable or at the transducer between the shield and one of the signal wires.

5. The location of the open or short can be determined by a loss of tone beyond the open or short circuit.

6. The following items may account for a weak tone at the transducer and must be taken into consideration when testing the system:

(a) Receiver potentiometers should be turned fully counterclockwise (left) so they do not attenuate the signal during the initial test of the system.

(b) On long cable runs, the transducers located close to the control unit generate a stronger tone than those at the end of the cable run. The strength of the signal will aid in determining whether additional transducers are needed for areas located far from the control unit.

7. After using the TRT-1 tester on a few systems, the experienced installer will be able to recognize what tone levels should be present in each area.

PULSE ALARM DETECTION SYSTEM

The solid-state Model 450 detection transmitter uses pulse tone coding to prevent false alarms and it is immune to tampering. The induced vibration of the protected object and the unit itself causes the transmitter to send a soundless, precisely defined signal to its companion receiver (up to 2,000 feet outdoors or 600 feet indoors). The transmitter operates consistently under adverse industrial environments, and the 16 gauge all-steel case will withstand severe weather conditions. The bracket assembly makes the unit completely portable. Any number of transmitters (Model 450) may be monitored by a single receiver (Model 150). Multiple areas may be zoned for closer identification and greater versatility.

This system is recommended for protection of trucks, trailers, boats, cars, airplanes, buildings and stationary containers. It may be used in conjunction with other alarm devices such as audio alarms, floodlights, dialers, cameras, etc.

Model 450 Transmitter Specifications (See Fig. 11-14)

Frequency:	11 meter band (27 MHz), plus or minus .01 percent
Subcarrier frequency:	Selected tone, 600 Hz to 9,500 Hz
Tone interrupt rate:	30 per second
Frequency control:	Crystal oscillator
DC power input:	240 milliwatts
Power Output:	90 milliwatts
Transistors:	Four
Operate temp:	-30 to +125 degrees F
Power source:	12-volt battery (Burgess TW2 or Eveready 732)
Alarm activation:	Two vibration sensors
Triggering sensitivity:	Adjustable
Dimensions:	7" high, 8½" long, 5¼" wide
Weight:	9 pounds
Remote triggering:	Normally open devices

Fig. 11-14. Vehicle protection transmitter. (Courtesy Pulse Alarm Detection Systems, Inc.)

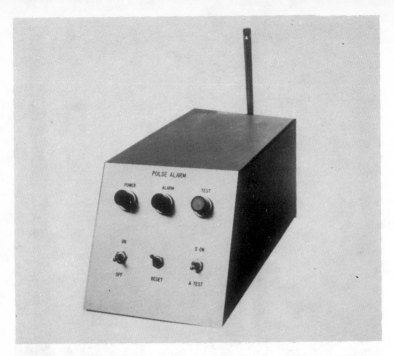

Fig. 11-15. Vehicle protection receiver. (Courtesy Pulse Alarm Detection Systems, Inc.)

Model 150 Receiver (Fig. 11-15)

Type receiver:	Single conversion superhet
Frequency:	11 meter band
Local oscillator:	Crystal control, plus or minus .01 percent
IF frequency:	455 kHz
Coding:	Fixed tone, selected subcarrier
Noise rejection:	Limiter, filter, level detector
Zone control:	Internal plug-in code control
Antenna:	18-inch fiberglass whip, optional outdoor
Output:	Solid-state switch (NO and NC, 5A)
Range:	2,000 feet outdoors, 600 feet indoors
Selectivity:	12 kHz at 6 db, 36 kHz at 60 db
Image ratio:	Greater than 30 db
Transistors:	12, plus 7 diodes
Power source:	117-volt AC, stepdown to 22v AC
	15 ma standby, 15 ma operate
Dimensions:	4⅝" high, 11½" long, 4⅝" wide
Weight:	7 pounds

SENSING TYPE VEHICLE ALARM

The Kalin Industries Model EKS-1000 and 1200 systems are triggered by specific electrical drains from the car or truck battery, with a switch to protect the engine compartment on cars not equipped with a hood light. This unique design eliminates the need for numerous switches which require hole drilling for wires. There are only three wires to connect—a gray ground wire to the negative ground (-), the black wire to the switch and the green wire for triggering. The unit has no moving parts—completely solid-state—and draws only 1 amp at 12 volts. An optional switch is available to mount inside the vehicle to enable the driver to signal for help in an emergency or as a panic alarm. Its midnight black finish avoids visual detection by car thieves. The EKSO-1200 has a 2-minute automatic shut-off and reset included. Any attempt to lift the hood, operate the ignition switch, open doors with courtesy lights, turn on direction signals, headlights, taillights, trunk light, etc., will immediately trigger the warning siren. Installation in the vehicle is fairly simple by following the step-by-step pictorial instructions included with each unit. No electrical or electronic skill is needed.

Manufacturers & Suppliers

Acron Corp.
1209 River Ave.
Lakewood, N.J. 08701

Adcor Electronics, Inc.
349 Peachtree Hills Ave N.E.
Atlanta, Ga. 30305

Advanced Devices Laboratory
316 Mathew St.
Santa Clara, Calif. 95050

Aerospace Research Inc.
130 Lincoln St.
Boston, Mass. 02135

Aerotron
P.O. Box 6527
Raleigh, N.C. 27608

Air Space Devices
P.O. Box 338
Paramount, Calif. 90723

Alarm Devices Mfg. Co., Inc.
165 Eileen Way
Syosset, L.I., N.Y. 11791

Alarm Products Int'l., Inc.
24-02 40th Ave.
Long Island City, N.Y. 11101

Alarmtronics Engineering, Inc.
154 California St.
Newton, Mass. 02195

American District Telegraph Co.
155 Sixth Ave.
New York, N.Y. 10013

AMF
1025 N. Royal St.
Alexandra, Va. 22314

Amptronic Controls
21 Fadem Road
Springfield, N.J. 07081

Applied Electronics Mfg., Inc.
443 Elm St.
Stamford, Conn. 06902

Arrowhead Enterprises, Inc.
P.O. Box 191, Diamond Ave.
Bethel, Conn. 06801

Artronix Surveillance
716 Hanley Industrial Court
St. Louis, Mo. 63144

A.T.A. Control Systems, Inc.
340 W. 78th Road
Hialeah, Fla. 33014

Auto-Matic Products Co.
3368 S. Parkway
Chicago, Ill. 60616

Beckman Research & Mfg. Co.
11 W. Ash Ave.
Burbank, Calif. 91502

Benedict Electronics, Inc.
506 State St.
Schenectady, N.Y. 12305

Benjamin Electronic Sound Corp.
Farmingdale, N.Y. 11735

Bourns Security Systems, Inc.
681 Old Willets Path
Smithtown, N.Y. 11787

BRK Electronics, Inc.
525 Rathbone Ave.
Aurora, Ill. 60538

Christy Industries, Inc.
1812 Bath Ave.
Brooklyn, N.Y. 11214

Cohu Electronics, Inc.
Box 623
San Diego, Calif. 92112

Concord Electronics Corp.
1935 Armacost Ave.
Los Angeles, Calif. 90025

Currier-Smith Corp..
P.O. Box 362
Bedford, Mass. 01730

Decatur Electronics, Inc.
715 Bright St.
Decatur, Ill. 62522

Delta Products, Inc.
P.O. Box 1147
Grand Junction, Calif. 81501

Design Controls, Inc.
75 Sealey Ave.
Hempstead, N.Y. 11550

Detection Systems, Inc.
211 Eyer Bldg.
East Rochester, N.Y. 14445

Detectron Security Systems, Inc.
P.O. Box 313A
Sag Harbor, L.I., N.Y. 11963

Detex Corp.
53 Park Place
New York, N.Y. 10007

Dialalarm, Inc.
7315 Lankershim Blvd.
North Hollywood, Calif. 91609

Eaton, Yale & Towne, Inc.
376 Halstead Ave,
Harrison, N.Y. 10528

Electronic Development Labs
357 Cottage St.
Springfield, Mass. 01104

Electrosonics International, Inc.
4120 Tower St.
Philadelphia, Pa. 19127

Electrospace Corp.
1717 Paterson Plank Rd.
North Bergen, N.J. 07047

Emergency Products Corp.
60 Lafayette St.
Newark, N.J. 07102

Fire-Lite Alarms, Inc.
190 Fulton Terrace
New Haven, Conn. 06504

A. W. Fruh & Co.
1815 North Orchard
Chicago, Ill. 60614

Functional Devices, Inc.
S. Union & Nashville Sts.
Russiaville, Ind. 46979

Gard, Inc.
207 Sandusky St.
Pittsburgh, Pa. 15212

GBC Closed Circuit TV Corp.
74 Fifth Ave.
New York, N.Y. 10011

GTE Sylvania Electronic Systems
Box 188
Mountain View, Calif. 94040

Heath Company
Benton Harbor, Mich. 49022

Holmes Protection Inc.
370 Seventh Ave.
New York, N.Y. 10001

Holobeam, Inc.
560 Winters Ave.
Paramus, N.J. 07652

Honeywell Inc.
Commercial Div. G2118
Minneapolis, Minn. 55408

Imperial Products Co., Inc.
37-08 Greenpoint Ave.
Long Island City, N.Y. 11101

Impossible Electronic Inc.
121 Coulter Ave.
Ardmore, Pa. 19003

James Electronics, Inc.
4050 N. Rockwell St.
Chicago, Ill. 60618

Javelin Electronics Co.
5556 W. Washington Blvd.
Los Angeles, Calif. 90016

John Colling Enterprises, Inc.
3997 E. Bayshore Rd.
Palo Alto, Calif. 94303

Johnson Service Co.
507 E. Michigan St.
Milwaukee, Wis. 53201

Kerux Systems, Inc.
6000 Stevenson Ave.
Alexandria, Va. 22304

Walter Kidde & Co., Inc.
Main St.
Belleville, N.J. 07109

Kolin Industries, Inc.
Box 357
Bronxville, N.Y. 10708

Lectro Systems, Inc.
131 State St.
St. Paul, Minn. 55107

Linear Corp.
347 S. Glasgow Ave.
Inglewood, Calif. 90301

Litton Systems
Poly Scientific Div.
1213 N. Main St.
Blacksburg, Va. 24060

Mallory Distributor Products Co.
Box 1284
Indianapolis, Ind. 46206

Matsushita Electric Corp.
200 Park Ave.
New York, N.Y. 10017

Metrotec Industries
33 Cain Drive
Plainview, N.Y. 11803

Mica Corp.
7735 Riverdale Rd.
New Carrollton, Md. 20784

Monroe Timer Co., Inc.
1960 Westchester Ave.
Bronx, N.Y. 10462

Morse Products Mfg.
12960 Bradley Ave.
Sylmar, Calif. 91342

Mosler Research Products, Inc.
9 South St.
Danbury, Conn. 06810

Motorola Communications, Inc.
1301 E. Algonquin Rd.
Schaumburg, Ill. 60172

Mountain West Alarm Supply Co.
4215 N. 16th St.
Phoenix, Ariz. 85016

Multi-Elmac Co.
21470 Coolidge Highway
Oak Park, Mich. 48237

Multra-Guard Inc.
1930 E. Pembroke Ave.
Hampton, Va. 23369

National Alarm Products Co., Inc.
291 Adams Blvd.
Farmingdale, N.Y. 11735

Nationwide Security Systems Co.
7415 Coventry Ave.
Melrose Park, Pa. 19004

Northern Electric Co.
5224 N. Kedzie Ave.
Chicago, Ill. 60093

Omni Spectra, Inc.
1040 W. Alameda Drive
Tempe, Arix. 85282

OMW Electronics, Inc.
4028 N.E. Sixth Ave.
Fort Lauderdale, Fla. 33308

On-Guard Corp. of America
350 Gotham Parkway
Carlstadt, N.J. 07072

Optical Controls, Inc.
Second Ave.
Burlington, Mass. 01803

Picture Proof
799 Roosevelt Rd.
Glen Ellyn, Ill. 60137

Pinkerton Electro-Security Corp.
275 Main St.
Webster, Mass. 01570

Pulse Alarm Detection Systems
5439 W. Fargo Ave.
Skokie, Ill. 60076

Pulse Dynamics, Inc.
5515 Westfield Ave.
Pennsauken, N.H. 08110

Pyrotector Inc.
333 Lincoln St.
Hingham, Mass. 02043

Pyrotronics, Inc.
8 Ridgedale Ave.
Cedar Knolls, N.J. 07927

Radatron Corp.
2424 Niagara Falls Blvd.
North Tonawanda, N.Y. 14120

Radar Devices Mfg. Corp.
22003 Harper Ave.
St. Clair Shores, Mich. 48080

Reeves Electronics, Inc.
7512 Santa Monica Blvd.
Los Angeles, Calif. 90046

Rusco Electronic Systems
953 S. Raymond Ave.
Pasadena, Calif. 91105

Schulmerich Electronics, Inc.
Carillion Hill
Sellersville, Pa. 18901

Seco Company
3018 Commerce St.
Houston, Tex. 77003

Securitron Corp.
P.O. Box 49875
Los Angeles, Calif. 90049

Security Systems of America
51st & A.V.R.R.
Pittsburgh, Pa. 15201

Sentrol, Inc.
14335 N.W. Science Park Dr.
Portland, Ore. 97229

Singer Company
Link Div.
Binghamton, N.Y. 13902

Sonar Radio Corp.
73 Wortman Ave.
Brooklyn, N.Y. 11207

Sontrix Distributing Co.
18455 Burbank Blvd.
Tarzana, Calif. 91356

Spies Electric Works
564 W. Van Buren St.
Chicago, Ill. 60607

Standard-Farrington Alarm Corp.
37 Terry Drive
Trevose, Pa. 19047

Systron-Donner Corp.
Security Devices Div.
6767 Dublin Blvd.
Dublin, Calif. 94566

Sylvania Security Systems
730 Third Ave.
New York, N.Y. 10017

Tapeswitch Corp.
320 Broad Hollow Rd.
Farmingdale, N.Y. 11735

Teledyne, Inc.
3401 Shiloh Road
Garland, Tex. 75040

Three-B Electronics, Inc.
5404 Eighth Ave.
Brooklyn, N.Y. 11220

3 M Company
Box 3686
St. Paul, Minn. 55001

Transcience, Inc.
17 Irving Ave.
Stamford, Conn. 06902

Trine Mfg. Corp.
1430-42 Ferris Place
Bronx, N.Y. 10461

Universal Security, Inc.
1315 E. Pratt St.
Baltimore, Md. 21231

Universal Sentry Systems
P.O. Box 1825
Vancouver, Wash. 98663

Video Control Corp.
3621 Wells Fargo
Scottsdale, Arix. 85251

Video-Eye of America, Inc.
1227 Enquirer Bldg.
Cincinnati, Ohio 45202

Glossary

Alarm, break—Alarm signal produced by opening an electrical circuit.

Alarm, cross—Alarm signal generated when the wires of an alarm system are shorted together.

Alarm, holdup—Device which generates an alarm when a concealed switch is opened or closed.

Alarm, local—System which causes a local bell or horn to sound when an alarm condition exists.

Alarm, nuisance—Any alarm signal caused by a factor other than an intrusion or circuit malfunction.

Annunciator—Device which provides visual and-or audible indications of the existence of an alarm condition.

Button, holdup—Button switch for activiating a holdup alarm.

Connection, police—Pair of wires connected to a monitor in a police station, in addition to the connection to a proprietary monitor or central station monitor.

Contact—Door or window switch which opens an electrical circuit when the door or window to which it is attached is opened.

Control, active-standby—Control used with constantly supervised security systems to allow normal traffic through a protected area during the hours of occupancy. This control renders the system inoperative, but allows tamper and line supervision to be maintained to prevent the system from being compromised during the hours of normal occupancy.

Control, day-night—Control which turns a security system on or off to allow normal occupancy and to provide protection during the hours of closure.

Detector—Any device which senses the presence of an intruder and causes an alarm indication to be given.

Detector, audio—System for detecting an intruder by the noise he makes; usually a microphone and amplifier are used to operate a relay. When the sound level rises by a preset amount above the normal ambient level, an alarm indication is given. Most systems of this type permit a guard at a remote station to listen to the sounds in the protected area, and some have an intercom feature.

Detector, capacitance—Device which protects a metal fixture such as a safe or filing cabinet by using the fixture as one plate of a capacitor and the earth or a metal mat as the other plate. Approaching or touching the protected fixture changes the capacitance in the circuit and this change in capacitance activates the alarm.

Detector, infrared—Photoelectric intrusion detection device which uses infrared light rather than visible light. (See photoelectric detector.)

Detector, heat—Thermostatic type switch designed for installation on metal doors. The heat from a cutting torch will open the switch, causing an alarm.

Detector, microwave—Detector which operates at microwave frequencies (above 2000 MHz) rather than lower radio frequencies. The unit detects apparent frequency shifts caused by the movement of an intruder in the protected area and generates an alarm indication.

Detector, photoelectric—Detection device which utilizes a beam of light projected into a photocell to detect an intruder. A

person walking through the light beam blocks the light from a photocell, which causes an alarm to be generated.

Detector, proximity—Device such as a capacitance detector which initiates an alarm if a person comes near or touches a protected object.

Detector, radar—Device which detects an intruder by his movement in a field of electromagnetic energy. Such a device may operate at microwave frequencies or lower radio frequencies. (See microwave detector.)

Detector, sonic—Device which sets up a field of sound waves in the air inside a protected area. A moving intruder causes an apparent frequency shift in the sound waves returning to the detector from the protected area. The detector senses this apparent frequency shift and generates an alarm indication.

Detector, vibration—Device which contains a pair of contacts that will open or close if the unit is jarred. Vibration detectors are used to protect soft walls, floors, ceilings and other critical areas against forceful entry. They are usually used in perimeter systems.

Detector, ultrasonic—Device similar in operation to the sonic detector, except that the frequency at which it operates is in the ultrasonic rather than the sonic range.

Double drop—Method often used in central station alarm systems where the alarm circuit is open, then crossed or shorted by the intrusion detection device to produce an alarm.

Fence, electromagnetic—A fence composed of wires which are electrically insulated from the fence posts. Electronic equipment is employed to set up an electromagnetic field between the wires. A person disturbing the field by going close to or through the fence causes an alarm to be initiated.

Foil—Very thin metal strips which are cemented to a glass window or door. The foil is connected into a closed electrical circuit or loop. If the glass is broken, it will break the foil and open the circuit, causing an alarm.

Instrument, control—Unit which contains the alarm relay, drop relay, day-night switch and sometimes a testing device in a local burglar alarm system.

Line, alarm—An electrically supervised pair of wires connected between the intrusion detection equipment in the protected area and the alarm indicating equipment for the purpose of transmitting alarm indications.

Line, reporting—Same as alarm line.

Line, security—Same as alarm line.

Loop, security—Same as alarm line.

Mat, contact—Rubber mat which has switches built into it. Contact mats are often used as floor traps where stepping on the mat operates a switch, which causes an alarm to be given.

Microphone, contact—Microphone which can be mounted directly on a protected wall, safe, etc. The microphone, usually insensitive to ambient room noises, detects the sound of the wall or safe being breached to activate an alarm circuit.

Monitor—Remote indicating device which provides audible and-or visual indications of alarm conditions.

Protection, area—Protection of the inner space or volume of a security area, rather than the perimeter of the area.

Protection, perimeter—System which protects the walls, doors, windows and sometimes the floors and ceiling of a security area against penetration.

Protection, object—System for protecting a specific object such as a safe or file cabinet by the use of a capacitance detector or similar device.

Protection, space—Same as area protection.

Protection, volume—Same as area protection.

Relay alarm—A high resistance, sensitive relay used in security equipment. Most burglar alarms have the relay held in by current through the alarm circuit. Opening the circuit de-energizes the relay, which usually pilots another drop relay. The second relay is equipped with heavier contacts than the alarm relay and operates an alarm horn, bell, etc., for local alarm systems. On more sophisticated systems, the alarm relay causes a line current change upon opening, which is detected by the monitor. The monitor then provides an alarm indication.

Relay, drop—An electrically latching relay which activates alarm indicating devices in a burglar alarm system. The operation of this relay is usually controlled by a low-current alarm relay, which has a coil connected in series with the foil, door, and window contacts used in ordinary burglar alarm systems.

Resistor, end-of-line—Resistance connected in an alarm line circuit to provide a required value of alarm line current. The more sophisticated security systems use a change in alarm line current rather than a simple break or cross indication to activate the alarm indicating device.

Resistor, termination—Same as end-of-line resistor.

Screen—Covering for a window or similar opening usually consisting of light wooden strips or dowels with fine wire cemented to the inside. The wire of the screen is a continuous circuit and is connected in series with the circuit of a burglar alarm. Cutting or breaking through the screen opens the circuit and activates the alarm.

Signal, trouble—Signal which indicates some defined abnormal condition or conditions, such as a circuit malfunction, loss of power, or tampering with alarm circuitry.

Supervision, electronic—Pertains to the supervision of the security equipment itself, rather than the alarm line. An electronically supervised security device incorporates failsafe electronic circuits to warn of equipment malfunction.

Supervision, line—Electrical protection of an alarm line. This is accomplished by having a continuous flow of current through the circuit. A change of current will be detected by the monitor. The monitor gives an alarm if the change exceeds the allowable amount for a given percentage of line supervision. (See percentage of supervision.)

Supervision, mechanical—Protection of security equipment against tampering by the use of tamper switches connected in series with an electrically supervised alarm line.

Supervision, percentage of—Percentage by which the supervisory current in an alarm line can be varied without causing an alarm. The lower the percentage of supervision, the more difficult the alarm line is to compromise.

Surveillance—Monitoring of equipment operation, boilers, industrial processes, etc., by means of an electrical connection to a remote indicating panel.

Switch, balanced magnetic—Magnetic door or gate switch which operates in a balanced magnetic field. This switch is built in such a manner as to make it difficult to compromise by the application of an external magnet. These switches usually consist of one or more reed switches held closed by a magnet on the protected door. Application of an external magnet causes a second set of contacts to close, causing an alarm to be given. Opening the door also opens the switch.

Switch, day-night—Switch used to deactivate a security system to allow access to the protected area during hours of normal occupancy.

Switch, door—A switch, usually magnetically operated, which opens its contacts when the door which it is protecting opens. The switch is usually mounted on the door frame and the

magnet which operates it is usually mounted on the door. The switch is connected in series with a closed alarm circuit, and opening the circuit causes an alarm to be given.

Switch, gate—This switch operates in the same manner as a door switch, and is usually enclosed in a weatherproof housing to permit outdoor use. (See door switch.)

Switch, tamper—A switch in security equipment enclosures which opens the alarm line circuit if the enclosure is opened, causing an alarm to be given.

System, active security—Security system employing a detector which generates the energy used to detect the presence of an intruder and receives the same energy when it is reflected back to the detector from the protected area.

System, central station—Alarm system connected to a central guard station. These are usually owned and operated by the installing company which also furnishes the guard personnel at the central station.

System, code transmission—A type of alarm system which has several customers premises on a single alarm loop connected to a central station. The circuit on each property sends a different coded signal to the central station upon alarm. Such systems are intended to minimize the cost of leased wires.

System, central alarm—Same as code transmission system.

System, combination central station and local alarm—Alarm system which sounds a local alarm such as a horn or bell and also transmits an alarm to a central station.

System, direct connected—Alarm system having an individual supervised connection to the central station or police headquarters or guard shack, etc.

System, direct wire—Alarm system connected directly to police headquarters.

System, electromechanical—Alarm system consisting of a closed electrical loop which runs around a protected area. In the loop are protective switching devices such as door switches, window foil, screens, etc. All of these components are connected in series and opening any one of them to enter the protected area breaks the circuit, de-energizes the relay and activates the alarm. The alarm may be either local or remote.

System, passive security—Security system such as an audio system which employs a detector that depends on audio or vibration energy produced by an intruder.

System, proprietary—Security system owned by the customer rather than by the installing company.

System, building security—Protective apparatus of a building. This can include electrical and electronic security equipment as well as a guard force. Equipment surveillance devices can also be included in the security system, along with the intrusion detection equipment. Security systems are generally more sophisticated than the simple burglar alarm and they provide more comprehensive protection.

Trap—This can consist of fine wire lacing in the opening of a skylight or similar opening. The operation is the same as that of a screen. (See screen.) A trap can also be a device which is installed within a security area to serve as secondary protection in the event that a perimeter system is successfully penetrated. It can be a switch operated by a cord placed across a likely path for an intruder, a switch mat hidden under a rug, a door switch on an inner door, etc.

Zones—Divisions within a security area. A zone can contain more than one intrusion detection device, but the detection devices are connected to a single monitor or monitor module providing an indication of the area of the building in which an intrusion occurs.

Zone, clear—Cleared area around an electromagnetic or capacitance fence. Its purpose is to minimize nuisance alarms resulting from falling limbs, blowing rubbish, small animals, etc.

Federal Crime Insurance Regulations

Following are excerpts from Chapter VII, Federal Insurance Administration, Department of Housing and Urban Development (Subchapter C, Title 24).

(1) Purpose of this subchapter is to inform the general public regarding the manner in which the insurance program operates, the States in which the insurance is sold and eligibility requirements for its purchase;

(2) to offer all licensed property insurance agents and brokers in eligible States an opportunity to sell Federal crime insurance and to set forth the conditions of the offer and

(3) to prescribe the rules and regulations for the general operation of the program, as well as the specific insurance policy forms that will be required.

A public hearing was held on June 11, 1971 to explain the crime insurance program in greater detail and to receive comments on the proposed regulations from approximately 150 persons in attendance. The regulations were adopted and became effective August 1st, 1971.

The principle changes from the adopted regulations originally proposed included slight changes in agents' commissions; rates were lowered for high limits of coverage; deductibles were lowered slightly; rules pertaining to cancellations and renewals were clarified; provision was made for nonprofit and public institutions to purchase coverage at premium rates based upon operating budgets; 12 States were determined to have a critical unresolved problem of crime insurance unavailability as of the effective date of the new regulation.

Subchapter C contains Parts 1930, 1931, 1932, 1933, and 1934.

Part 1930—Description of Program and Offer to Agents

1930.3 (b) No Federal crime insurance Policy issued by or on behalf of the insurer shall be subject to any State or local tax or insurance tax or regulation.

(c) Nothing in this section shall be construed as authorizing or denying any State or subdivision thereof the right to impose any income or other tax on fees, commissions, or profits earned by agents, brokers, or servicing companies solely for their own account.

Part 1931—Purchase of Insurance and Adjustment of Claims

1931.1 (b) On the basis of information available to date, the Administrator has concluded that the following States have an unresolved critical market unavailability situation which will necessitate the implementation of the Federal crime insurance program within such States: California, Connecticut, District of Columbia, Illinois, Maryland, Massachusetts, Michigan, Missouri, New York, Ohio, Pennsylvania, and Rhode Island.

(c) If any of the States listed in paragraph (b) adopts a suitable program under State law to make the standard lines of crime insurance available within that state at affordable rates, or if such insurance becomes generally available through the normal insurance market at affordable rates, then in either case the eligibility of such State for the subsequent sale of crime insurance under the program will be promptly terminated by the insurer.

Part 1932—Protective Device Requirements

Subpart A—General

1932.1 Definitions.

As used in this subchapter, the term:

(a) "Baffle" means a piece of metal that covers the opening between a door and its frame at the area of penetration of the bolt or latch to deter the insertion of tools and prevent the exertion of pressure against the bolt or latch;

(b) "Central station, supervised service alarm system" means a silent alarm system that is constantly in operation, which signals (upon any breach of a door, window, or other accessible opening to the protected premises) at a private sentry or guard headquarters that is attended and monitoried 24 hours a day; that dispatches guards to the protected premises immediately upon the activation of an alarm; that periodically checks the operation and effectiveness of the system, and that notifies law enforcement authorities as soon as the breach of the premises is confirmed;

(c) "Dead bolt" means a locking device using a fixed bolt that, when in the locked position, cannot be retracted by a door knob or handle or other normal door opening device or by the application of force against the penetrating end of the bolt;

(d) "Dead latch" means a locking device, usually spring-operated, that incorporates a feature to render the latch rigid in its locked position and incapable of release by prying or by the turning of an outside door knob or handle or similar door opening device;

(e) "Dead lock" means a locking device incorporating a lock that cannot be pushed or retracted into a door or window by the use of tools inserted between the frame of the door or window and the door or window itself. Except as otherwise indicated, a dead lock may be equipped with a dead bolt or dead latch;

(f) "Double cylinder dead bolt lock" means a dead bolt lock that can be released from its locked position only by a key, whether on the inside or the outside of the door;

(g) "Local alarm system" means an alarm system that signals (upon any breach of a door, window, or other accessible opening to the protected premises) by means of one or more tamper protected sounding devices mounted on the exterior of the protected premises;

(h) "Silent alarm system" means an alarm system that signals at a location other than the premises where it is installed (upon any breach of a door, window, or other accessible opening to the protected premises) without giving warning at the location of the breached premises that it has been activated; and

(i) "Throw," when used in the context of a locking device, means the distance penetrated by that part of a bolt or latch on a door or window that actually penetrates into the fixed bolt or latch receptacle on the door or window frame.

1932.2 Purpose of protective device requirements.

(a) Section 1231(b) of the Act (12 U.S.C. 1749bbb-10a(b) provides that no Federal crime insurance shall be made available to a property which is deemed by the insurer to be uninsurable or to a property with respect to which reasonable protective measures to prevent loss, consistent with standards established by the insurer, have not been adopted.

(b) It is the intention of the insurer to require at the inception of the program only those protective devices generally in use or readily available for particular types and classes of properties at the present time. As the program progresses, however, the insurer proposes to amend these requirements from time to time to enforce a higher and more effective standard of protection against ordinary property crimes than now exists. Such revised requirements are not expected to be published more often than once a year and will be applicable only to crime insurance policies issued or renewed after their effective date.

1932.2 Classification of properties.

The protective devices required under this part fall into two broad categories, residential and commercial. Requirements for residential properties are expected to remain relatively stable and are not likely to vary by classes. The protective devices required for commercial and industrial properties will vary greatly by the type of risk involved and will be changed periodically as experience and knowledge are gained under the program and from studies being undertaken by other public and private agencies.

1932.4 Lack of protective devices voids policy.

(a) Each property owner applying for Federal crime insurance shall be personally responsible for meeting the protective device requirements applicable to the type of property for which he seeks insurance. Ignorance of such requirements shall not be deemed an excuse for any lack of compliance with the protective device requirements of this subchapter, and any person who is doubtful as to whether the protective devices existing on his premises at the time of application meet such requirements should seek competent technical advice before actually making application.

(b) Although agents and brokers are expected to assist and advise property owners as to the requirements for and adequacy of protective devices, no agent or broker shall be authorized to approve or disapprove on behalf of the insurer the adequacy of any required protective devices, and any representation to the contrary is false and shall be void.

(c) Premises found upon inspection to lack installation of the required protective devices shall be deemed to have been misrepresented at the time of application, and no insurance coverage shall be deemed to have been attached, regardless of the length of time the policy ostensibly has been in force, unless the property owner can clearly establish that a removal of the protective devices actually occurred subsequent to the insurance of the policy, in which event the policy shall be deemed cancelled by the insured as of the date of such removal.

(d) The insured shall promptly notify the servicing company of any malfunction or breakdown or protective devices and supply it with all relevant facts at the time the deficiency occurs. If such deficiency is corrected within the time specified by the servicing company, no lapse in coverage will result.

(e) Premises found upon inspection to be deficient in meeting the then currently applicable protective device requirements because of the uncorrected inadequacy, inoperability, or malfunction of existing protective devices shall, in the absence of evidence of fraud or misrepresentation, be deemed to have been ineligible for coverage from the date of the most recent application or renewal, whichever is applicable, and no coverage under the program shall exist with respect to such premises, regardless of the length of time the insured may have had coverage prior to such invalid application or renewal.

Subpart B — Residential Properites

1932.21 Minimum standards for residences and apartments.

In order to be eligible for Federal crime insurance, a residential property shall be equipped either with (a) a baffle-protected, self-locking latch and a dead bolt or (b) with a self-locking dead latch on every exterior door and every door leading into garage areas or public hallways, except that each sliding door shall be equipped with a dead lock device of any kind. All first floor and basement windows, and all windows opening onto stairways, porches, platforms, or other areas affording easy access to the premises, shall be equipped with locking devices. All dead locks required by this section shall have a minimum throw of one-half inch or have interlocking bolts and striker.

Subpart C — Nonresidential Properties

1932.31 Minimum standards for industrial and commercial properties.

The following requirements shall apply to all nonresidential properties as a condition of eligibility for Federal crime insurance:

(a) All exterior doors shall be equipped with dead latches with at least a ½-inch throw. Except where expressly prohibited by applicable laws pertaining to protection against fire, all exterior doors shall also be equipped with heavy duty, double cylinder, dead bolt locks, whose bolts extend at least one inch into the frame of the door, or which have interlocking bolts and striker.

(b) All exterior grate or grill-type doors shall be secured by one or more padlocks with heavy duty, case-hardened steel shackles, having a minimum 5-pin tumbler operation and an unremovable key when in an unlocked position.

(c) All exterior doors shall be of heavy gauge metal, tempered glass, or solid wood core construction, not less than 1³⁄₈ inches thick, or else shall be covered with metal sheeting of at least 16 gauge (one-16th inch thick) or its equivalent, or with grillwork, to give like protection;

(d) Outside hinge pins shall be welded, flanged, or screw-secured, non-removable pins;

(e) Except where expressly prohibited by applicable laws pertaining to fire protection, accessible openings exceeding 96 square inches in area and 6 inches in the smallest dimension,

shall either meet the standards for doors, or else shall be protected by inside or outside iron bars one-half inch in diameter, or by flat steel material spaced not more than 5 inches apart and securely fastened, or by iron or steel grills of ¹⁄₈-inch material of 2-inch mesh, securely fastened.

(f) The following types of establishments whose inventories pose a particularly heavy risk shall, as a minimum, be protected by the type of alarm systems indicated. If the system specified in subparagraph (1) of this paragraph is not available in the community in which the premises are located, the type of system specified in subparagraph (2) of this paragraph shall be permitted.

(1) Central stations, supervised service alarm systems shall be required for the following: Jewelry manufacturing, wholesale, and retail; gun and ammunition shop; wholesale liquor; wholesale tobacco; wholesale drug; and fur store.

(2) Silent alarm systems shall be required for the following: Liquor store; pawn shop; electronic equipment store; wig shop; clothing (new) store; coin and stamp shop; industrial tool supply house; camera store; and precious metal storage facility.

(3) Local alarm systems shall be required for the following: Antique store; art gallery, and service station.

Part 1933 - Coverage, Rates, and Prescribed Policy Forms

Subpart A — Residential

1933.1 Description of residential coverage.

Policy reimburses the insured for a loss from burglary and larceny incident thereto, robbery (including observed theft), or attempt threat, of personal property from the premises or in the presence of an insured, and for damage to the premises caused by any such attempt. It also covers damage to the interior of the part of the building occupied by the named insured's household at the described premises, and to the insured property both therein and away from the premises, caused by vandalism or malicious mischief: Provided that an insured is the owner thereof or is liable for such damage to the building. The policy is subject to the exclusions set forth therein. Policy shall be written only for an individual or for a single family or household, living in a one-to-four family house or as tenants in separate living quarters in an apartment building or dormitory. Others are not eligible under the residential policy.

1933.2 Limits of residential coverage.

The limits of coverage may not exceed $5,000 for each insurable premises, or be for less than $1,000.

1933.3 Amount of residential policy deductible.

The amount of deductible is $100 for each loss occurrence, or 5 percent of the gross amount of the loss, whichever is greater.

1933.4 Residential crime insurance rates.

The premium rates vary according to the territory in which the insured premises are located as set forth in Part 1934. Annual premiums for policy limits of $1,000, $2,000, $3,000, and $5,000 in each of these territorial classifications shall be as follows:

(a) Territory 01 (low risk): $30, $40, $50, and $60;
(b) Territory 02 (average risk): $40, $50, $60, and $70;
(c) Territory 03 (high risk): $50, $60, $70, and $80.

Subpart B — Commercial

1933.22 Limits of commercial coverage.

The limits of coverage may not exceed $15,000 for each premises, and the limit of coverage may not be increased by insuring several departments of a single business or institution at one premises as separate premises. Each $1,000 of insurance, or fraction thereof, shall be charged the applicable rate for the full $1,000 of coverage.

1933.23 Amount of commercial policy deductible.

The amount of deductible shall be subject to the following amounts for each loss occurrence, or 5 percent of the gross amount of the loss, whichever is greater, in accordance with the categories established in 1933.25(b) (3): Category I, $100;

Category II, $150; all other categories, $200. Nonprofit or public property risks shall be subject to a $200 deductible for each loss occurrence, or 5 percent of the loss, whichever is greater.

1933.24 Classification of commercial risks.

Classification of risks determined by the kind of business conducted by the insured at that location; if no specific kind, then the kind of merchandise inventoried and held for sale governs. Such risks take the classification of the merchandise or inventory comprising the majority value of the contents. For example, a candy store carrying an incidental line of tobacco is still classified as a candy store. Individual concessionaires operating within a premises take the same classification as the business premises in which they operate unless concessionaire's classification is higher, in which case the concessionaire's classification shall be used. The following classifications are applicable:

Class:	Statistical Code
1 All risks not otherwise classified, including nonprofit and public properties	01
3 Amusement enterprises (not otherwise classified)	02
2 Automobile sales & service	03
2 Billiard & pool parlors	04
2 Bowling lanes or centers	05
3 Cameras & photographic supplies	06
3 Clubs	07
3 Dance halls & pavillions	08
2 Drug stores & druggists' sundries	09
3 Dry cleaners	10
2 Electrical appliances, sales & service	11
3 Furriers	12
2 Garages	13
3 Gasoline service stations	14
2 Golf & other sports professionals	15
2 Grocery stores & delicatessens	16
3 Gun & ammunition shops	17
3 Jewelry stores	18
3 Laundries	19
3 Liquor stores	20
2 Meat & poultry dealers; butcher stores	21
2 Men's & students' clothing, 14 years and over	22
3 Pawnbrokers	23
2 Radio & television, sales & service	24
2 Restaurants	25
3 Small loan & finance companies	26
3 Taverns	27
3 Theaters	28
2 Tobacco dealers	29
2 Women's & junior teens' clothing, 14 years and over	30

1933.25 Commercial crime insurance rates.

The following procedure shall be used to determine the annual rates applicable:

(1) The risk classification and territory rate shall first be determined in accordance with 1933.24 and 1934.2 of this chapter;

(2) For risks having gross receipts of less than $2 million annually, the base rate for the first $1,000 of coverage shall be determined in accordance with the following table:

Class

01
02
03

Territory

01	02	03
$70	$80	$100
80	100	120
100	120	130

For risks having gross receipts between $2 million and $4,999,999, the base rate is 0.0002 of such gross receipts. For risks having gross receipts of $5 million or more, the base rate shall be 0.00025 of such gross receipts.

(3) The base rate determined in subparagraph (2) of this paragraph shall be multiplied by the appropriate multiplier from the following table, as determined by the applicant's Federal income tax return for the most recent taxable year, in order to obtain the actual premium for the first $1,000 of coverage. If the applicant is a nonprofit or public entity whose gross receipts constitute less than its operating budget, its operating budget shall be used in lieu of gross receipts to determine the appropriate multiplier.

Category	Gross Receipts	Multiplier
1.00		I
1.50		II
2.00		III
2.50		IV
3.00		V
3.50		VI
4.00		VII
4.50		VIII
1.00		IX

Less than $25,000
$25,000 - $49,999
$50,000 - $99,999
$100,000 - $299,999
$300,000 - $499,999
$500,000 - $999,999
$1,000,000 - $1,499,999
$1,500,000 - $1,999,999
$2,000,000 or over

(4) Rates for higher limits of coverage shall be determined by applying to the premium base derived in accordance with subparagraph (3) of this paragraph the appropriate higher limits factor from the following table for the applicable amount of coverage:

Rate for applicable amount of coverage	Higher Limits Factor
$1,000	1.00
$2,000	1.95
$3,000	2.85
$4,000	3.70
$5,000	4.50
$6,000	5.25
$7,000	5.95
$8,000	6.60
$9,000	7.20
$10,000	7.75
$11,000	8.25
$12,000	8.70
$13,000	9.10
$14,000	9.45
$15,000	9.75

(5) The product derived in accordance with subparagraph (4) of this paragraph shall then be rounded to the next higher dollar above 0.49 to obtain the chargeable annual policy holder premium.

1933.26 Required commercial policy form.

(b) Commercial Crime Insurance Policy form:

FEDERAL INSURANCE ADMINISTRATION COMMERCIAL CRIME INSURANCE POLICY

The Federal Insurance Administrator, herein called the Insurer, agree with the insured, named in the Application made a part hereof, in consideration of the payment of the premium and in reliance upon the statements in the Application, and subject to (1) the provisions of Title VI of Public Law 91-609 and Subchapter C, Chapter VII, Title 24 of the Code of Federal Regulations, and (2) the limits of insurance, exclusions, conditions, deductibles, and other terms of this Policy with respect to the following criminal acts:

Insuring Agreements

I. Robbery, including observed theft, inside the premises. To pay for loss by robbery or observed theft of money, securities, merchandise, furniture, fixtures, and equipment within the premises.

II. Robbery, including observed theft, outside the premises. To pay for loss by robbery or observed theft of money, securities, and merchandise, including the wallet or bag containing such property, while such property is being conveyed by a messenger outside the premises, but no payment shall be made for any loss in excess of $5,000 except when an armed guard accompanies the messenger.

III. Safe burglary. To pay for loss by safe burglary and larceny incident thereto, of money, securities, and merchandise within the premises, but no payment shall be made for any loss in excess of $5,000 except with respect to loss by safe burglary of a Class E safe securely anchored to the floor.

IV. **Theft from night depository.** To pay for loss by theft of money and securities within any night depository in a bank.

V. **Burglary; robbery of watchman.** To pay for loss by burglary and larceny incident thereto or by robbery of a watchman, while the premises are not open for business, of merchandise, furniture, fixtures, and equipment within the premises. Under this insuring agreement, the actual cash value of any one article of jewelry shall be deemed not to exceed $50.

VI. **Damage.** To pay for damage to the premises, and to money, securities, merchandise, furniture, fixtures, and equipment within the premises, by robbery, burglary, safe burglary, robbery of a watchman, or attempt thereat, provided that with respect to damage to the premises, the insured is the owner thereof or is liable for such damage.

VII. **Policy period, territory.** This Policy applies only to loss which occurs during the Policy period within a State.

Exclusions

This Policy does not apply:

(a) To loss due to embezzlement or to any fraudulent, dishonest, or criminal act by any insured, a partner therein, or an officer, employee, director, trustee, or authorized representative thereof while working or otherwise and whether acting alone or in collusion with others: *Provided,* That this exclusion does not apply to safe burglary or attempt threat by other than the insured or a partner therein;

(b) To loss due to war, whether or not declared, civil war, insurrection, rebellion, or revolution, or any act or condition incident to any of the foregoing;

(c) To loss of manuscripts, records,, or accounts;

(d) Under Insuring Agreements V and VI, to loss occurring during a fire in the premises;

(e) To loss due to nuclear reaction, nuclear radiation, or radio-active contamination, or to any act or condition incident to any of the foregoing;

(f) To any loss if the premises are not equipped with the protective devices required as a condition of eligibility for the purchase of this Policy by the regulations of the Federal Insurance Administration, as published at the time of the inception of the current term of the Policy in Subchapter C, Chapter VII, Title 24, Code of Federal Regulations.

Conditions

1. Definitons.

(a) **Money.** "Money" means currency, coins, bank notes, and bullion; travelers checks, register checks, and money orders held for sale to the public.

(b) **Securities.** "Securities" means all negotiable and non-negotiable instruments or contracts representing either money or other property and includes revenue and other stamps in current use, tokens, and tickets, but does not include money.

(c) **Premises.** "Premises" means the interior of that portion of any building at a location designated in the Application which is occupied by the insured as stated therein, but shall not include (1) showcases or show windows not opening directly into the interior of the premises, or (2) public entrances, halls, stairways. As respects Insuring Agreements I and II only, the premises shall also include the space immediately surrounding such building, provided such space is occupied by the insured in conducting his business.

(d) **Custodian.** "Custodian" means the insured, a partner therein, an officer thereof, or any employee thereof who is in the regular service of and duly authorized by the insured to have the care and custody of the insured property within the premises, excluding any person while acting as a watchman, porter, or janitor.

(e) **Messenger.** "Messenger" means the insured, a partner therein, an officer thereof, or any employee thereof who is in the regular service of and duly authorized by the insured to have the care and custody of the insured property outside the premises.

(f) **Robbery.** "Robbery" or "robbery, including observed theft" means the taking of insured property (1) by violence inflicted upon a messenger or a custodian; (2) by putting him in fear of violence; (3) by any other overt felonious act committed in his presence and of which he was actually cognizant, provided such other act is not committed by an officer, partner, or employee of the insured; (4) from the person or direct care and custody of a messenger or custodian who has been killed or rendered unconscious; (5) from within the premises by compelling a messenger or custodian by violence or threat of violence while outside the premises to admit a person into the premises or to furnish him with means of ingress into the premises; or (6) from a showcase or show window within the premises while regularly open for business, by a person who has broken the glass thereof from outside the premises.

(g) **Robbery of a watchman.** "Robbery of a watchman" means a felonious taking of insured property of violence or threat of violence inflicted upon a private watchman employed exclusively by the insured and while such watchman is on duty within the premises.

(h) **Burglar.** "Burglar" or "burglary and larceny incident thereto" means the felonious abstraction of insured property from within the premises by a person making felonious entry therein by actual force and violence, evidenced by visible marks upon, or physical damage to, the exterior of the premises at the place of such entry.

(i) **Safe burglary.** "Safe burglary" or "safe burglar and larceny incident thereto" means (1) the felonious abstraction of insured property from within a vault or safe, the door of which is equipped with a combination lock, located within the premises, by a person making felonious entry into such vault or such safe and any vault containing the safe, when all doors thereof are duly closed and locked by all combination locks thereon, provided such entry shall be made by actual force and violence, evidenced by visible marks upon the exterior of (a) all of said doors of such vault or such safe and any vault containing the safe, if entry is made through such doors, or (b) the top, bottom, or walls of such vault or such safe and any vault containing the safe through which entry is made, if not made through such doors, or the felonious abstraction of such safe from within the premises.

(j) **Jewelry.** "Jewelry" means jewelry, watches, gems, precious or semiprecious stones, and articles containing one or more gems.

(k) **Loss.** "Loss," except as used in Insurance Agreements I through V, includes damage.

(l) **Class E Safe.** "Class E Safe" means a steel safe having walls at least one inch thick and doors at least 1½ inches thick, or a vault of steel at least ½ inch thick or of reinforced concrete or stone at least 9 inches thick or of non-reinforced concrete or stone at least 12 inches thick, with steel doors at least 1½ inches thick.

2. Ownership of property; interests covered. The insured property may be owned by the insured or held by him in any capacity, whether or not the insured is liable for the loss thereof.

3. Joint insured. If more than one interest is named in the Application, the insured first named shall act for every insured for all purposes of this Policy.

4. Books and records. The insured shall keep records of all insured property in such manner that the Insurer can accurately determine therefrom the amount of loss, and if the insured maintains cash funds for the purpose of check cashing, a complete record of each check negotiated shall be kept by the insured showing the names of the maker, payee and drawee bank, and the date and amount of the check, and such records shall be maintained in a receptacle other than used for money and securities.

5. Limits of liability; settlement options. The Insurer shall not be liable on account of any loss unless the amount of such loss shall exceed the amount of the deductible, and then only for such excess over and above the deductible, subject to and within the limit of insurance covered by the Policy.

Part 1934 - Classification of Territories

1934.1 Method of classifying territories.

(a) Because rates are related to urban population concentrations rather than to State boundaries, the insurer has determined that the interests of the public will best be served by classifying territories for the purposes of the Federal crime insurance program on the basis of statistics applicable to entire Standard Metropolitan Statistical Areas, generally referred to as "SMSA's."

1934.2 List and classification of territories.

(a) Territories shall be classified for statistical and rating purposes as set forth in the insure's Crime Insurance Manual, which shall apply to all crime insurance policies written under the program. Such manual shall be supplied by the servicing company on behalf of the insurer to all eligible agents and brokers within an eligible State.

C. **Grading.** Each SMSA and each remainder of State is classified into one of three territories for rating purposes:

Territory 3: high risk
Territory 2: average risk
Territory 1: low risk

Index